C000200246

MONKEY BUSINESS

MONKEY BUSINESS

The Memoirs of General Sir Cecil Blacker

Quiller Press
London

ISBN 1 870948 87 4

First published 1993 by
Quiller Press Limited
46 Lillie Road
London SW6 1TN

Line illustrations by Joan Wanklyn

Produced by Book Production Consultants
25–27 High Street, Chesterton, Cambridge.
Typeset by Cambridge Photosetting Services.
Printed by St Edmundsbury Press, Bury St Edmunds, Suffolk.

Title page: *Cartoon by Molly Bishop (Lady George Montagu Douglas Scott, wife of a fellow squadron leader) drawn before a 23rd Hussars party at Whitby 1941.*

Contents

Contents

Preface

At luncheon at a racemeeting Woodrow Wyatt, the chairman of the Tote, asked me how I proposed to occupy myself after I retired from the post of the Jockey Club's deputy Senior Steward, which I was about to do.

I said that I had a tentative idea of writing some memoirs. In his leg-pulling and jocular style he commented, 'Oh, but generals don't have interesting enough lives for that.' And compared with his remarkable career described in his *Confessions of an Optimist* he had a point. Nevertheless I decided to try.

I like to feel that there is a difference, however subtle, between a book of memoirs and an autobiography. Whether I am right or wrong I have used the presumed distinction as an excuse for picking and choosing incidents from my life, and even making the confusion worse by starting halfway through it.

Although I spent 40 years in the army this is far from being a military memoir. My life as a soldier had for much of the time to fit in participation in steeplechasing as an amateur jockey and in international sport, and after I retired in the administration of racing and of equestrian activities. Indeed during my 40s I found myself leading almost a double life.

An army officer has to be interested in people because he spends his time working with them, working under them, working on their behalf and occasionally commanding them. In my case this interest spilled over into the personalities whom I met, competed against and worked with in racing and in the equestrian world, and who have helped me with my painting. It is the cast of characters in this narrative which may make it, I hope, worth reading. I fear that anyone searching for a serious 'message', military or otherwise, will be disappointed.

My thanks are principally due to my old friend John Weiner, who took my narrative by the scruff of its neck and shook it into some form of order. To another old friend, Joan Wanklyn, I am most grateful for her skill and helpfulness over the illustrations. I also thank Chris Pharazyn for the maps. Three books about the Second World War, J.R. Colville's *Man of Valour* and Major J.J. How's *Hill 112* and *Normandy; The British Breakout* were most valuable sources of information, which I acknowledge. I have also taken the liberty of extracting a short passage from the history of the 11th Armoured Division (see page 94).

CHAPTER ONE

Two Field Marshals (1958–60)

From the seat behind me in the aircraft the Field Marshal said peevishly to a stewardess, 'I am sorry, but I do most particularly dislike Chicken Maryland.' I glanced round and glimpsed the enormous and discontented frame of Frankie Festing, his usual sense of humour well submerged. Before taking off we had for some reason been stuck on the Hong Kong runway for an hour in the broiling sun with no air conditioning. The Chief of the Imperial General Staff, attired in his usual touring garb of thick corduroy riding breeches and leather gaiters, had suffered more than most.

He had unbuttoned himself as far as was decently possible, his snuff box had been upset down his front and, as he fretfully discussed with the stewardess the least unpalatable alternative to Chicken Maryland, various salads and condiments were rolling off the tray into his lap.

As his keen Military Assistant the thought did cross my mind that on our arrival in Singapore this dishevelled figure would shortly be inspecting an immaculate guard of honour, but I had previously discovered that attempts to tidy him up were not welcome. On this occasion my sole contribution to his turnout on our arrival, as he was about to descend the aircraft steps, was to pluck from his collar a label stuck there on which was clearly marked 'Unsuitable for stowage in the luggage rack'.

The Field Marshal's turnout at all times did leave to the military purist much to be desired, but his lifelong tendency to scruffiness had by then become so much a part, indeed a controlled part, of his persona that if he had suddenly appeared in shiny boots and a Savile Row uniform it would have been a let-down. In any case his formidable frame and demeanour, and the amazement generated by those extraordinary breeches and gaiters, with the large rubicund face topped by a faded Greenjacket beret, made his hosts at once appreciate that they were privileged to behold probably the last of the senior eccentrics of the British Army.

He had been Commander-in-Chief of the Far East before taking over as CIGS. Whilst appreciating his promotion to the head of the army he had left the Far East with reluctance. He enjoyed his comforts and he had been all too aware that the life-style of Whitehall was a good deal more austere than the proconsular splendour of his Singapore establishment, as well as providing him with a good deal more work. To make himself feel at home he had brought back with him as many of his personal staff as he could.

I had been the sole survivor of the previous regime, having served his predecessor, Gerald Templer, for the past year, and I was, so to speak, taken over with the job. Indeed, I soon discovered, I was lucky to have survived at all, for Frankie had developed a liking for being surrounded by faces he knew. He had no scruples about removing officers if they were strange to him, as I was, if he thought they were going to bore him, and his boredom threshold was extremely low. Somehow I managed to pass muster.

Field Marshal Sir Francis Festing was, as by now will have been gathered, a 'character'. I believe he was of Viking descent, and this was not difficult to credit. Exchange the Greenjacket beret for a helmet, his staff car for a long-boat, and his normal cheerful expression for the scowl he wore when in a bad mood, and the picture is all there. Even his easygoing personality had something elemental and primitive about it, and it was not hard to believe a story which had followed him back from the Far East.

John Cornell, his ADC, had been with him when, as Commander-in-Chief Far East, he visited South Korea. The Koreans took him and the American general stationed there to shoot deer. At the end of the day the last victim's throat was cut and a bowl filled with its blood was proffered to the two guests. The American turned green and declined, thus losing a lot of face. Frankie seized the bowl, quaffed the contents with relish and offered it back with a grin.

During the war in Burma he had proved to be a highly effective and formidable commander in battle. 'Front-Line Frankie', he had been called. In peacetime he displayed a marked preference for visiting troops to sitting in his office. So for that matter had his predecessor, Gerald Templer, but there the similarity ended.

Field Marshal Sir Gerald Templer was probably the outstanding soldier of the post-war years – energetic, highly-strung and immensely hard-working. The War Office staff had grown used to being galvanised by the dynamo on the second floor. Their role had been to provide the facts and the options for him, and then stand trembling before him waiting to be told what to do.

Now the War Office staff had to deal with a CIGS who, typically, had made up his mind to be as different from Gerald as he could be. He made a point of working much shorter hours than Gerald had. He disliked reading papers and only did so in the sketchiest of fashions. He preferred being briefed verbally, and only then by officers congenial to him.

The change was not well-received by his earnest briefers and a wave of disapproval swept through the War Office. The intelligent, conscientious and competent officers there soon formed the impression that he was not very bright.

They could not have been more wrong. In fact he had a natural quickness of mind and an intellectual depth which in my personal judgement have not been surpassed by any of his successors. Only part of his mind and attention, however, were occupied by military problems, and he resolutely declined to be a dedicated soldier. Plans to acquire a sought-after Japanese Samurai sword – on which subject he was an international expert – or to augment his collection of duelling pistols and other antiques were often uppermost in his thoughts. His besetting sin was idleness. His powerful mind was wayward, and if he was not interested in a subject, however relevant to his duties, he could hardly be bothered with it.

Nevertheless, his intuition, common-sense and wisdom, combined with vast experience in war and peace and an ability to see the wood for the trees, made him a much better CIGS than he will ever be given credit for. He was liked and trusted by politicians, his fellow Chiefs of Staff and by our Allies. He was robust in his defence of the army and bowed his head to no-one. His religious faith – he was a Roman Catholic – was profound. He never missed a weekly Mass if he could help it and avoided public engagements during Holy Week. Whitehall was rocked by his retort when the Prime Minister, Harold Macmillan, unexpectedly asked him to attend a Cabinet meeting – 'I'm not going to allow the Prime Minister to bugger up my Holy Week', followed by a blank refusal.

He had within him all the attributes needed for success in his new role but seemed to go out of his way to conceal them. The 'character' which he decided to impersonate in his later years was that of a bluff, down-to-earth infantry warrior, caring nothing for his appearance or what people thought of him, spending as little time as possible in his office and as much as possible with soldiers in the field. For much of the time he was of course putting on an act. There was no need to wear those acutely uncomfortable breeches and gaiters, nor to be so scruffy. He succeeded in coming across as a 'character' and as an eccentric, but he overplayed his part. Unfortunately he fooled a number of people into believing that he really was the fuddy duddy he made himself out to be.

One of Frankie Festing's many contributions as CIGS was to lower the temperature in the relations between his office and Duncan Sandys, the Defence Minister. Gerald Templer, since he had reluctantly to remain on speaking with Duncan Sandys, had contrived to make their exchanges as acerbic as possible and never made the slightest effort to conceal his deep dislike and distrust of the Minister. Frankie deliberately adopted a more emollient attitude and while he was no more successful than his predecessor in frustrating what the War Office regarded as the knavish tricks of their political chief, relations none the less became more agreeable.

One of the Minister's policies had been the belief that the nuclear deterrent would have the effect of reducing the size of the conventional forces. Thus, during the Templer period, the National Service Army had begun to contract into a much smaller professional one, and this resulted in the loss of many famous regimental names and identities. Frankie's response was as always to combine his love of the traditional regimental system with realism, and thus he was in many ways the ideal man to console, to comfort and, if necessary, to straighten out the many who were moved to protest against what he regarded as the inevitable.

He kept a critical eye on the personalities running the various headquarters and establishments worldwide. If in his view they were not up to the mark, changes were ruthlessly made. It was not long before his eye fell on the Royal Military Academy Sandhurst. This establishment was unlucky enough to harbour two 'moles' in the persons of his sons Michael and Andrew who were not finding their lives as officer cadets to their liking. Frankie's suspicions of the place were fanned by their complaints and in due course he decided to launch what was little less than a punitive expedition. 'Now,' he said to me one day, 'I want to visit Sandhurst but you are not to tell them till the evening before or they will have time to prepare. I'm told the food is disgusting, so I want to lunch with the cadets, but again you are not to tell them.' So the conspiracy was set in train, in the guise of an informal short-notice visit.

I arrived at the Festing's flat to pick up the CIGS and, as I waited for him to ready himself, I saw on the hall table several notes scribbled by the moles to bring their father up to date. 'Food *revolting* again' read one, and another 'Once more stopped from riding with the Drag – what's the point of keeping a horse here?' – and more in the same vein. When the Field Marshal appeared he was obviously in a fault-finding mood and I kept quiet on the journey down.

On entering Camberley from London you pass the Staff College entrance, which from that direction provides the shorter access to the RMAS than by turning into the Sandhurst gate further on. Not unreasonably, but perhaps unwisely as the visit was supposed to be informal, the Sandhurst staff had thought to welcome the CIGS by providing as guides two land rovers complete with smartly dressed staff officers and red-hatted military policemen poised expectantly and deferentially at the Staff College gate.

Inside the Rolls, which was so elderly and stately that it was called Queen Mary, there was an explosion. 'Bloody fools," said the Field Marshal. 'Do they really imagine that I don't know the way into Sandhurst – drive on, Sergeant Baker, drive on. Drive on down the road and don't take any notice of these silly buggers; go in through the proper gate.' Sergeant Baker, a charming man with a great sense of humour – an indispensable trait in that particular job and who was allowed, typically, to break the Whitehall headgear rules and continue to wear his airborne beret – duly proceeded down the main road. The land rovers, without a backward glance and assuming the great man was in tow, drove insouciantly through the Staff College entrance.

We turned into the Sandhurst gate, and crossed the main square to the headquarters, altogether outflanking a group of officers headed by the Commandant who, not surprisingly, were pointing in the opposite direction. The resulting embarrassment clearly gave the CIGS much pleasure.

At the ensuing conference the Field Marshal ran over the main criticisms he had of Sandhurst; the Commandant defended his charge and so matters proceeded until 12.45, when it was suggested we should repair to the officers mess for luncheon. 'Oh no," said the Field Marshal mendaciously. 'Haven't you been told – you certainly should have been. I particularly want to lunch with the cadets.' There was a horrified pause. A staff officer came to the rescue, 'I'm afraid it's too late for that, sir, the cadets finish their meal in a few minutes.' It was a good try but it failed. 'Well then,' said the CIGS, 'all the more reason to hurry and just catch them before the dining room closes down.'

We rose and trooped down to the cadets' mess where we were received with dismay but in due course seated round a distinctly uninviting table. There were about ten of us – rather a lonely group – as the last of the cadets were trickling out, looking astonished at the appearance of so much high brass. Reluctantly and ungraciously the civilian staff began to dish out the food, and here the CIGS scored a bullseye, for that meal ranks high amongst the nastiest I have tasted.

By the time the pudding had arrived the civilian staff were fed up with us. We had considerably delayed their departure and they clearly felt it was time this nonsense ended. Two of the scruffiest in their ranks seized buckets and a mop, sluiced water lavishly over the floor, and began to propel mini-waves of dirty liquid round and under our table. As the Chief of the Imperial General Staff's feet became awash, I caught his eye. It conveyed a glimpse of devilish triumph.

I was beginning to feel sorry for the Commandant who was, in fact, a very nice man though perhaps not ideal for his present job. He bore his ordeal with calm and courtesy, but it was not over yet because, before he left, Frankie insisted in interviewing all the senior staff one by one. This, of course, took a long time as well as completely disrupting the Academy's afternoon programme. Nor did it go well. At the close the Commandant wore the resigned expression of one all too aware that the wind of change, of which he would be the first victim, would shortly be blowing.

It was indeed to blow. The next Commandant was Geordie Gordon Lennox, a Grenadier of striking looks and personality who, by the time he handed over, had transformed the place. The wind also blew me, promoted to brigadier, into his Assistant Commandant's role. So I found myself bidding 'au revoir' to Whitehall – but certainly not farewell.

During my two years there I had managed to avoid becoming entirely office-bound. The Festing regime, unlike the Templer one which had preceded it, allowed time for a luncheon interval. This I spent in picture galleries, occasionally buying a picture which gives me pleasure to this day. Before I came to work I would prepare my show-jumper, Workboy, for the next competition. He was an old friend from my racing days and, when he was no longer sound enough for racing, he developed an astonishing talent for the less demanding sport of show-jumping.

In 1959 he had lifted me into the British show-jumping team. This was an honour that had been hard won and in no way was I prepared to allow my duties as Military Assistant to the CIGS unduly to cramp my style. Both the Field Marshals whom I served were only too pleased to allow me to travel with the team to the continent and once to South America. Indeed they seemed rather tickled by the idea of having an international show-jumper on their staff.

Of course this relaxed attitude on their part depended on my ability to do the work to their satisfaction. I never had any illusions during my time as an amateur steeplechase jockey and later as a show-jumper, that the job I was paid for came first. Luckily I was a quick worker and my assistants, first Dick Jefferies and later Alastair Neilson, were more than capable of temporarily taking over. I admit, though, that my double life brought with it some hard work, some close shaves and many hours of catching up at distinctly unsocial hours. But it was worth it.

Careful planning was necessary together with some split-second timing. I once rode out of the show-jumping arena at Barcelona at one a.m. and caught the next available aircraft for Heathrow. Waiting for me was my uniform and a great deal of paperwork. By eight a.m. I was again the Military Assistant standing respectfully outside the VIP lounge to greet the CIGS, to bring him up to date with the relevant news and fly off with him to Berlin.

At luncheon there the brigadier, Miles Fitzalan Howard (now the Duke of Norfolk and whom at that time I had not met), heard my name and politely enquired, 'Are you by any chance a relation of the Blacker who rides in shows?' – a good question to which by that time I could hardly remember the answer.

I particularly recall that trip because the CIGS went to pay his respects to the Mayor of West Berlin, Herr Willy Brandt, the future German Chancellor. He duly disappeared, gaiters and all, into the mayoral parlour. When he emerged and re-entered his car, I followed in a second car. The Field Marshal's drove off, with the Mayor politely waving goodbye but as my car, slightly delayed, passed Herr Brandt I was amused to see that his expression had changed into one of hilarious bafflement and he was turning back to his staff convulsed with disbelieving mirth. Clearly he had never before met anyone like our Frankie.

It was a strange double life that I led then, and I suspect now, although the world-wide commitments of the British Army are vastly reduced, it would be regarded as inconceivable for the Military Assistant to the CGS (the 'I' having been dropped) to act as an international sportsman as well. In later years the work load seemed steadily to increase in inverse proportion to the scale of British world responsibilities. Military office life became more intense and humourless. Officers took themselves and their duties more and more seriously, and often actually created unnecessary work.

I started my military life with no particular ambition other than to do each job I was given as best as I could and to enjoy myself as much as possible in the process. If I ever thought about such things, I expected to occupy my time mainly with active, low level or regimental duties, and then to retire and find myself something else to do, probably connected with the horse. Thus, when I finished commanding my regiment in Germany in 1957, it was a shock, though a pleasant one, to find myself selected as Military Assistant to Field Marshal Sir Gerald Templer, the CIGS.

Having enjoyed many books on the political and military personalities of the past 50 years, who had inhabited a world quite unrelated to any I seemed ever likely to become part of, it was a thrill actually to find myself in the office next to that of the Chief of the Imperial General Staff. I would daily enter the room in which the great Lord Alanbrooke had grappled with the problems of the Second World War as Churchill's right hand man, and often find myself in the stately chamber where Kitchener had sat in the First World War as Secretary of State. It was quite a change from Sennelager Camp on the North-West German plain.

Now I had, anyway for a year or two – if I survived – a role in the corridors of power. They lived up to expectations – wide marble staircases above the entrance, rising smoothly and portentously to the door of the Secretary of State's office; tall marble pillars; high ceilings; ceremonially attired porters – all conveying a cold Victorian grandeur and a strong sense of Britain's history. Even now in the days of the modern Ministry of Defence and, with the original building somewhat contemptuously called the Old War Office, with chattering typists crowded into the former CIGS's office and with *sic transit gloria* echoing from every corner you turn, it still retalns its dignity if not much else.

Soon after he became CIGS in 1955 Gerald Templer had walked straight into the Suez crisis; indeed probably no-one in Whitehall, other than Anthony Eden himself, had carried a heavier load of responsibility during it.

When it was over Anthony Head, whom he liked, had been replaced as Defence Minister by Duncan Sandys, whom he quickly grew to loathe. This was not surprising, for the new Minister at once made it clear that he had no time for the conventional forces or for their Chiefs; he was concerned with the development of the nuclear deterrent and the reduction of all three Services, particularly the army. Inevitably this led to an immediate confrontation and a clash of two strong personalities.

By the time I arrived in 1957 therefore, Gerald Templer had endured nearly two years of strain and conflict exceptional even for the notoriously testing post of CIGS. This period had closely followed the completion of his historic role in Malaya. He was far from being an easy-going man, able to relax. It had often been said, 'Of course Gerald lives entirely on his nerves; he won't last very long; he'll soon burn himself out.' In fact, he lived on well into his 80s, positive and forceful to the last.

Probably the reason for this unexpected longevity was his altogether exceptional will-power. This literally made him indomitable. He never admitted defeat until the cause was utterly lost, or gave in to physical weakness. The saying about mind over matter might have been invented for him. His resilience was extraordinary. I have often seen him almost tottering with exhaustion as he left the office after seven p.m., return home, and after two gins and tonics be the life and soul of a subsequent dinner party.

In appearance he was slight, saturnine, with a thin black moustache – a description which fitted scores of other officers. But even his back view marked him out as a person of consequence. Personality emanated from him in waves, intensified by his voice, incisive, harsh, almost menacing. He had been well named the Tiger of Malaya. If, in jungle terms, Frankie was the elephant, outwardly placid but capable of ferocious menace, Gerald was the carnivore. Even in his most avuncular and jovial moods, one could not help being fascinated by very sharp teeth which the friendly smile failed to hide.

He had an insatiable appetite for work, almost a mania. He would invariably come to the office on Saturdays. Luckily for me my predecessor as MA was Chris Sinclair, a Rifle Brigade officer of marked good sense and of a temperament which would now be called 'laid back'. He had firmly declined to come in himself on Saturdays or let any of his staff do so except for the duty clerk. On Saturday mornings this clerk would dump mounds of paper, mostly of no consequence whatever, in front of the Chief who would sit there contentedly ploughing his way through them. As a result he was tiresomely well informed on Monday mornings.

When I arrived in my appointment the battles over the 1957 Defence White Paper were over but the War Office was still smarting. Its distrust of the Ministry of Defence, particularly the Minister himself, had if anything increased. From Gerald's point of view the White Paper had been a disaster, ignoring as it did the need to rectify the many shortcomings which the Suez operation had painfully made clear. Instead it concentrated on an independent nuclear deterrent and the consequent need to reduce our conventional forces. The resulting programme of regimental amalgamations and disbandments had been agony for so intense a regimental soldier as Gerald. His distrust of Duncan Sandys began to verge on the paranoic. Now the Minister was producing the 1958 White Paper. 'That bugger Sandys will pull another fast one, and this time he bloody well won't get away with it if I can help it.'

Duncan Sandys was a strange man. He gave the impression that he genuinely did not care whether people liked him or not. He even seemed to go out of his way to make them actively dislike him. He worked, spoke, and apparently thought, very slowly – 'the mills of God' is the painfully unoriginal quote which springs to mind. He worked, if he wanted to, all hours of the day and night – literally. The drafts of the 1958 White Paper would be churned out in a continuous process in chunks of three or four pages, the time of completion of each chunk stamped with a little clock sign in the top right-hand corner – 2230, 0130, 0300 and so on right through the 24 hours. The drafts would have to be cleared or commented on within a few hours of their arrival at the War Office and their other Whitehall destinations. If no comment was received by the deadline it would be too late – agreement would be assumed. This tactic was perceived by the CIGS as an all too typical trick to slip something unpalatable past the unwary – which it probably was. He instructed me that each instalment was to be shown to him immediately it was received.

So we used to sit in the War Office very late indeed. Then the Field Marshal was laid low with flu and made to go to bed. A croaking voice would ask me on the telephone, 'Where are the latest drafts? Bring them round to me at once.' So I would go round to No. 10 Wilton Street where her ladyship would receive me very frostily indeed. 'No, you can't possibly disturb Gerald. He's far too ill.' Then a hoarse shout of 'Show him up' and in I would go. The papers would be seized, scribbled upon, criticised with a fierce intensity, and flung back at me. I would then run the gauntlet of Peggie Templer's disapproval on my way out. After a few of these excursions she could bear it no more and complained to the Vice Chief that the new MA was badgering Gerald with papers when he was ill. It made no difference, and I cannot remember which ended first – the little clock signs or Gerald's illness – but, whichever it was, it was a relief.

The 1958 summer was a long, hot one, as we say nowadays. The first White Paper was succeeded by a second, which dealt with the reorganisation of the higher defence system, but the agitation this engendered was soon eclipsed by a first-class crisis in the Middle East. This was provoked by a military coup in Iraq – then a Baghdad Pact ally – in which the King, Crown Prince and the Prime Minister were all killed and the British Embassy burned and looted. Lebanon and Jordan asked for military assistance which both the British and the Americans were contracted to give.

Gerald was extracted from a dinner party to attend a Cabinet meeting and by the early hours of the morning two parachute battalions were in the air for Amman. American marines had already arrived in Beirut.

On the following morning the CIGS was in his element. A crowd of expectant senior officers was summoned to his office, most of them ignorant of what had happened during the night. At the centre, glowering and volcanic behind his desk, crouched the Tiger, probing, questioning, rapping out orders, lucid, incisive, totally in command. Officers having received their instructions shot out of the door on their way to comply; others came running down the corridor to be sucked into the whirlpool.

Unfortunately in all the nocturnal excitement too relaxed a view had been taken of the little matter of permission to overfly Israel. The Israelis were not proving cooperative. Some of the aircraft had arrived in Amman; others were held up in Cyprus; others returned. Meanwhile the Israeli cabinet deliberated. At one p.m. they broke up, and luckily the answer was 'yes'.

Towards the end of this somewhat tense morning, an elderly officer wandered vaguely down the corridor, clearly one of the few who had not yet found a role in the current drama. He looked in through my door with an air of mild curiosity, 'Is this rumour true? Have we really sent troops to Jordan?' He was the Director of Public Relations, as usual in Gerald's regime the last to hear about anything, such was the Field Marshal's loathing of the Press.

The next few weeks were spent by Ministers and Chiefs of Staff frantically trying to decide what they should do next about Iraq. Julian Amery, the War Office Under Secretary of State, was determined that somehow we should 'intervene'. He and Christopher Soames, the Secretary of State, portentously unrolled large maps of the Middle East, and would stand before them looking dynamic and statesmanlike. 'We should of course invade Iraq. I see a brigade moving up through Syria' – and here the right hand would sweep through several Middle Eastern countries – 'supported by perhaps a division landing at Basra' with the left hand jabbing upwards some hundreds of miles from the other. Their advice was not taken. The CIGS was tempted for instinctively he was anxious to 'do something', but as always his head overruled his heart.

After several trying weeks the excitement died down. A complication from my own point of view was that the crisis inconveniently clashed with the International Horse Show at the White City, but my assistant, Dick Jefferies, was more than capable of holding the fort in my absence. Although once back in the office I would have many hours of catching up to do, I felt much refreshed, particularly as I sometimes returned with a rosette, and very slightly the richer.

At least during this crisis I was aware of what was going on and could get on with my job. This could not be said about the high level manoeuvring which preceded the second Defence White Paper of the year, concerning a reorganisation of the Chiefs of Staff Committee. Duncan Sandys, while conceding that the time was not ripe for a centralised Ministry of Defence – which occurred in 1963 – proposed that the existing post of Chairman of the Chiefs of Staff should be replaced by a much more powerful Chief of Defence Staff, with his own central staff and reporting direct to the Minister. With hindsight and with over 30 years of this system working without noticeable disaster, it is surprising to recall the horror with which this idea was greeted in some quarters at the time.

The CIGS was passionately opposed, and found a strong ally, as he did on most subjects, in the Chief of the Air Staff, Dermot Boyle. The First Sea Lord, Lord Mountbatten, while paying lip service to their objections, was suspected of speaking with a forked tongue, because he would be the man to take on this new job and was reputed to want it badly. But surprisingly they found a wholehearted ally in Mountbatten's Vice Chief, Caspar John, son of Augustus, who in this instance was at cross purposes with his master. Not surprisingly, with the Prime Minister behind him, Sandys won. Gerald was desolated, but the Iraq crisis soon took his mind off it.

Of course his fears about a central staff, whilst not entirely groundless, were much exaggerated. On this one issue Gerald Templer's two main weaknesses were exemplified – his inability to see the political side of a question and a traditionalism born of a passionate loyalty to the British Army which made him instinctively recoil from change, however inevitable. Although his head always ruled his heart in the end, it was no walkover and the battle between them would cause him much mental anguish.

His relations with politicians recalled the 'frocks versus brass' situation of the First World War. He respected some, but not many. He held the – alas – old-fashioned view that politicians should tell the army what to do and then stand back. This was expecting too much and was almost unrealistic as the futile protest, often heard, that politics and sport should not mix.

Over the Suez affair he was passionately pro-Eden and strongly supported the whole venture, even after it had failed. He felt that but for the lily-livered and interfering politicians it would have been a success and would have transformed the Middle East to our advantage. Whether he was right or wrong will never be known. But Suez reinforced his dislike of politicians and set the tone for his whole tenure of office.

His sense of tradition and his love affair with the British Army meant that his time in office, coinciding as it did with the beginning of the inevitable reduction in the army's size, was a long, and to him, agonising struggle for the survival of the values with which he had been brought up and for which he carried the responsibility on the army's behalf. The idea of actually ordering the disbandment of historic regiments and battalions was more than even his nerve could stand but the alternative of amalgamation caused enough trouble, mainly, not surprisingly, from retired officers. One even protested beyond the grave! Gerald would point to a picture in his office of a former CIGS, Sir Charles Douglas, who was a distinguished Gordon Highlander, and would recall a meeting which he held there to discuss the amalgamations that might be necessary in the Highland and Lowland Brigades. When in the course of it Gerald said, 'Well, let's look at the Gordon Highlanders again,' there was a loud crack on the wall and, lo, the glass on the picture of Sir Charles was cracked in twain. Gerald ordered that it should remain unrepaired.

The infantry amalgamations were mainly dealt with by the ingenious solution of 'large regiments' or 'brigades' as they were initially called. The advantage was that in, say, the Light Infantry of four battalions, the necesssary reduction from four to three could be achieved without the agony – or the public outcry – of ordering the disbandment of the junior one, the celebrated Durham Light Infantry. The remaining three were then called the 1st, 2nd and 3rd Light Infantry. This enabled the authorities to say that no-one had been disbanded;

the regiment had simply contracted. But not all regiments would agree to relinquish their historic titles and were allowed to spurn the 'large regiment' concept. This, as some of us suspected at the time, laid up trouble for the future and in 1991, when our forces were again cut back in 'Options For Change', the chickens came home to roost. Gerald knew that logically he should have pushed this idea much further but he could not bring himself to do it. Knowing the intensity of feeling at the time, I for one cannot blame him.

Gerald Templer may have been too resistant to change but I have no doubt that in those troubled years, during which the army was literally cut in half, he was the man for the hour. Duncan Sandys was rough, tough and formidable and, if an opponent was not up to his weight, he would walk all over him. The intensity of Gerald's argument and the strength of his personality undoubtedly mitigated or deflected some of the Minister's more drastic proposals. Almost certainly it was the opposition of the CIGS which caused a welcome modification in the absolute priority being given to the independent nuclear deterrent.

Gerald Templer was a battler but an attractive side to his character was that his battles were never fought for himself – his own personal advantage never seemed to enter his head. He led from the front, with everything firing. From his subordinates he expected perfection, and reaching for his standard of excellence was the most draining task that I ever had to undertake. To use a racing simile, with him I was always half a length down and 'off the bit' – and with my natural speed of working I had never encountered this before and very seldom since.

He could not help creating tension. In the second floor offices of the War Office the staff, working outwardly calmly behind their desks, were inwardly keyed up, not for any particular reason but because it was in the air. He did not mean to have this effect on people. He would come into the 'outer office' in a jovial mood – for he had a strong sense of humour of the teasing, leg-pulling variety – and suggest it was quite time we had some leave, we mustn't work too hard, must have some fun, and so on. He refused to go on leave himself because, he said, he wanted to keep his eye on the Minister. If truth be told the idea of leave bored him. When we did once persuade him to go fishing on the Test for a week he would be on the telephone every morning. After three days he had had enough of it and was back behind his desk.

You might have thought that so dedicated a soldier as he was would, when he retired, have faded away as old soldiers are supposed to do. Not a bit of it – his mind and interests were far too active and wide ranging for that. He flung himself into successful business pursuits and provided the driving force and the expert knowledge in the realisation of his dream of a National Army Museum. This strange man, this slave-driver as many thought him – particularly the wives of those who served him – was capable of inspiring great devotion. When that frail, exhausted figure tottered away down the War Office corridor for the last time, I watched that back receding with a lump in my throat.

After he had left he wrote me a most charming letter thanking me for the enjoyment which he said he had had in working with me, not only from the professional but from the personal point of view.

He concluded – and here I am already breaking the rule I made for myself not to quote from complimentary letters in these pages – 'You will go from strength to strength and I shall enjoy watching it from the sidelines. Thank you so very much.'

Many years later, and only a few months before he died, I was able in a speech at a dinner which he attended to say publicly to his face what I and so many of my contemporaries felt about him. I said that the post-war years had seen all too few great men, but that Field Marshal Sir Gerald Templer had without question been one of them.

CHAPTER TWO

Almost another world (1916–39)

One teatime at Sandhurst in 1934 I was sitting with some friends at a table in the dining hall and we were chatting merrily about the horses we had ridden that afternoon. An elderly instructor, an intelligent and somewhat eccentric Sapper major, who was sitting at our table, leaned across and said, 'You know, Blacker, I can just see you in the years to come when you join your regiment, hour after hour, day after day, your sole subject of conversation will be your polo ponies or whatever horses you had ridden that afternoon.' At which he relapsed into his normal lugubrious silence.

This was a salutary warning, which I have since tried to heed. Nearly all my friends and my family, if they were not talking about sport, talked about horses. In the world outside there were millions of unemployed, hunger marches and strikes; the international scene was threatening; the arts were there to be enjoyed, but our consciences and senses were impervious to these events. None of them concerned us. All we were interested in was our life at Sandhurst, sport, parties, and trying to imitate Fred Astaire.

No doubt this was deplorable. But we were young and not much given to reflection. Many of us had been to schools where little effort had been made to educate us out of our philistine ways, and we came from homes still recovering from the agony of the First World War. In 1934 Armistice Day was only 16 years behind us. The 1920s and the 1930s saw most parents, particularly those likely to produce future Army officers, doing their best to catch up with all they had missed during those years of war which had engulfed their world and almost destroyed their generation. Sport and parties, parties and sport – anything to forget what they had been through, and above all nothing earnest or serious – had provided the background for our childhood and adolescence. Deplorable, perhaps. But those who had never had to walk through the furnace of the Great War, as our parents so recently had, should temper their scorn.

To anyone possessed of a reasonable level of intelligence, Sandhurst then was, intellectually, an almost complete waste of an important 18 months of his life. There were plenty of physical, but no mental challenges. As far as I was concerned, its sole achievement was to convert me from an immature schoolboy to an immature subaltern just capable of commanding my soldiers when I joined my regiment.

I made many friends but, since my Sandhurst intake was destined to provide the platoon and troop commanders in 1940 and the majors and upwards from 1941 onwards, not many survived until 1946. The irrepressible Kim Muir, killed with the 10th Hussars in 1940, thought I looked like an ape and would screech 'Monk, Monk' at me while scratching his armpit. I have been known as 'Monkey' ever since. I suppose as nicknames go it could be worse – better anyway than having to go through life known as 'Crackers', 'Bolo', 'Splosh' or 'Ugly' as other unfortunate officers have had to do. This army habit of saddling officers with embarrassing nicknames seems to have died out – a good thing.

I had no need to do much work at Sandhurst because I had already been accepted for the 5th Inniskilling Dragoon Guards. All I had to achieve was a pass in the final exam, preferably higher for reasons of seniority than the other regimental candidate. I soon established that neither task would be hard. So, from having passed into Sandhurst fourth, I viewed with the utmost unconcern a passing-out place considerably lower. I have since deeply regretted that I did not attend university and, much later in life, dealing with highly-educated civil servants and officers with degrees, I was made to realise what I had missed.

It had been much the same at Wellington – not clever enough to join the academic élite but not stupid enough to have a problem with the required exams. I had been to a preparatory school with a high academic standard and just missed a scholarship to Wellington. Thus I started in a class quite high up the school and soon discovered that, since I was destined for the army, my target in the four years that lay ahead was the easily attainable Army Lower Sixth. This I reached with two years to spare.

I am sure the school was only going through a temporary patch, but at that time Wellington College did not seem to me to be a good choice for the would-be army officer. Although it had the reputation of being a 'military' school and produced more army officers than any other, the then Master appeared, rather perversely it might be thought, to have the utmost contempt for the army, and Sandhurst in particular. I am not sure if Dr Malim was the Master who described Sandhurst as 'that little hell over the hill' but it easily could have been. Those whom he found to be aiming at an army career were simply provided with enough education to pass the army exam; no effort was made to arouse any intellectual or artistic interests in them.

No doubt the army entrants should have had the personal initiative not to accept this state of affairs; it is too easy to blame the school entirely for leaving us so bereft. The opportunities were there but, except for music which was, I believe, brilliantly and imaginatively taught to those gifted enough to profit, no attempt was made to interest us in them. My subsequent passion for painting and pictures remained well submerged in my schooldays. In art classes the drawing of all those square boxes soon ensured my early escape.

The army at this period took as officers a large number of Wellingtonians who were instantly recognisable as such. There were many honourable exceptions, many intelligent and distinguished products of Wellington both in the Services and in civilian life, but a high proportion of Old Wellingtonians wore porkpie hats, talked heartily about rugger, and in early middle age became portly and red-faced, still talking about rugger without ever having had an original idea in their lives. Initiative and independence of thought were discouraged; to conform was all. We lived by a strict and predictable programme of work and play, and most Wellingtonians – certainly this applied to me – consequently emerged young for their age and very wet behind the ears. When I was there the school was still easily recognisable as the establishment which had housed J.D. Marstock in Harold Nicolson's evocative chapter in *Some People.*

By the 1930s however some of the more enterprising and independent boys had started to rebel. Two of my friends disappeared one night through the skylight of their dormitory and were never seen again. A celebrated rebel was Esmond Romilly, of whom my only recollection is of his remarkable scruffiness, even by schoolboy standards. As may be remembered he ran off with Jessica Mitford, wrote a rude book about Wellington and departed to fight for the Communists in Spain. The rest of us, more conventional and much less enterprising, were outwardly shocked but inwardly rather envious.

The Blackers were a long-established protestant Irish family, with branches scattered all over Ireland, north and south. By the end of the 19th century the main family house was Castlemartin, near the Curragh in County Kildare, and now the home of Tony O'Reilly of Irish rugby and Heinz Baked Beans fame. My grandfather had been brought up in Castlemartin but as the younger son had moved to a house nearby when he married.

There he raised three sons and one daughter. In common with similar families all over the British Isles at that time they were brought up in the peace, tranquillity and confidence of the Edwardian era, blissfully unaware of the abyss ahead. The Irish gentry, in particular, were immersed to the exclusion of all else in sport and social life, horses and shooting. They lived surrounded by pictures of Punchestown races and of fox-hunting; by photographs of heavily moustached and thickly clad gentlemen, usually mounted; of ladies in long riding habits and unbecoming bowler hats on the side-saddle, by Victoriana of all kinds, and above all by peace and plenty.

In 1914, still not believing that war with the Germans could cause more than a temporary check to their way of life, the three sons went off to battle. Their parents remained in Ireland until the Troubles after the war. These were the last straw for my grandmother. She was a lady of character, a daughter of the Sir Joseph Bazalgette who designed the London sewage system. She had, I suspect, not been quite so enchanted by her life in Ireland as had the remainder of the family. She lost no time in removing my grandfather from Ireland and establishing him, of all contrasting places, in Leatherhead. There, deprived of all his interests, and not the man to take up new ones, he soon died, no doubt mainly of boredom.

I hardly remember him, or my paternal grandmother, except that she had a most engaging personality, which my father inherited. When I recall my two grandmothers I see old ladies in long black dresses and a good deal of lace, almost permanently reclining in an armchair or presiding in stately fashion at the head of a tea-table, with a gentle walk round the garden the height of their day's activity. This picture contrasts with their present descendants as grandmothers, usually clad in huskies, jeans and rubber boots, still capable of delivering calves, breaking young horses, proceeding rapidly down a mountain on skis, and outwalking most of their grandchildren. Times change.

My generation, and still less later generations, never really comprehended the true horror of the experiences which our fathers went through in the First World War. In our household after it was over the war was never mentioned so I suppose our ignorance was not surprising. The Second World War, except no doubt on the Russian front, did not compare, unpleasant though it was, with the First. My father, young and inexperienced in any life other than the carefree one he was leaving, departed to France in 1914. Within weeks his twin brother, Cecil, to whom he was devoted, was killed with the Connaught Rangers in the retreat from Mons. He then went through four years in the trenches of the Western Front, the mud, the gruesome carnage, the constant likelihood of death, the responsibility of asking his men for sacrifice after sacrifice. He had two short spells away wounded, during one of which he married my mother, and ended the war as a lieutenant-colonel of 28 with a DSO and an MC.

Nothing would induce him to refer to his experiences subsequently; he appeared completely to close his mind to the past. Like most of his generation, while the scars remained within and without, he was able to lead a happy and normal life. But memories of the Great War, though outwardly ignored, retained a ghostly presence in the background, materialising particularly in those wartime songs, those poignant, chin up, desperate songs like 'Pack up your troubles in your old kit bag and smile, smile, smile', 'It's a long way to Tipperary', 'Keep the home fires burning'. I still cannot hear them without emotion.

By the end of the war my father had had enough of the army. Like so many he took up chicken farming. Like so many he did not succeed. We moved from place to place ending up near Bicester in Oxfordshire. There he set up a livery yard, which was soon full of the horses belonging to rich Londoners who wished to hunt with the Bicester hounds. He was made secretary of the hunt, and was at once a resounding success, charming the farmers into accepting the devastation to their land and fences which the passage of the hunt had caused and being particularly welcoming to the visiting Oxford undergraduates. Many elderly gentlemen have told me how as young men they had appreciated his kindness and remember what fun he was to go hunting with.

Our family and social life was based very largely on horses and hunting – family because it was my parents' all-consuming interest and social because all our friends hunted. The members of the hunting field ranged from the skilful and brave through the keen but timorous to the frankly terrified. But anyone who aspired to be a member of the local gentry followed hounds – even if, as we did, they came into the category described by Trollope as 'us second-class gentry with our £800 a year'. It was the 'done thing' in the parts of the United Kingdom with fashionable packs and little less so in the unfashionable areas.

Victorian novels make it plain how much foxhunting was a part of country life in their time, but with the arrival of the motor car, and as importantly the motor horse-box, the 1920s and the 1930s probably saw the sport reach its apotheosis. The bookshelves of the country houses groaned under volumes of hunting fiction, hunting memoirs, hunting lore and hunting statistics, Surtees, Nimrod and uncountable other portrayers of the chase, whimsical Irish tales by Dorothea Conyers, John Masefield's 'Reynard the Fox', and children's books often featuring Reynard in human guise. If the household was not up to inheriting Ferneleys and Herrings, Lionel Edwards and Cecil Aldin prints filled the walls. Hunting diaries were written up; alas, they do not now make enthralling reading.

In the summer holidays my sister and I would rise at five a.m. for the cubbing. I still cannot smell the scent of tobacco flowers without in memory crossing our garden on those fresh lovely mornings on the way to the ponies. We would clatter down the roads in the dawn light to local coverts which we helped to surround, beating our whips on the flaps of our saddles to deter the unfortunate cubs from escaping. We enthusiastically submitted to the practice now condemned as barbaric, that of 'blooding' – the bloody end of a severed fox's paw would be smeared on our cheeks as part of our initiation to hunting.

A very good reason for all this enthusiasm was that in those days a run across a stiffly fenced grass country, on a good horse and with hounds screaming along in full view, with unpredictable hazards and decisions presenting themselves in quick succession, with the element of competition far from absent, together provided a sporting thrill which in my experience was second to none. A really good hunt on a star horse generated a feeling almost of exaltation. Nothing I have experienced in sport has made me so conscious of sublime enjoyment at the time. Riding round Aintree, for example, is a thrill but quite a different one; a high proportion of the enjoyment is retrospective, and in the race you look forward to passing the winning post intact and as soon as possible. But in one of those pre-war hunts you longed for it to go on for ever.

Not only was it fun, but exposure to the 'image of war with ten percent of its danger' was good for one too. I am sure it does good to be mildly frightened every so often; it sharpens one up. Later in life I would observe officers move from an office or normal regimental job to one in which they had to jump out of aeroplanes with parachutes – indeed I did this myself. After a few weeks their step was brisker, their attitude more decisive and their whole demeanour livelier.

It was the season of 1938–39, with real war – not just its hunting image – manifestly over the horizon which instilled a 'what the hell' feeling in most of us, that I remember best. The Bicester hounds had at the time reached a peak of excellence. Bob Field-Marsham, a born amateur huntsman, was the Master and hunted hounds on two of the four days. He was not only superb at his job but had the essential ingredient for success in the hunting field; he made the day fun. My father as field master had the same gift. On the other two days hounds were hunted by the professional, Clarence Johnson. He was one of the great huntsmen – brilliant. By then he was physically past his best but his skill, instinct, and knowledge of hunting lore remained unsurpassed and only equalled by a very few. He was understandably not quite so brave across country as he had been. He was apt to halt in front of a forbidding obstacle and, when one of the young thrusters arrived, he would be exhorted to 'Go on, sir, go on, sir' to give the great man a lead and hopefully reduce the size of the fence in doing so.

Distance may lend enchantment but in that season we rarely went home without a memorable hunt. The gateway before the first draw was packed with over a hundred riders, and as the hounds first spoke the horses would congeal into a straining, steaming mass as we tried to achieve the advantage of a good start, which was all-important in that highly competitive field.

With much cursing and shouting the cork would come out of the bottle and the field career forward to the fences ahead. My father was inevitably in front, often riding one of Lord Bicester's magnificent ex-chasers. These would arrive from his lordship in a steady stream, for his trainer had the unhappy knack of souring them for racing early in their careers, which they fortunately concluded in the hunting field with my father. With him was usually Daisy Lyon, so pretty and charming that every male foxhunter was in love with her, and a superb horsewoman, Tinker Gilbey, immaculate on a side-saddle, relaxed and with apparently all the time in the world, together with a collection of young men, some cool and collected, others hot and uncollected, but all determined not to let the others get in front of them. I remember an invasion from the neighbouring Grafton Hunt, when a contingent headed by Neil Foster and Mary Rose Fitzroy arrived obviously intending to show the Bicester the way the Grafton went. The temperature rose, there was much crashing of timber, and the invaders were not, I believe, entirely successful in proving their point.

But despite the competitive edge, there was a splendid camaraderie in our hunting field. Everyone was kind to young people like myself, and when I became a junior subaltern the more senior soldiers in the field went out of their way to be friendly. Sadly, few survived the war. Malcolm Erskine, immaculate Scots Guardsman and a good man to hounds, a few years later as a brigadier flew out one day over the Malayan jungle in his light aircraft and was never seen again. Major-General Beckwith-Smith – Becky – was a grand little man, always cheerful and encouraging, with a resounding laugh which would take the chill off the keenest wind. He was destined to arrive in Malaya with his division just as resistance to the Japanese collapsed, to be forced to surrender without firing a shot and later to die in a Japanese prison camp. He would have enjoyed watching the success of the grandson he never saw, Nicky Henderson the trainer.

So many tragedies and horrors were hidden round the corner in early 1939, and our half-formed apprehension about the international situation never approached the reality of what was about to happen to us. We had no conception that our conventional, light-hearted and ordered life would in a few months begin to disintegrate and then totally vanish, for ever. 'Pre-war' is now another world, almost a dream.

Towards the end of a day's hunting thoughts of the homeward journey would surface. Before we could afford a motor horsebox, or even after if there was no room for me in it, the only way was to hack home. We had sometimes ridden 14 miles to the meet, which meant an early start, and there was a tendency for the heart to sink if during the day hounds ran away from home and added another four or five miles. Clip-clopping slowly on a tired horse mile after mile after mile in the gathering gloom is one of the less pleasant memories, but at the end of it there was the blessing of a lighted stable-yard, grooms coming to take my horse and by the time the adhesive Bicester clay was being removed from its coat I would be indoors hungrily eating a late tea.

These teas were often enlivened by the owners who kept their horses with us and whom we would refresh before they were swept back to London in their chauffeured limousines. I remember particularly an enchanting lady called Claire Shakespeare, sophistication personified. In India, we understood, she had married a Colonel Shakespeare, but he had long since disappeared into the limbo of forgotten things as she moved – elegant, vivacious but with background obscure – into London society. In due course she became Mrs Vincent Dunkerly, but later captivated the Duke of Sutherland and ended up a Duchess. Fascinated, I would observe how her lipstick left large crimson marks on her teacup, and await with glee the inevitable 'My dear, how simply TOO, TOO divine.'

My parents were happier during this period than at any other time in their lives. We never seemed to have any money, and I only achieved the basic minimum private means on which it was possible to survive in a cavalry regiment through my ever generous grandmother. If our home life was modest, so were our ambitions. Competitiveness in the hunting field was an instinctive reaction, but otherwise we were not competitive in a serious way. Of course we preferred to win in any competition in which we might be taking part, such as tennis, and parents naturally hoped that their offspring would 'do well' at school and in their subsequent lives. But to excel seriously was considered not only rather pushy but beyond the realms of realism. In racing the winning of a point-to-point would be all that could be expected of people like ourselves, and the idea of riding in a professional steeplechase, or show-jumping at Olympia, was only dreamed of, usually as far as I was concerned during the sermon at the village church.

It was always understood that I would go into the army. There was no discussion about this. I just went along with the decision that had been made for me, just as I found myself at Wellington without having been asked if I would have preferred Winchester, my mother's choice. In the army my parents hoped that one day I might achieve the rank of lieutenant-colonel, like my father, but the prevailing note was struck by my Uncle Billy who on hearing of my commission wrote to congratulate me, ending his letter with 'But don't get ambition – it's fatal'. Why he went out of his way to say this I am not sure but I have a feeling that I was already suspect in his eyes.

At home, various subjects were taboo. Weather forecasts which heralded frost and so the suspension of hunting were ignored and not spoken of. When the ground did freeze up my father behaved as if we were in mourning. To enjoy oneself by skating on the local pond was regarded in the same light as fraternising with the enemy. Another utterly taboo subject was the obvious approach of the Second World War. To my mother and father the thought of returning to the purgatory of 1914/1918 was so appalling that they just closed their minds to the ever-worsening news; they would neither hear nor speak about it.

When war was eventually declared in September 1939 they bowed their heads in anguish and knew in their heart of hearts that the best part of their lives was over. They were right. What a tragic and fated generation theirs was, to have to endure, as active adults, two world wars. My father was called back to the colours as a colonel, and my mother busied herself with evacuees and war work. Then in 1940 my father was promoted to command a regular brigade stationed at Portsmouth as part of our defence against invasion. Shortly after he took over, the new Commander-in-Chief, Southern Command, appeared on a tour of inspection. General Montgomery, having enquired my father's age – he was 50 – and background, instantly sacked him. No doubt Monty used words which later became familiar to those who worked for him 'Too old. Quite useless. He must go'.

And go he did – demoted to colonel – disgruntled, bitter and unable from then on to hear the word Monty mentioned without a flow of wide-ranging invective. After the war he decided that post-war hunting was not his scene and my parents withdrew to Norfolk for the rest of their lives.

In January 1936 I travelled to the Cavalry Barracks, Colchester, to join the 5th Inniskilling Dragoon Guards. I found the camp almost deserted. Nearly every officer was away hunting and the men were on leave, apart from the minimum needed to look after the horses, a good many of which were away hunting too, with the officers. Yes, we were, three years before the outbreak of the Second World War, preparing to fight the enemy on horseback and we continued in this role until 1938, the year of Munich. Not that we could have fought anyone very effectively at the time. We were so undermanned that in 1937 we could only muster one mounted squadron out of an establishment of three. Rifles were the only weapons we possessed. We were supposed to have some machine guns but when we were required to use them on maneouvres we sat down and waved red flags. This period – the locust years as Churchill called them – saw the British Army at its lowest level of effectiveness in living memory. One shudders to think of what would have happened in 1938 if we had not been reprieved by Munich and had had to go to war then.

I had been told at Sandhurst that when you first joined your regiment no one spoke to you for several months. This was not my experience. The very few officers in the mess were welcoming, though in rather a distant fashion. But so little was happening at Colchester that I went home and continued hunting, driving back and forth in my bull-nosed Morris, which had cost eight pounds and was surprisingly reliable.

Later the mess began to fill up and I met a few more of my colleagues. Gerald Kildare would fly back and forth from Ireland in his private aeroplane, usually arriving with a traveller's tale to tell. He was a first-rate pilot but small aeroplanes with one engine were unpredictable conveyances in the 1930s. On one occasion a head wind made him so short of fuel that on his last pint he just made the beach on the western tip of Wales. On another in a thick fog he lost his way to Cheltenham races and only found it by swooping down on railway stations and reading the name on the platform. Dick Vigors, with a strong sense of humour and a liking for fast cars, became another friend.

One day the mess waiters looked unusually alert and began to bustle about. Obviously something was about to happen and I asked what. Sergeant Heward's voice dropped in respectful awe, 'Captain Ansell is coming for the night, sir. He's on his way back from playing polo in India and intends to go off to hunt tomorrow.' And there in the mess in the evening was the already celebrated Mike Ansell, tall, hawk-featured and radiating energy, holding court on the fender. He was an international polo player, an international show-jumper and an officer to whom command and leadership came completely naturally. At the time he was unquestionably the cavalry's rising star. He was friendly to me but soon turned to talk to someone more interesting. It was indeed rather like sighting a rare bird because, at that period of his life, almost the only time he appeared in barracks was to put his name in the leave book for another six months sporting absence.

Another celebrated absentee was the adjutant, Perry Harding. Short, squat and tough, he was probably the best amateur ever to ride over fences – in fact amateur only in name. Nothing about him was in the least amateur either in appearance – for he looked just like a professional – or in the way he conducted his racing life. In the summer he would be seen briskly entering the adjutant's office – soon leaving it to play polo – but from October to April the Cavalry Barracks was simply a place which could be an occasional convenience but no more. The exiguous winter duties of the adjutant would be handed over to someone else and he would be based, as far as we could understand, mainly on the Hammam Baths in Jermyn Street. There he and his professional cronies would combine reducing their weight with – if the 'Cap', as the racing Press called him, was to be believed – hatching plots to enrich themselves at the races on the next day.

I suspect the stories improved with the telling, but the enjoyment he obtained from bending – an understatement – the rules of racing became well known and did him no good in the long run. The fellow amateurs and owners who had suffered at his hands, or thought they had, became leading members of the Jockey Club after the war. The name of Perry Harding was anathema to them, despite his distinguished war record, and although he would have been a most useful member, of the poacher turned gamekeeper type, he remained irretrievably blackballed.

Percy Legard, blond and well-built, was half-Swedish and was, exceptionally, much keener on skiing than hunting, spending his winters on the snow. Long before Eddie the Eagle of modern ski-jumping fame was hailed, incorrectly, as the first British ski-jumper, Percy was jumping regularly, with, I suspect, rather more success than the Eagle, and certainly more glamour, for he was very good-looking. He was extremely versatile, and spoke several languages; a natural athlete, he played regularly in dance bands and painted in oils. But he had no powers of application; he was so relaxed and so anxious to rush off to the next party that he really never became more than a jack of all trades. However the Modern Pentathlon might have been invented for him, and he was in the British team for the 1932 Los Angeles and the 1936 Berlin Olympics.

The delightful and intelligent university graduate, John Anderson, was obviously destined to become a general one day, a destiny which he fulfilled. Alec Scott was a brilliant horseman who won a bronze medal in the Three Day Event in the 1936 Berlin Olympics. All in all it was a lively and enterprising officer's mess and most, with their wives and offspring, became friends for life. The loyalty and instinctive togetherness of those who have served in my regiment have always been a joy to me. It is genuinely comparable with a family, in a way which civilian life, in my observation at least, can in no way match.

During the winter there was no question of doing any soldiering. This was not as remiss as it sounds. Other than keeping the horse fed and exercised there was nothing militarily useful that could have been done, in view of the pitiful shortage of men and equipment. It was understood that every officer would depart for two months to hunt, taking with him his two chargers plus one or two troop horses hired for the winter, together with his own horses if he had any, and as many soldier grooms as were needed to look after them. Apart from paying for the horses' keep, hiring the troop horses for fifty shillings a week each, and settling his hunt subscription, his winter's enjoyment was mainly funded by His Majesty's government.

The soldier grooms had to agree to provide their services. There was no shortage of volunteers because life at the various hunting centres was a good deal more comfortable and interesting than the routine in a cold and deserted barracks. They had joined the cavalry to ride and look after horses, and happily became part of their officer's domestic staff during the winter months.

In spring the regiment reassembled. The riding school became active, troop training began and we rode in point-to-points. The officers had to appear each day in shiny brown riding boots and spurs, clean breeches with smart lemon-coloured strapping, and a well-tailored tunic set off by a gleaming Sam Browne belt. Our soldier servants – no hang-ups then about using that word – had their hands full preparing all that kit for us. Most became friends for life with their officers. I still hear from mine, Arthur Ward, 55 years later.

Someone had to look after our chargers too, and he was the 'second servant'; again most remained permanent friends. Perry Harding's second servant was Trooper Whelan, now as 'Boggy' Whelan a well-known character and ex-trainer at Epsom. To modern eyes the whole pre-war cavalry set-up may seem grotesque, but then to be required to go into battle in the late 1930s as a horsed cavalry regiment was a grotesque idea in any case. In fact the organisation and method of the cavalry year was a thoroughly practical assessment of what was necessary, useful and realistic given our circumstances.

Training on the Berechurch area of Colchester continued throughout the summer and I soon discovered that commanding a troop of horses was excellent for developing a tactical instinct. One moment you were manoeuvring at a brisk trot or gallop to outflank; the next, with horse concealed in rear, you were on foot acting as infantry. The soldiers were hard, dyed-in-the-wool cavalrymen and first-rate. I soon found, though, that it was necessary to do the map reading personally. Efforts to delegate would too often result in furious shouts and gesticulations from an enraged squadron leader in rear. On one occasion, my troop sergeant, charming but not very bright, expostulated memorably, 'Can't understand it, sir. I insulted my map before leaving.'

Training in the morning, polo in the afternoon and hectic visits to London at night occupied the summer months. Then in autumn came the climax of the year – cavalry maneouvres. We would ride from Colchester to Salisbury Plain, passing in column down a deserted Oxford Street at five a.m. On arrival the horses were staked out in picket lines surrounded by tents. All available cavalry regiments would try to outsmart their rivals in tactical maneouvre or in the appearance of their lines. On our return to Colchester we started to wind down for the winter.

This routine was being carried out by the cavalry and horsed artillery throughout the army in this country at the time, and it might seem to have been a somewhat inadequate preparation for armoured warfare two or three years later. Strange to say it turned out to be quite a good one. We did what we had to do very professionally and this professionalism became second nature, to be applied rigorously to whatever changes in role that might confront us.

It was, also, understood that every officer must risk his neck in some sport or other, and these sports were hard and competitive. Anyone who hunted seriously – as we all did – or competed on a horse, found himself having to make quick decisions which only he could make, to assess rapidly the best way across a piece of country, and to get used to hard knocks and unpleasant accidents. The many cavalry and horse artillery officers who rose to high positions as commanders in the war were very often those who had stood out as competitive horsemen in the 'locust years'.

After two years of this life at Colchester I was becoming restless. Some will regard this as absurd. Here I was, with very little money, playing polo, hunting, escorting girl-friends in London and Colchester, with work that was far from testing and anyway enjoyable, and here was I restless after only two years of this paradise. But now and again, with increasing frequency, I asked myself, 'Surely there must be more to life than this?' Perhaps a spell in the Somaliland Camel Corps or a stint in the Trans-Jordan Frontier Force might be considered, though neither idea was very original. If there was a war I could perhaps prepare myself for a special role in it?

I conceived the idea, from my readings of the First World War, that a key country in another war might be Turkey. I resolved to learn Turkish, collected books of Turkish grammar and embarked on a correspondence course. In due course I could see myself, fluent in the Turkish language, the indispensable participant, a key figure, in secret talks and operations vital to the safety of the Empire, in true John Buchan style. No chance. Just as I had reached the point at which I could have informed any Turk interested that the maiden had taken the pitcher to the well, I was sent to Catterick to learn the mysteries of the Number 1 Wireless Set. This was followed by Munich, then by mechanisation, then by war – in France, not Turkey which remained throughout the war firmly on the sidelines.

I learnt the morse code from Sergeant McMahon, the excellent regimental signal sergeant, and set off for Catterick, returning some months later as regimental signal officer. I found the atmosphere and tempo of life at Colchester quite altered. At last we were to be mechanised and equipped with light tanks and armoured troop carriers. We were also under new management.

Colonel 'Ugly' Martin was large and ungainly and one could see how he got his nickname. He was rightly convinced that within a very short time we would be at war and was determined that his regiment would be ready. Some other cavalry regiments accepted mechanisation with an air of resignation. Ugly fell upon it like an ardent lover and clutched it to his bosom. One of my first requests, made somewhat perfunctorily to the new commanding officer, was for leave of absence to ride in a point-to-point on a working afternoon. I could hardly believe my ears when I was told to remain at my duties. I reeled out of Ugly's office, outraged. The old order had changed with a vengeance. For ever.

CHAPTER THREE

We'll hang out the washing on the Siegfried Line (1939–40)

The year of 1939 had opened in traditional style in the hunting field. For a few months our sporting life was no more than mildly inconvenienced by the new regime. Our troop horses had disappeared in 1938 but the government, in a fit of most unusual generosity, had allowed officers to keep one of their two chargers.

My charger was an extraordinary character. He was enormous, with vast limbs and a great coffin-shaped head, and had been named Big Ben. Although it would not have surprised anyone to learn that a carthorse featured prominently in his pedigree, he had the body of an athlete and the hindlegs of a steeplechaser, though twice the size.

What was remarkable about this very common-looking government horse was his success in point-to-points. That season I won five on him. Since he was a magnificent jumper and stayed for ever I badly wanted to run him in the Liverpool Foxhunters, then run over the full Grand National distance of four-and-a-half miles, but could not bend the rule which prevented government horses from running in steeplechases. I bought him out, but too late – by then we were at war. Although he then wasted the rest of his life in a field at home, at least my faithful servant was spared service in Palestine and the fate which ultimately awaited so many of those old cavalry horses which had given so much pleasure.

It took more than an imminent world war to stop polo. The Colchester grounds reverberated twice a week to the oaths and shouts of the participants, for I soon discovered that the mildest of officers would on the polo field become incandescent at the smallest provocation. Ugly Martin, despite his preoccupation with preparations for war, joined in with gusto. He was an excitable officer with a very short fuse and on one occasion contributed to the spectacle of two commanding officers – one himself and the other the commander of the neighbouring gunner regiment – galloping the length of the ground belabouring each other with their polo sticks.

No one enjoyed such scenes more than the watching wives, for the lot of the 'polo wives', as they ruefully called themselves, was not to be envied. They were expected invariably to be seated along the side of the ground, lines of colourful dresses, dark glasses, and hands bobbing over knitting, watching the players swiping inaccurately and abusively at the ball, week after week from May until September. Though inclined to be tedious, it was at least more peaceful than their point-to-point role, watching their husbands anxiously through field-glasses, with the ever-present likelihood that soon they would find themselves running down the course towards an unconscious figure lying somewhere out in the country.

Some of the wives were only superficially interested in horses but in the 1930s the cavalry ladies were expected to be in support of their husbands at riding events, and in that comparatively conventional and submissive era they dutifully fell into line. Other wives were expert horsewomen themselves and needed no persuading. Indeed a few talked of little else. A newly engaged couple dancing together at a party were once eavesdropped by a mischievous young officer anxious to overhear the sweet nothings that were doubtless passing between them. All he received for his pains was the lady murmuring, as she danced cheek to cheek, 'Well, whatever you say, I always much prefer a double bridle to a snaffle.'

As the summer of 1939 wore on the wives saw less of their husbands as the tempo of preparations increased. We were to become a light reconnaissance regiment – the divisional cavalry. Two troops of each of the three squadrons were to be equipped with the new Mark VIB light tank, and four troops with the armoured bren carrier, which was intended to carry riflemen from place to place for the same purpose as the horse had done. This was a tracked three-ton armoured vehicle, open at the top.

The Mark VIB weighed five tons and accommodated three men, the commander, the operator and the driver. Its armour was too thin to keep out anything but rifle fire, it was armed with two machine guns of which one fired armour-piercing bullets with singular lack of effect, and its suspension was so bad that cross country travel was acutely uncomfortable for the crew. Its sole advantage was the speed with which it could proceed down the road or over flat country. It was a deplorable vehicle, but most of us were delighted with it for want of anything better. As we were to discover later the Mark VIB was sadly to be only the first of the many British and then American tank models to be badly outgunned and outstripped by our German opponents.

Some of the cavalry soldiers flung up their hands in horror at the sight of these new-fangled machines and left for other tasks, but the remainder became instructors in driving and maintenance, signals and gunnery. Tom Williamson was put in charge of educating us mechanically, supposedly on the grounds that he drove a rather sporty car and gave the impression that he understood how and why it went. I had been taught the morse code and had actually mixed at Catterick with the Royal Corps of Signals, so obviously I became the signal officer. We received our first tanks only nine months before war broke out and, since no one provided us with any equipment to use for training, we bought our own out of regimental funds. No one from above the regimental level made any attempt to supervise our training. We used our own initiative and got on with it.

Later we had good reason to be grateful to Ugly Martin for his single-minded determination to see that his regiment was fit for war. In the space of 15 months he succeeded in converting us from an under-strength horsed regiment to an up-to-strength and adequately trained mechanised one, overcoming in the process attitudes of mind as well as every kind of material difficulty. It was, admittedly, very fortunate that in the event we had seven months of more training in France before May 1940, but the solid base, created almost entirely by Ugly, was there.

The cavalry have long suffered from the gibe about the officer who was so stupid that even his brother officers noticed it. Whilst our conversation and breadth of interests were certainly limited, it was our background and upbringing rather than stupidity that made them so. Our profession, sport and way of life had centred round the horse, and from our earliest days we had moved and socialised with people of similar interests. Our brains had never been exercised or extended beyond certain restricted limits. For some of us that came later.

The regiment's pre-war regular officers could never have been classed as typical cavalry officers, whatever that may mean. All were markedly individual. John Anderson was far cleverer than any of us but used his charm and wit to conceal it. Mike Ansell was a volcano of energy and enterprise. Percy Legard and Tom Williamson kept us all amused with their guitars. Gilbert Monckton, son of Sir Walter, hid a variety of talent and intelligence under a wildness that sometimes bordered on eccentricity. Perry Harding was shrewd and tough. I could go on.

On the verge of the war's outbreak the regular officers were reinforced by the supplementary reserve officers, comparatively elderly subalterns such as Frank Stockdale, Humphrey Philips, Edward Paget, Mick Murland and Edward Barran. Then there were the 'dug-outs', officers who had served in the regiment in the last war. Even making allowance for the generation gap, we found them astonishing; agreeable, amiable old gentlemen but conversationally capable of little more than grunts until after a few strong whiskies their mental processes had limbered up enough to manage reminiscences of polo matches of long ago. A few whiskies later and they would suggest debagging the second-in-command, whom they still saw as the unpopular subaltern he had been in their day. They were speedily dispersed to suitable tasks elsewhere but one remained, the admirable Bill Barraclough, fatherly, imperturbable and the perfect choice for command of the Headquarters squadron, which was designed for administration and included the supply vehicles.

The best of the rank and file, old-style cavalrymen, were readily adaptable to mechanisation. They had the sense to realise that the tactics of a mechanised regiment would be much the same as those of the cavalry, with horses replaced by machines about which they now had to learn. They were regular cavalrymen of many years service, for whom the regiment was their life. Their devotion and loyalty rendered all doubt superfluous; their regiment wanted them to make this change in their lives; it was the best cavalry regiment in the army and now they would make it the best mechanised regiment.

They had the authority and personality to instil the same feeling into the new arrivals, militia men – for the government had at last nerved itself to introduce National Service – and reservists. All over the British Army the same example was doubtless being set by its non-commissioned officers. In my regiment I particularly recall Jack Clayton, Corporal Clayton in the first troop I commanded. Loyal, tough and brave, humorous and compassionate, he earned a Military Medal and became regimental sergeant major. Men like him won us the war.

As officers our relationship with the men was a good deal more formal and distant than it could ever be now because we lived very different lives. The men did not expect any other attitude from us, and were shocked if an officer became too familiar – but they had very definite ways of indicating that their officer was not finding favour with them. They soon divined whether an officer was up to his job and was interested in looking after them and if he passed the test the prevailing atmosphere was a joy to experience – team spirit at its best, lightened by much leg-pulling and joking and often resulting in friendships that endured.

The word man-management was not in our dictionary. If care of our men was not an automatic impulse, the lesson was soon learnt from our superiors. There is no reason to feel particularly smug about this. The officer/man relationship of the 1930s simply reflected the prevailing social attitudes. But at least in our regiment, and doubtless elsewhere in the army, we tried to display these attitudes at their best.

Just over 15 months after we had paraded for the last time on horses we paraded again as a mechanised regiment, this time for formation training with the 4th Division at Shorncliffe. After two days at camp the news of the Hitler/Stalin pact broke and we returned to mobilise for war. Reservists – old dogs not all capable of learning new tricks but in surprisingly high good humour – poured into the barracks. Ugly Martin departed on promotion, and Jack Anstice, with whom I was to be closely associated, took over. Mike Ansell became second-in-command. Soon we were listening to the reedy voice of Mr Chamberlain telling us on the officers mess wireless set that we were at war with Germany.

My generation did not share the gloom of our parents. Officers with wives and families were subdued and thoughtful, but the unmarried young, though they tried to assume a sober and portentous bearing, were inwardly excited. We discounted the oft-quoted story of the British motorist in Germany who had run into a German tank and found it to be made of plywood, and at the back of our minds we accepted the prevailing view that bombs and poison gas would soon be raining down upon us. We had to admit to ourselves that the future might be unpleasant and dangerous, but with the optimism of youth we set off into the unknown with the same excitement, enthusiasm and merciful lack of imagination that, I expect, most young professional soldiers feel as they go off for the first time to war.

The British Expeditionary Force assembled with commendable despatch in France. By the end of September we were clattering along in our troop train, singing 'Roll Out The Barrel', to our destination, a village on the outskirts of Lille. Here we settled into a countryside peopled with ghosts from Flanders fields, rattling in our tanks and carriers through villages which had once been melancholy household names – La Bassée, Armentières, Vimy, Aubers. There were reports of panzer divisions concentrating across the frontier, alarmist rumours from neutral Belgium, reconnaissance flights by German aircraft – quite enough to keep us on our toes.

We were much luckier than the infantry, who had to combine their training with belated and only moderately successful attempts to prolong the Maginot line along the Belgian frontier. It was not possible, with the best will in the world, to become particularly enthusiastic about this project, for it was well known that as soon as the 'balloon went up' we were to leave these defences far behind us and advance to engage the Germans in the open country of central Belgium. In the event, to few people's surprise, these defences played almost no part in the battle later on.

At night the officers of the BEF converged upon the fleshpots of Lille. The soldiers could not afford the taxis and had to be content with the occasional military 'passion wagon'. The way was thus left clear for all too many officers to demonstrate that the British consider good manners are for home consumption only; 'abroad' is different. Officers resembling Captain Mainwaring of Dad's Army , normally paragons of respectability, could be seen reeling lasciviously about the bars and nightspots, and the Lillois began to realise that they had bitten off more than they could chew. It was not long before the authorities imposed a curfew and required the Services to be out of Lille by midnight.

We did not take much notice of this curfew, merely ensuring that wherever we went the doors were firmly locked behind us. One night Gerald Kildare and I were still in one of our favourite establishments long after we should have been, when there was a loud knock on the door. The military police, suspicious, demanded entry. Madame engineered our exit through a trap door on to the roof before she allowed the red-caps to enter. They did not take long to discover our escape route, and clambered through the trap door to effect an arrest. We fled away across the rooftops, with our pursuers loudly demanding our surrender, but we were more agile round the chimney pots and over the hazards of 'les toits de Lille' and in due course evaded them. Some thirty years later, when I had the honour of being the Colonel Commandant of the Royal Military Police, I considered on one social occasion telling them this story, but on the whole decided not to.

I managed a few days at home. The Bicester hounds were still hunting but the atmosphere was sadly changed. My father and Bob Field-Marsham were away soldiering, the field was much depleted and Clarence Johnson, though pleased to welcome me back, had the air of one whose life's work was almost over. Even the wonderful sounds that he could conjure from his horn seemed to have a tang of melancholy.

The local young ladies had been swallowed up by war work. Some had repaired to Caversfield House where they drove the dashing young RAF officers from Bicester aerodrome. They found many of these officers all too glamorous. Many years later, when serving in the Ministry of Defence, I was talking to a very senior air marshal when Caversfield was mentioned. 'Did I know Miss X?' he asked somewhat diffidently, and when I said I knew her well and still saw her occasionally, a look of alarm crossed those distinguished features and he changed the subject. Some of the local girls took up more serious war work. One of the mothers told me, lowering her voice confidentially, 'Oh yes, of course, Delia is doing something hush-hush at Blenheim.' It was all much changed, and I was not as sorry as I might have been to return to Flanders.

We had meanwhile been moved to a village much further from Lille than the last one, and taxis had become too expensive. For one expedition, which had unfortunate consequences, I managed to persuade the padre to lend me his car. Gerald Kildare was again my companion.

We were returning, for once perfectly sober, when a car driven by a Frenchman crashed violently into us. I can say with a clear conscience that the accident was in no way my fault, but the French car was a write-off and the padre's car, though still a runner, was much the worse for wear. Gerald had had his hand resting at the point of impact and it was badly injured. Obviously he must go immediately to hospital.

The French driver, a young man of about my own age, was not injured, but obviously could not be left where he was, so I invited him to accompany us to hospital before reporting the accident. He was not cooperative, indeed abusive, and a swift right to the jaw deposited him on his bottom in the road, where he lay moaning. I bundled him into the car and we drove off.

We stopped at an estaminet to ask the way, and Gerald, who was being very gallant but in great pain, came in and lay down on a settee. The Frenchman followed us and then refused to leave, so I left him there, delivered Gerald to hospital and reported the accident.

I then had to break the news to the commanding officer and the padre. Unsurprisingly neither were pleased. Nothing happened for a few days, though Gerald had to have a finger amputated and was sent back to England. It was the calm before the storm. I was accused by higher authority of inflicting grievous bodily harm on a French national and, even worse, attempting to shoot him. Apparently a couple of revolver rounds had fallen out of one of our pockets, probably Gerald's as he lay on the settee. After we had left the estaminet they had been picked up and used to fabricate a case against us, though neither of us had been carrying a pistol.

In my trouble I now felt the full benefit of the regimental maxim that as far as the outside world was concerned none of its members could be in the wrong. Any misdemeanour would be dealt with by the regiment and within the regiment. After that the matter was closed; any accusations levelled by outsiders against a member of the regiment were not only false, but an insult to it. I also saw a new side to Mike Ansell. I had always greatly respected Mike because of his powers of leadership and achievements, but now he went to endless personal trouble to see that the charges against me were disproved. He drove miles to interview witnesses, lobbied the authorities and meanwhile was kindness itself in helping to boost my bruised morale. His support and his energy on behalf of one of his subalterns revealed a facet of the character of this remarkable man which not many people knew existed.

Try as he might, I looked likely to face a court martial. It was not too difficult to disprove the shooting accusation since we were not armed, but that right to the jaw was another matter. To assault a French national, given the sensitive relations between the BEF and its hosts, was regarded as a serious matter. And so the case was assembled and submitted to higher authority at BEF rear headquarters at Amiens. Unsurprisingly nothing was heard for several weeks. Meanwhile the German Army took a hand by marching into Amiens where presumably – for nothing more was heard of the matter – amongst their booty were the relevant papers. So the great cloud of the Blitzkrieg had one tiny silver lining. It was for me the first of several occasions throughout my life when the Almighty has bestowed the most remarkable good fortune upon his unworthy servant.

So unconcerned was my commanding officer with this cloud on my horizon that he made me his adjutant. I had had only three years service by then and remained a lieutenant, but no longer was I ' one of the boys' and indeed never was one again. I became the third member of the regimental triumvirate with the colonel and the second-in-command. Shortly after this Mike Ansell left on promotion to become the youngest cavalry commanding officer. He took command of the Lothian and Border Horse in the 51st Highland Division, but all his high hopes and military ambitions were later extinguished at the débacle of St Valèry, where he was blinded and taken prisoner. Bill Bovill succeeded him as our second-in-command; he had been my first squadron leader and I knew him well.

Jack Anstice, the commanding officer, was one of the most complex characters that I have ever met. In his subaltern days he had been ridiculed, teased, abused and nicknamed 'Lucy'. He had developed an inferiority complex which he never lost; he was prickly, defensive and acted on the assumption that everyone disliked him. I found him kind-hearted and considerate, though a hard man to work for. He had fully earned his right to his present command for he was clear-headed, competent and, as the regiment was soon to discover, tactically brilliant. He was a product of the old cavalry school which held that an officer's place was with his regiment, and that the Staff College was only patronised by shits. Nevertheless his staff work was meticulous, neat, concise and clear. On principle he disliked those set above him and would sometimes treat them in an embarrassingly caustic fashion. He was fortunate to work under wise and broadminded commanders for most of his career but later on, when he became a brigadier, he met his match in the formidable 'Hobo', Major-General Percy Hobart, and came badly unstuck for a while.

In the spring of 1940 the regiment was lent to the 3rd Division for its manoeuvres. This division was commanded by Major-General Bernard Montgomery, then very far from being a popular figure, but even my commanding officer did have to admit that the general seemed to know what he was about. He was prescient enough to base the exercise on the tactics of withdrawal.

It was interesting for the first time to see a cross-section of the BEF operating in the field. It has been said that its tactical training was more related to the previous war than the present one, but since at the time we were not equipped for modern war it is hard to see how we could have trained for it. It is true that the BEF was more motorised than either the French or the Germans; behind the panzers plodded infantry almost entirely supplied by horse transport and the French also relied to a large extent on the horse. We had no horses, mercifully, but neither were we in any way equipped for armoured warfare.

In May 1940 there existed one British armoured division, but it was not ready for operations and was still in England. It only appeared south of the Somme in late May after the BEF had been evacuated. In the BEF were about 60 Matilda Ones when the battle began. Their armour was thick, but their top speed was no more than a fast walking pace. A single machine gun was their sole armament. They could support infantry against other infantry, but were helpless against enemy tanks. The Matilda Twos were only just coming off the production line. With their two-pounder gun they were a great improvement, but when fighting began there were far too few in France to make much impact. The light tanks of the four divisional cavalry regiments were only fit for reconnaissance. The BEF was therefore basically an infantry army supported by artillery, much as it had been in 1918.*

The German Army was closely supported by its dive-bombers. We hardly saw the RAF. British fighter aircraft were intended for shooting down other aircraft, not enemy troops on the ground. The bombers, somewhat irrelevantly it might be thought, were targeted far away from the battlefield. Land/air cooperation was, again, no further advanced than it had been in 1918.

Whatever its shortcomings in equipment and tactical thinking, the leadership ability of commanders at all levels in the BEF was on the whole very good. My regiment went into action harbouring five future wartime commanding officers

*In May 1940 the BEF consisted of three corps (1,11,and 111) of two or three divisions each, together with three untrained territorial divisions.

and one wartime brigadier. Doubtless many other regiments or battalions could match or exceed this potential. Senior BEF commanders included Alanbrooke, Alexander, Montgomery, Dempsey, Horrocks – to name only leading wartime figures. The evacuation from Dunkirk was itself a miracle owing much to the weather with which it was blessed, but if Lord Gort, the Commander-in-Chief, had not taken the final decision to retreat to the coast against the wishes of the French High Command and of the British government, there would have been no evacuation at all.

The capture by the Germans of the bulk of the British Army of the day, with all the talent and potential contained therein, was at one moment not a possibility but a probability. If this had happened it seems likely that either the British government would have been forced to sue for peace, or Hitler would have nerved himself to invade and once ashore there would have been little to stop him. In fact, but for the successful evacuation from Dunkirk, we would almost certainly have lost the war within nine months of its beginning. We tend to forget what a very close-run thing this was.

In the spring of 1940 there were very few signs that such dramatic events were only a few weeks away. Indeed our life was singularly undramatic and enthusiasm had begun to wane. 'No war in the West' proclaimed the *Daily Express*, and when there began to be talk of starting polo, some of us began to be restless. Then, this time with no warning at all, the Germans really did strike, on the morning of 10th May.

Belgium and Holland, pathetically fearful of offending the Germans, had not allowed us to reconnoitre the positions we were to occupy. The plan was to advance to the River Dyle, beyond Brussels and astride Louvain, and to await the Germans after they had disposed of the Belgian frontier defences. By the evening of 10th May we were crossing the frontier on our way to our first battle.

The BEF, cocooned within its regimental and battalion families, was confident and cheerful. When we looked outside those cosy enclaves, however, a whiff of fear and defeat was already in the air. Even during the march across Belgium we were constantly hampered by Belgian soldiery and horse transport proceeding firmly away from an enemy still far distant on the frontier with Germany. When we arrived on the Dyle the first refugees were beginning to appear.

The approach of 'les Boches' for the second time in 26 years had induced such a feeling of panic that Belgian families had abandoned their homes and farms and taken mindlessly to the roads. If they owned a car it was crammed with the family and strange shapeless belongings, invariably topped by a canopy of striped mattresses tied to the roof. Cyclists, with their machines festooned with packages, wound their way through the column, together with farm wagons drawn by teams of great Flemish horses. Aged peasants trudging along on foot.

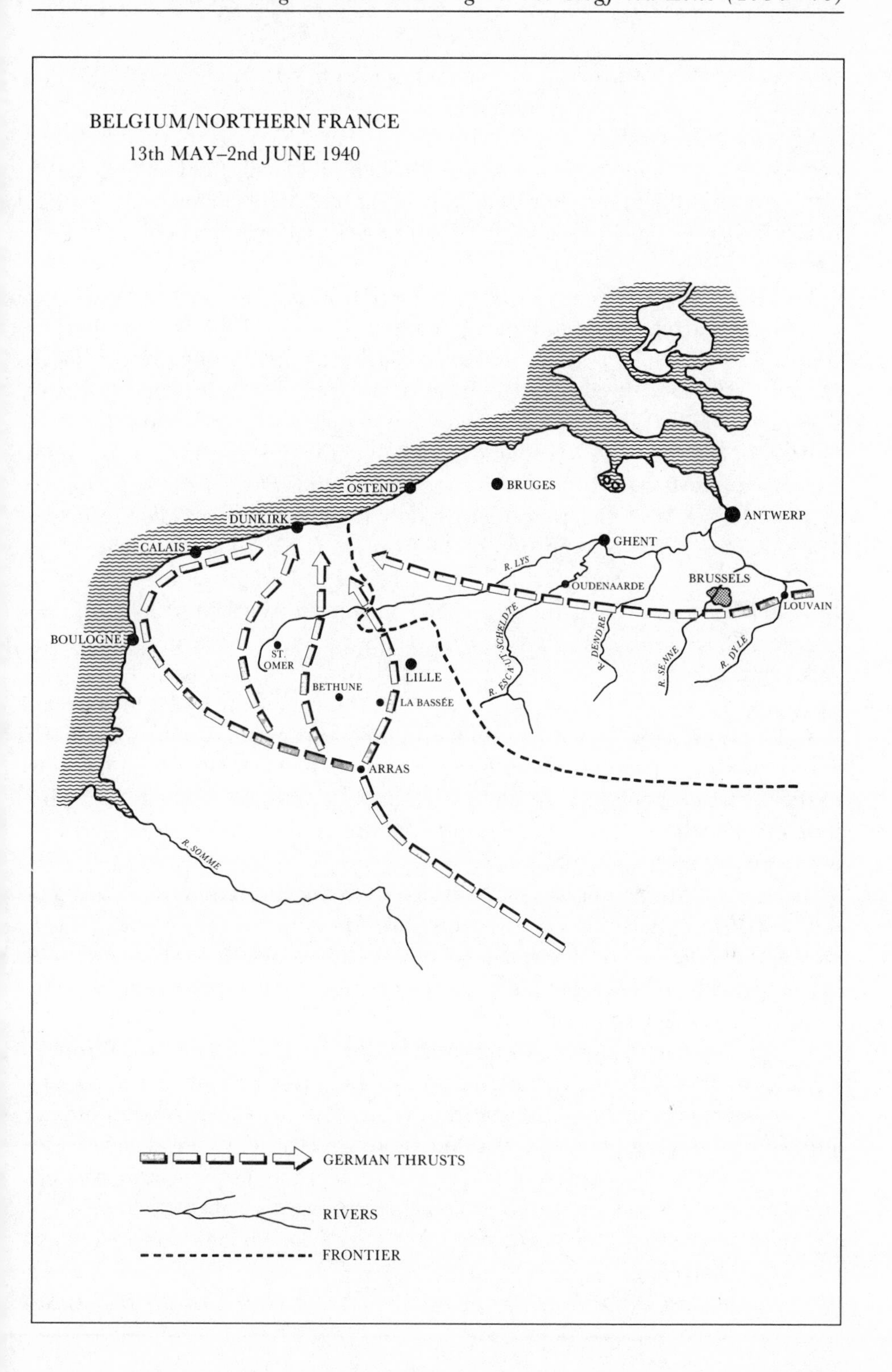
BELGIUM/NORTHERN FRANCE
13th MAY–2nd JUNE 1940
OSTEND
BRUGES
ANTWERP
DUNKIRK
GHENT
CALAIS
R. LYS
OUDENAARDE
BRUSSELS
LOUVAIN
BOULOGNE
R. ESCAUT-SCHELDTE
R. DENDRE
R. SENNE
R. DYLE
ST. OMER
LILLE
BETHUNE
LA BASSÉE
ARRAS
R. SOMME
GERMAN THRUSTS
RIVERS
FRONTIER

All were impelled by a quiet, pervasive terror inspired by memories of 1914 and countless invasions over the centuries.

Very soon these refugees were joined by Belgian soldiers, first in a thin thread entwined amongst them, then in a steady trickle, and finally in a flood of cavalry, horse-drawn artillery and horsed infantry transport. They made it quite clear that they had no further intention of fighting the Germans, whose arrival was imminent.

We had a comparatively gentle introduction into battle on 14th May. First came reports from our neighbouring regiment the 15th/19th Hussars that the enemy were ten miles away and advancing upon us. As evening drew on came sporadic rifle fire directed at us from across the river and some not very damaging shellfire. Finally, as the enemy closed up to the river, battle was joined.

It was not at first a very severe engagement, but the Coldstream Guards, whom we were supporting, started to suffer casualties and for the first time we had to accustom ourselves to hearing that personal friends had been killed in battle. The situation, at least on our part of the front, remained under control.

We were of course being duped. The Germans had not been sorry to see the BEF and its two flanking French armies moving forward into Belgium. We believed in our innocence that we were facing the main thrust of the German Army but, as we were exchanging fire with infantrymen across the Dyle, the panzers were striking through the Ardennes well to our south and into our rear.

Suddenly on 16th May we were told, with no reason given, that the whole BEF was to withdraw first to the Brussels canal, then to the River Dendre, and finally to the Escaut/Scheldte where it was to stand and fight. The divisional cavalry were to cover the withdrawal of the infantry, which was to be achieved partly in buses and partly by marching.

Just as we were digesting this somewhat bewildering information, the Germans put in a serious attack on the Dyle position. At one point they got across the river and although they were gallantly counter-attacked by the Coldstream with our help, the Belgians on our left departed in a hurry. A general withdrawal had in any case to begin forthwith.

On our way back to Brussels as rearguard the Coldstream marched through us. They had been through a rough few days, and I remember particularly one of their subalterns marching at the head of his platoon. I had last seen him at a deb dance in London, elegant, willowy and languid. Now he was clearly out on his feet, but equally clearly he was determined not to show it. His weary step and the cut of his shoulders were still elegant; the imperturbable and languid charm was still evident; willpower had taken over from anything so common as fear and exhaustion.

We passed through a Brussels apparently quite unmoved by the retreating columns of British and Belgian troops or by the approach of the German Army. Why the terror of the refugees from the countryside was not shared by their capital remains a mystery. We stopped on the outskirts of Brussels and a conference was called by our superiors.

Jack Anstice and I crammed ourselves into a small room in a villa with a number of red-tabbed officers poring over a confused jumble of maps on their knees or on the floor. They were putting pieces of talc over the maps and were marking with chinagraph pencils the routes back to the Dendre which the various units were to take. The lights were dim, the chinagraphs kept slipping. All too conscious that very soon I would find myself marking the maps of our own squadron leaders, I crawled into the melée and started writing the routes down in a pocket book, the scruffy and tattered pages of which now repose in the regimental museum. Just as I had completed this fresh orders arrived and all the routes were changed, so we had to start again. We emerged only just in time to position our squadrons along the Brussels canal as dawn broke and the infantry started to withdraw.

Everything went wrong from the start. We had been given two routes back to the Dendre. The 15th/19th were on our left, with the Belgians on their left. On our right were the 13/18th Hussars of 1 Corps. They had for some reason been given orders by their corps to withdraw an hour earlier than we did, thus exposing our right flank. This did not in the event matter but on our left the 15th/19th were soon reporting what they took to be large columns of Belgian infantry and armoured cars withdrawing and exposing their left flank. Soon after they discovered that these were not Belgian at all – long since departed – but German. Their flank was not only exposed; it was being turned.

Although the main German offensive was much further south, the enemy advancing against us were enterprising and aggressive. They had no tanks, and their spearhead consisted of nothing more formidable than armoured cars, anti-tank guns and infantry on bicycles or on motorcycles with sidecars. They were, however, used most skilfully and greatly outnumbered our little force of light tanks and carriers.

The 15th/19th were soon in serious trouble. Our squadrons commanded by Alec Scott and Tom Williamson began to be attacked as well, sustaining some casualties. These would have been much greater but for the effectiveness of our training – everything, wireless, guns, tactics, machines – all worked as they had done in those countless exercises during the past year. We had however been so outflanked from the left that the Germans were able to drive down the Dendre behind us and capture the two bridges over which the 15th/19th were to withdraw. Meanwhile the third bridge out of the four available to our two regiments was discovered to have been blown.

We remained on our position with some difficulty. An attempt by Perry Harding's squadron to move north towards the 15th/19th was firmly repulsed by nests of anti-tank guns, and he could do no more than remain protecting our left flank. When the infantry were all back over the river we withdrew to cover our southernmost and only remaining bridge. Eventually one squadron of the 15th/19th, commanded by Harry Floyd, extricated itself and wound its way back through our position. Behind them the road remained empty. A faint message, almost inaudible, came through from their regimental headquarters saying they were surrounded and would try to fight their way out. The dilemma, so familiar in every retreat, now presented itself; how long to wait before making the decision to blow the bridge and sacrifice those on the far side? Wait too long and you risk the worst of both worlds.

The shadows lengthened and the infantry battalion charged with holding the ground behind the river, commanded by my delightful Sandhurst company commander, Colonel Grant-Taylor, began to feel it was time the bridge was blown. Still we held our hand and hoped. Across the river the green and leafy landscape was lifeless. I borrowed a bren carrier and, not without some trepidation, drove over the bridge and down the road ahead. The silence and the total lack of any sign of life and movement were eerie. After a mile or so I reckoned I had gone far enough and stopped to look and listen. Through my field-glasses some vehicles on the skyline were visible and all too clearly they were not the 15th/19th Hussars. I returned and soon afterwards the bridge went up. Although there was never any chance that we could have come to the 15th/19th's rescue – and indeed only escaped the same fate ourselves after some determined fighting – it was a desolate moment.

And so, but for one squadron, the 15th/19th Hussars were surrounded and taken prisoner. The second-in-command, 'Looney' Hinde, swam the river and escaped to distinguish himself later in the war. Anthony Taylor, the adjutant, slipped out of the POW column, made his way to the coast and crossed the Channel in a French fishing boat. He was to command his re-formed regiment on its return to France in 1944 with the utmost dash and ability.

Before leaving the Dendre on the following day, we twice had to move our headquarters out of the way of some very accurate shelling and we were forced to realise that the Germans were being so ungentlemanly as to listen in to our broadcasts. So we decided that it would be wise to veil our speech, disguised so that the person addressed and not the enemy could pierce the veil. For example if you were trying to give Perry Harding your own position you might tell him you were in a village with a name rather like that of the winner of the last Champion Hurdle, hoping that the listening German did not have a Chaseform handy.

We now repeated the same manoeuvre back to the River Escaut/Scheldte with the difference that we had to cover double the frontage. Some of the infantry's buses were delayed, we became more and more dispersed and, by late afternoon, we could only communicate by using morse code. Sergeant MacMahon, the signal sergeant, tirelessly tapped out messages from the top of the colonel's tank while Jack Anstice fumed impotently beside him. It was a particularly tiring and frustrating day and not good for the colonel's temper. But as darkness fell the regiment had somehow struggled back over the bridge at Oudenarde.

The town and its surroundings were one large traffic jam. The Escaut/Scheldte was the line on which the BEF was to stand and fight. The rear elements of our corps, II Corps, had been joined by the leading elements of III Corps, who were expecting to go into action on the next day. There were also crowds of disorganised Belgian soldiery, expecting no such thing. The commander of our wheeled vehicles, Bill Barraclough, firmly wedged in the tumult, was the only calm individual in sight and strongly advised that we should seek harbour elsewhere.

So we motored out of this confusion for some 15 miles. There we found a large house with a park-like garden into which we drove, forcing our tanks and carriers under trees and into bushes. Inevitably there were soon furious screams from an upstairs window, from which leant a large lady with bosoms overflowing from her nightdress. We may perhaps be forgiven to have ignored her; none of us had slept for the past 48 hours.

I woke to find everyone else around me unconscious except for one figure, immaculate and walking thoughtfully round the garden – the colonel. I got up and greeted him but did not join him. His mind was clearly far away, pondering the decisions he might soon have to make, and assessing as far as he was able an increasingly uncertain future, a lonely man, never one for confidences or for sharing his worries with anyone.

It was by then 20th May, much later than we realised. Further south the panzers were approaching Arras, until recently the headquarters of the BEF. The War Cabinet was telling our commander-in-chief that the whole BEF must march south through the gap which the Germans had torn and link up with the main French armies. Lord Gort, with his regular divisions lined up along the Escaut/Scheldte under heavy attack, was unable to do more than launch a limited offensive south and ask the French to fight their way northwards towards it, which they never did.

The wide sweep of von Rundstedt's panzers was turning north, the hammer intended to smash us against von Bock's anvil spread across the Belgian plains. So far we had faced the anvil. Now we were switched to the path of the hammer, which was being opposed by untrained and ill-armed territorials, fighting with the greatest gallantry. Facing south and west along the canals of Northern France, these territorials were joined by every man who could be found in the back areas of the BEF, men returning from leave, medical orderlies, clerks, a mobile bath unit – reputed to have fought with much bravery. It has even been said that a 'posse of padres' went into action to defend a bridge.

We moved back into France, aiming for one of our more comfortable billets of the 'phoney war'. At the frontier post, ironically named Risquet Tout, two panic-stricken columns of refugees had met head-on. The French column had been propelled on to the roads leading north by disastrous news from the south, and consisted of terrified rich from the Lille area – large, glossy chauffeur-driven limousines containing large, glossy businessmen accompanied by large, purple-lipped wives, all in a high state of agitation. The Belgian column had taken to the roads because of disastrous news from the north and looked much the same as the pathetic rabble we had seen at Louvain. Both columns were at a standstill, screeching at each other. It was not, mercifully, our job to sort them out, and we took to the fields to bypass a scene which must have given thought to the least imaginative.

We found ourselves in corps reserve and for two days were able to relax. We even managed an evening in Lille. No panic amongst the restaurateurs – shortly afterwards they were doubtless just as welcoming to their German customers. It was a pleasant change, but our cheerfulness was somewhat forced. Although by now the news was very bad we still took refuge in what was then a widespread but totally misplaced confidence in the French Army – the feeling that soon it would counter-attack, as it had on the Marne in 1914.

One sunny morning the colonel assembled his regiment in the park outside the mansion in which we were billetted. He gathered us round him in the shade of a large beech tree – a slim, erect figure, fair hair turning grey, face calm and set, living what was certainly, despite later successes, his finest hour. A deep sense of occasion settled upon us all.

He started by thanking us for what we had done so far and described as far as he was able the dangers ahead. At this time there was no thought of evacuation; the possibility was not mentioned. He was sure that victory would come somehow, some day, and that the regiment would play a part in winning it. But it soon became clear that he was preparing us for what he believed at the time the fate most likely to befall us – encirclement. He was no great orator and he made no attempt to dramatise. All complexes submerged he spoke from a bedrock of simple courage, simply expressed in his closing words, 'And if we go down, as we may, I know that I can count on you to go down as the naval chaps do, with guns firing and flags flying.' From now on we were under no illusions.

We had left behind on the Escaut/Sheldte line the regular divisions of the

BEF. Heavily outnumbered, they continued to fight a brilliant defensive battle without which no evacuation would have been possible. By 23rd May we were on the other flank, charged with supporting the territorials, in particular the 46th Division, whose equipment and training were nothing less than a national scandal. They had been sent to France for labour duties and to train; they were armed with nothing but rifles, and had not even been taught section drill. The officers and men were magnificent, which only made it worse.

Now they were charged with defending the La Bassée canal against von Rundstedt's panzers and his supporting aircraft. Indeed we lost several men from bombing before we even reached them. We then had to fend off German tanks which our machine-guns could not penetrate. We resorted to bluff, to rattling round in the darkness in the hopes that the Germans might believe that we were an armoured division. On several occasions about 30 tanks advanced upon us. Our squadrons gave battle, doing little damage but not without some effect. On one occasion regimental headquarters found itself alone in a village with nothing between us and German tanks except one elderly French anti-tank gun manned by reluctant French gunners.

The fact that this gun never had to go into action, and that the regiment, though taking casualties and greatly outnumbered, was never overwhelmed, must say something about the lack of enthusiasm with which the German armour was operating. A really determined attack could have motored straight through us. They had of course come a long way and were getting tired. Anyway the northern battle was obviously won and they may have been anxious to avoid more casualties. Judging from an intercepted broadcast, our ruse may have worked as they obviously believed that a large force of British tanks was indeed operating in the area. Soon after this von Runstedt halted his panzers and left it to his infantry to finish us off. I have little doubt that without that decision not many of us would have reached Dunkirk; the Germans would have got there first and there would have been no evacuation.

The 2nd Division had now arrived to reinforce this flank and conduct what was to be the final defence of the La Bassée canal, with our squadrons to cover their withdrawal. Two battalions – the Cameron Highlanders and the Dorsets – were overwhelmed in a fury of flame and dust, most being captured. We were heavily attacked by medium tanks. The troops of Robert Crockett and Humphrey Philips took severe casualties, and Neville Usher and his crew were wounded and captured. Sergeant Bevan was also captured. Although severely wounded he later made an escape through Gibraltar which is a saga of guts and courage.

By the late afternoon the Germans paused for breath. Through the smoke and dust emerged a scene for a picture by Terence Cuneo – burning farmhouses the background for wounded and exhausted infantrymen struggling back, our surviving carriers bringing in more wounded and in the distance dive-bombers swooping down from a cab-rank to demolish a small town; each plane in turn rising vertically like a wood-pigeon in spring before flicking over to howl downwards and deliver its bombs. As evening fell it began to rain, very heavily.

It was on that night, 27th May, that, at least on our front, the retreat became a rout. The road on which we had been told to withdraw to our next position was already crammed with French – on foot, on horseback, in camions. 'Sauve qui peut' ruled. No one was the slightest bit concerned about anything but their own safety, and took no notice of anyone. At one moment, in pitch darkness and with rain bucketting down, the head of our column, already double-banked with French vehicles, met another horsedrawn column moving in the other direction. Amid the gesticulations and the furious Anglo-Gallic oaths the unfortunate horses stood, patiently waiting for their masters to tell them what to do. It was dawn before we shook ourselves clear.

We were then told that Belgium had capitulated and that the whole BEF was to withdraw to Dunkirk and embark. This time there was to be no Marne, no counterstroke, just defeat. Everything that could not be carried in our tanks and carriers was to be dumped in ditches; our wheeled vehicles, other than those that were to carry dismounted men, were to be destroyed. There was no question of a planned withdrawal by stages; we were simply ordered to make for the coast.

Everyone else had apparently been given this order and no other, for the road was packed with lines of vehicles from, it seemed, every unit in the BEF, all trying to pass each other and getting jammed in the process. Whenever attack from the air threatened, most drivers without hesitation bailed out into the ditch, bringing everyone else to a halt. Sitting ducks, we were a perfect target for the Luftwaffe, which it missed almost completely. As darkness fell it was clear from the flares going up on our flanks that the Germans were keeping pace with us, and we were all too aware that there was nothing to stop them cutting us off whenever or wherever they wished. Why they made no attempt to do so I have never understood. Dunkirk was a red glow in the distance, and as I, for about the twentieth time, got out of my tank to push an abandoned lorry into the ditch, I did not give much for our chances of reaching it.

Up to now it had been a disorderly rout, now it became a panic-stricken rout, affecting the British as well as the French. This unhappy campaign produced many examples of sustained and devoted courage, but there was another side to the coin. It was horrifying to see so many British soldiers in such a state of fear and indiscipline that their sole consideration had become their personal safety. Comrades, vehicles, weapons, all were abandoned. As we approached Dunkirk the road became wider; on both sides stood hundreds of deserted trucks filled with every conceivable type of military supply. No effort had been made to destroy them or their contents; some still had their engines running.

Of course, if civilians with little or no military training are called up to drive supply wagons; if their officers are equally untrained and probably unsuitable anyway; if after a few months since they donned uniform, they find themselves being bombed and shelled and see comrades killed; if they are told nothing and no one is in control, there is bound to be panic. The fault lay not with these unfortunate men, but with the authorities who sent them into action not as trained soldiers but as civilians in uniform. The picture was very different when the real soldiers appeared, but not everyone was a 'Dunkirk hero' by any means.

Before we had set off for Dunkirk we had been formed into a composite regiment, commanded by Jack Anstice, with two of our own squadrons, the 15th/19th squadron dismounted, and the remaining squadron of the 4th/7th Dragoon Guards. This included a subaltern who looked sixteen but was apparently a year or so older – Ian Gill, chirpy, competent and a future major-general. On our arrival we were spread out round the thinly-held perimeter protecting the embarkation. Bully beef, which I have disliked ever since, seemed to be the only available ration.

We were much better off in the perimeter than on the beaches, which were a frequent Luftwaffe target. However we did have to contend with infantry attacks, becoming more persistent as the days went by, as well as a general indecision about our future. At one time we were told that almost certainly the troops on the perimeter would have to be left behind, to hold off the Germans while the evacuation was completed without us. It was surprising how little this news affected us. By that time we were so used to having everything go wrong that could go wrong that, although outwardly we remained our normal selves, inwardly we were resigned, resigned to almost anything. Partly this was due to shame. We had been part of what we believed to be the most shameful disgrace ever suffered by the British Army in all its long history; how could we show our faces at home after this?

Every day for the next three – from 29th May to 31st – we were told that this was going to be the last. Every day the German attacks on the perimeter grew fiercer. Several more of our men were killed. Alec Scott and Perry Harding, at what was perhaps the grimmest moment of the evacuation, were told to report to the commander of the 46th Division, General Curtis, who was planning a counterattack. Before the conference began, some bottles of port were miraculously produced and glasses were raised to the general's toast 'The continued success of foxhunting'. Thus fortified they all went into battle.

The whole of the latter part of the withdrawal from the Dyle had been marked by extraordinary good fortune – that is, if one had been lucky enough not to have become a casualty. The British troops who had guarded the northern flank against von Bock experienced by far the worst fighting, but they comprised high quality regular divisions which withdrew in comparatively good order. The southern and western flank was our 'soft underbelly', where General Ad Hoc was in charge, and any determined German thrust could not have failed to have rounded us up. Now, having caught up with us again and given us some anxious moments, the Germans suddenly seemed to lose interest.

The attacks died down, the bombers went away. On the penultimate day of embarkation – 1st June – the troops on the perimeter were able to wend their way down to the beaches and sit there gazing hopefully out to sea, not without an occasional backward glance because by then the Germans could have walked down to the beach behind us. If this was an anticlimax, we did not complain. As I helped my crew smash up as far as we were able our faithful little Mark VIB, which had carried us for so many miles since it landed in France in 1939 without ever letting us down, I felt a pang. This disappeared altogether when I reminded myself of how I would have been feeling if it had been Big Ben that I was leaving behind on the beach of Dunkirk.

Early next morning there were cheerful British voices out to sea, hands helping us into boats, and no fire directed at us from the shore. Someone had been watching over us.

CHAPTER FOUR

Black and charging bull (1941–44)

'It's perfectly all right to be a stationary nude, but if you move, it's rude.' So sang Naunton Wayne at the Café de Paris, ridiculing the existing laws of public decency, one of the countless cabaret ditties with which, in our comparative idleness during the winter of 1940/41, we were regaled. My regiment was then located reasonably near London and we spent a good many evenings there on the tiles.

Girl-friends were plentiful in that twilight period before the gloom and restrictions of total war descended on the country. The young ladies local to our station in Northampton were reinforced by the sisters and relatives of the officers of the surrounding regiments, many of them operating with the same motive as the pre-war 'fishing fleet' in India, but with less restraint.

The Berkeley Hotel, then in Piccadilly, became a kind of officers club where parties assembled and drank champagne cocktails to provide a springboard for the evening ahead. Then off to the Four Hundred, the Café de Paris, the Embassy – semi-darkness, cheek to cheek, warm and expensive drinks, Rex Harrison being sick in the gents, and the music throbbing, often to the Cole Porter tune which so exactly caught the mood of the time:

It was just one of those things,
Just one of those crazy things...
So goodbye, dear, let it end,
Here's hoping we'll meet now and then,
For it was great fun, but it was just
One of those things.

It was all too easy in that steamy atmosphere to become more involved than was wise. When a lady friend began to ask whether it wasn't time she met my mother, the red light shone clearly through the haze of drink and sex. Emotional stress was by no means confined to the single. Many married couples became infected by the prevailing mood of 'anything goes' and danced off into the night with a new partner, for good.

The mood was hardly caused by the 'eat, drink and be merry' syndrome for the fate of 'tomorrow we die' was most unlikely at the time to befall any of the revellers. It resulted more from uncertainty, from a loss of direction, and from a very natural inclination to make hay while the sun shone. I made hay with the best of them, but it was not a period of which I am particularly proud.

After a period in which the regiment had trundled about in vans with slabs of armour fastened to their sides, we were to become an armoured regiment equipped with cruiser tanks, which in early 1941 had slowly started to arrive. Although they were much bigger than the Mark VI B there was little more to be said for them. They were thinly armoured, under-gunned, and the early versions, named the Covenanter, were highly unreliable mechanically.

There was also an influx of wartime officers, and these included three steeplechase jockeys imported by Perry Harding – George Archibald, Jack Bissill and Bryan Marshall. George was a well-known and stylish jockey who had recently won the Cheltenham Gold Cup; Jack had also made his name; the least known of the three was the very Irish Bryan Marshall. I first became aware that he was something out of the ordinary when he took part in a motor-bike race against some expert regimental riders. It was staged round a very muddy field. Bryan had hardly sat on a motor-bike before, but after a truly hair-raising and acrobatic ride he won it. Later, of course, he became one of steeplechasing's all-time greats.

I ceased being adjutant and went as second in command to a squadron*. We were now part of a new armoured division, the 9th Armoured. Its divisional sign

* The armoured (tank) regiments during the war consisted of three squadrons, A, B, and C, of four troops of four tanks each, with three tanks for squadron headquarters. Regimental headquarters was mounted in four tanks. Headquarters Squadron housed the administrative and supply vehicles.

was the head of a panda. This unwarlike symbol proved all too appropriate, for the division never went to war. There is not a truer saying, in my experience, that everything starts at the top. It certainly applied here. The division included battle-experienced regiments like my own with first-class officers and men. All these regiments, when they were belatedly given a chance to return to the battle, performed extremely well. They deserved a better fate than they got.

The leadership, at least in the early days of which I have knowledge, was relaxed in the extreme. The attitude seemed to be 'We have very good regiments in the division; they know what to do; let them get on with it'. This the regiments did, but the tempo of the normal working day remained at peacetime level only slightly stepped up; we jogged along competently enough but without much urgency. The hours were gentlemanly and could be managed easily however bad one's hangover. We needed galvanising from the top down and we never were.

By mid-1941, restless as ever, I had become convinced that the panda would never go anywhere. For once I was prescient. In future years, when armoured divisions were required for service overseas, the 9th Armoured was invariably passed over and a more junior division sent. After D Day it was disbanded and its regiments used to reinforce other divisions in France. This was however well into the future.

Meanwhile I was offered a posting which proved to be by far the most rewarding military experience of my life. A wartime regiment had been formed in late 1940 and called the 23rd Hussars. Its commanding officer had suddenly been posted in late 1941 to command his own regular regiment in the desert. He had taken with him one of the 23rd Hussars squadron commanders. Our Perry Harding was now appointed as the new commanding officer and he asked me to come with him to command the vacant squadron.

Though I never had the slightest doubt that I would accept, leaving the regiment and all the friends and loyalties of the last five years was neither easy nor happy. My officer colleagues were not impressed by what they saw as my desertion; they did not appear to be as restless or as dissatisfied with the present regime as I was. It turned out to be a much longer absence than I had bargained for. Apart from a period of a few months after the war ended, I did not return for 13 years, and then as commanding officer. My faithful soldier servant, Arthur Ward, now nicknamed 'Oscar', gallantly volunteered to accompany me to what he suspected was a vastly inferior set-up, and he never returned at all.

Together, one day in September 1941, we set off for Whitby in Yorkshire where the 23rd Hussars were stationed. I found my new squadron, C Squadron, eating their evening meal in a wood. After a day with them in the field I felt homesick for the practised skills and soldierly attitude of the regulars I had left behind.

Everyone was friendly and welcoming but unmistakably and unashamedly civilians in uniform.

The 23rd Hussars was one of the new armoured regiments which the War Office had formed in late 1940 by a stroke of the pen. These regiments had no history, no background, no 'old comrades', no tradition. One day they did not exist, the next day there they were. A major in the 10th Hussars and well known in the world of racing, Roscoe Harvey, had been promoted to be the 23rd Hussars commanding officer and provided with a small cadre of regular officers and NCOs with which to create his new regiment. One of the contributing regiments produced such a mediocre selection that very few remained after a year, and almost none after three. Ninety-five per cent of the 23rd Hussars who eventually went into action in Normandy had been civilians with no military experience before 1941. Most of these had been 'called up'.

In the January of that year the first of these recruits could be seen walking up the drive of a large deserted mansion in Staffordshire, the headquarters of the regiment to which they had been told to report. They came in whatever clothes they felt appropriate for such occasion – cloth caps, pullovers, overcoats, baggy grey trousers. They had been drawn haphazardly from all walks of life and from every corner of the British Isles. They were of all ages. Indeed a high proportion were in their middle or late thirties, or even early forties. There were decorators, carpenters, cobblers, clerks, farm labourers; some were small businessmen or shopkeepers used to exercising authority and to being treated with respect; others were men who had stood in the dole queue. They were a cross-section of Great Britain at war – unmilitary, peace loving, not motivated by any burning zeal – indeed far from keen to expose themselves to danger but united in a resigned determination to do whatever they were asked to do as well as they could.

To these men the regular army was something quite strange and weird. They had heard about it of course, but if they thought about it at all they had regarded it as rather a joke, useful naturally in an emergency but meanwhile nothing to do with them. On their visits to the cinema they had seen army officers and, particularly, sergeant-majors portrayed on film often as figures of fun, and now suddenly these people were real, and what was worse, in charge of their lives.

The nine months for which the 23rd Hussars had existed before I joined them had not been wasted. Like other similar regiments and some yeomanry (territorial) regiments – but no regular regiments – they had been formed into the 11th Armoured Division. Its commander was one of the war's 'characters', Major-General Percy Hobart of the Royal Tank Regiment. 'Hobo' had been one of the pioneers of the tank since its earliest days.

He was also of a quarrelsome disposition. This had caused his removal from command of a division in Egypt and his transfer to the Home Guard in the rank of lance-corporal. Winston Churchill, however, had heard of his forceful reputation and on coming to power had unerringly restored him to divisional command. In 'Hobo's eyes cavalry officers were highly suspect – too often languid, usually ignorant, insufficiently energetic, and – even worse – had sometimes been heard to express their distaste for tanks. He, an old man in a hurry, proceeded ruthlessly and vehemently to set about this army of civilians, commanded mainly by cavalry officers, with the aim of converting them into the finest armoured division in the British Army. Far more senior and qualified commanders than I would agree with me that he succeeded.

In appearance he was of medium build, trim, grey-haired and florid, with a hawk nose and hard eyes. Often these intimidating features hide a soft streak; it may well have been that 'Hobo' was sentimental about children and soppy with dogs, but if so we never knew him well enough to discover. What the officers in his division saw of him was in the image of his divisional sign – a black and charging bull that had come to rest in front of them and was asking awkward and probing questions, metaphorically pawing the ground.

It was all too clear to his target that behind his quickfire questions was a powerful and incisive mind, estimating whether or not you were up to your job. The general's bark was bad, but his bite was far worse. If he decided an officer was not good enough, he went at once. After every divisional manoeuvre a sizeable bag of commanders from brigadier downwards would find themselves surplus to 11th Armoured Division's requirements and be on the train to somewhere else. It was interesting to see how quickly all signs of languor dropped from those officers of the original cadres who survived the first year of the Bull.

The officers and men who had lately been civilians were never allowed to feel that they had been dragged from their homes and occupations in order to idle their time away in some unattractive military camp. They were made to appreciate that they were making a contribution, through training for armoured warfare, to national survival; that they were doing something worth doing, and doing it as well as it could be done. They began to work as a team, to develop a corporate loyalty, a regimental spirit which was to carry them through some very testing times.

Perry Harding was ideally suited to command this civilian regiment. Indeed for the past few years he had spent a good deal more time in the civilian world of racing than he had in the military. He conformed in no possible way with anyone's idea of a stage colonel and his mode of expression was derived more from the weighing room at Kempton Park than the Cavalry Club. Some of the snootier of the regular officers from the original cadres disapproved of this lowering of the tone and were apt to look down their noses at him, but in a couple of years most had been moved out and replaced by former civilians. They, and the soldiers of the regiment, conceived a respect and admiration for Perry which after a few weeks in Normandy had developed into worship. He had the quality – essential for a commander in battle and which he possessed to an outstanding degree – of inspiring confidence. Whatever he required his soldiers to do no doubts ever entered their heads. Their colonel wanted it done that way, therefore it must be the right way, and of course they could and would do it. This ability to inspire confidence was evident from the first few weeks of his command.

I myself was initially not so successful because I tried too hard to make my squadron react as if they were regulars. The regular cavalry habit of rapping out orders and then shouting if they were not immediately obeyed was a complete failure; it simply got backs up. But soon C Squadron, secretly to its gratification, became quite military, and the blinkers began to drop from my eyes.

My officers helped me in this for they were as diverse as the men. Some of my troop leaders were older than I was. The most impressive was Peter Walter, in normal life an actor. His repertory trained memory was capable of retaining simultaneously three major roles in three major plays. He looked out upon the world with humour toughened but never made cynical by the repertory circuit, with a smiling, reassuring kindness and helpfulness. His high competence included – surprisingly for one of his profession – skill as a mechanic together with a willing readiness to get his hands dirty. I never once saw him lose his temper, always a smile whatever his physical discomfort.

His troop revered him. His fairy godmother, however, while lavishing all these gifts on him, had left out that of personal ambition. After the war, as long as he had a happy life, which he had with his wife, Victoria Hopper, once Basil Dean's leading lady, and with his friends, and as long as he earned enough money to make a modestly comfortable living, which despite leaving the stage he did, he was perfectly happy. My Uncle Billy would have understood this attitude; I confess I found it a great waste of talent.

Peter's best friend was Bunny Jones, who ran a garage. Most evenings would find them both in the Whitby pubs, chatting up the barmaids. Bob Clark, who was a corn-merchant, would often join them, but the two younger officers were seen there less often. One was Jock Addison, who as John Addison has become a very distinguished composer of music for the cinema and television, with an Oscar to his name. He was then extremely young, extremely unsure of himself, extremely modest and extremely socialist. Another young squadron officer was Felix Hookham, whose sister was Margot Fonteyn. Not surprisingly the interests and conversation of this group of officers were somewhat different from those of a regular cavalry mess.

Another officer was Jock Addison's political mentor, Bill Shebbeare. This modest little figure concealed a remarkable if unmilitary character. Small and slight, with a head that seemed too big for his body, complexion pasty, his full lips could break into a most charming smile which lit up his whole face. He looked very like a garden gnome.

Bill had been President of the Oxford Union and was considered brilliant, both intellectually and as a speaker. Although the child of conservative country gentry he had become a socialist at 16, worked as a journalist for the *Daily Herald* and for his Trade Union, and was a Labour parliamentary candidate. He kept this innocuous if unusual background a closely guarded secret from all but Jock Addison. Presumably he felt that a regiment run by regular army officers would be bound to disapprove. The more percipient could penetrate the charm and wit of this engaging little man, and sense beneath them a formidable brain and a determined will. Although he and I became close friends he could never bring himself to discuss politics with me and clammed up as soon as the subject was mentioned.

I discovered later that he had a secret which at that time probably did need concealing. He was a member of the Communist Party. Now that we know that Denis Healey and other contemporary socialists who later became prominent were also members at the time this was, to use a modern phrase, no big deal. But at that period public knowledge could have risked his commission.

Another 'character' was our medical officer George Mitchell, who later became an eminent surgeon in Edinburgh. He was young, brisk and extremely fit. One day the physical training instructor thought he would take him down a peg and challenged him to a boxing match. George won it so decisively that whenever a return was suggested the instructor always found himself indisposed. George stood no nonsense with his patients. He certainly never indulged in the modern military technique of 'counselling', nor did he ever contemplate providing soldiers who had been exposed to stress with 'mental therapy'. A few brisk words from the medical officer were more than sufficient to calm quivering nerves and the impact of his personality was all the therapy they needed.

The 11th Armoured Division was initially equipped with three-man Valentine tanks, stoutly armoured and with a two-pounder gun, but slow. We trained on the North Yorkshire moors, which were strewn with concealed bogs. We spent many nights floundering about in mud attaching cables to recovery vehicles. It was not an ideal area but it served.

In the summer of 1942 we moved south to Sussex. The squadrons were scattered about in empty farmhouses and Perry's office was appropriately located in the weighing room of Plumpton racecourse. C Squadron's farmhouse was idyllic, with the South Downs looking benevolently upon it, and with an apple orchard in which to conceal the tanks from the Luftwaffe. The officers lived in the farmhouse and the men under canvas. This gave Jock Addison a problem with his social conscience. He insisted in living in a tent with his men rather than in the modest officers mess which we had established in the farmhouse. Fond as they were of Jock, his men found it a great bore to have their troop leader constantly with them. Eventually by some mysterious democratic process Jock's conscience was appeased and he joined us in the farmhouse.

Bill Shebbeare had become adjutant, and this released the previous adjutant, Chris Seymour, to become my second in command. The word 'gentleman' describes Chris exactly, considerate, charming, amusing and competent. He and Honor became life-long friends. It was a happy period, though it was still necessary to keep a watchful eye out for the Bull. There was a story that he had appeared unexpectedly one Sunday afternoon at a squadron camp (of another regiment) to find the officers lying about in the sun, and that fearful retribution had followed.

I had been grooming the brightest of the civilian soldiers to occupy senior positions in the squadron instead of the regulars with whom we were from time to time supplied. These were usually cast-offs and on the whole uncongenial. Indeed I only narrowly restrained myself from taking one particular NCO behind a bush and personally and physically sorting him out. In the end a very few remained. An honourable exception was Bill Shipton, who became sergeant-major of A Squadron and was eventually and deservedly commissioned. My sergeant major, Hartwell, had been called up into the 10th Hussars as a militiaman and was young for the job but excellent. Of the civilians, Don Smith, a shrewd and lanky Yorkshireman, was on his way to becoming a sergeant, as was the cheerful Glaswegian, Don McIntosh. Other personalities preferred not to be promoted, the most entertaining being young 'Mush' Wright, a London taxi-driver of unquenchable Cockney humour and a master of repartee.

We all, officers and men, began to know each other so well that the enforcement of discipline became unnecessary; indeed the word was never used. Our armoured skills were becoming high. All the squadron took a pride in knowing their jobs and not letting their comrades down – a pride based on trust, mutual confidence and relaxed but thorough military skills.

By mid-summer of 1942 we were suddenly issued with modern cruiser tanks and, almost imperceptibly, we became aware that something was up. In August we were packed off to Norfolk. There in November we heard that we were to be mobilised and sent abroad as part of Operation Torch, the invasion of North Africa. This was intensely exciting but we were to be bitterly deflated. Our tanks reached Birkenhead and were loaded. Then we were told it was all off – no more armour needed in North Africa. We returned to Newmarket with our tails between our legs. After Exercise Turnabout – as we called our abortive expedition – we were left gloomily wondering whether the fruits of all those years of training were ever going to be garnered.

Night life in Newmarket centred round the flat owned by Audrey Balding (later King). She was already semi-detached from her husband, who appeared only occasionally, and her small apartment seemed to be mainly furnished with low, comfortable sofas with accompanying tables on which to place the glass of gin. She was tall, dark and seductive, with long thin legs, and a natural hostess. Most of the 23rd Hussars officers would find their way to 'Audrey's' in the evenings and so did many of the Newmarket young ladies. She succeeded in making a particularly dreary period of the war fun for a great many people and if memories of parties there do not remain very clear, perhaps it is better sometimes that 'old men forget'. One of my troop leaders, Bob Clark, cheerful and likeable, even found a wife there, the attractive Diana Darling, daughter of Sam Darling, the trainer.

In July 1943 we moved again, back to Yorkshire, this time to Bridlington. We were to train across the Yorkshire Wolds, desecrating the East Middleton Hunt's fences and walls by driving our tanks straight through them. Many of the holes survive to this day. We were now to be equipped with the American Sherman tank, the victor of the desert battles.

Indeed we began to hear a lot about the desert. Bronzed and self-confident officers were sent to lecture us on tank gunnery, and there was an influx of desert commanders. Our new divisional commander was the 36-year-old Pip Roberts, the youngest major-general in the Army and preceded by a formidable reputation in the desert. Our new brigadier was our old friend and founder of the 23rd Hussars, Roscoe Harvey, fresh from a brigade command in Eighth Army. Both were vast improvements on their predecessors. Hope began to grow that something might really happen this time.

The Sherman was a five-man tank with a 75 mm gun and, like our commanders, a great improvement on its predecessor. In my own crew my right-hand man was Sergeant Bert Horrobin; in my long life I still have met no one more competent. In his twenties, from Manchester, with a maturity and presence well beyond his years, the role of squadron leader's wireless operator was child's play. He was also a very nice man. Oscar Ward, anxious for a more active role than batman, became my corporal gunner. In the driver's seat was Trooper Sam English, a tough and combative London bus-driver in his early thirties. Sam was one of those soldiers with quite enough personality and authority to be promoted, but every time he was given a stripe it ended in tears, usually because someone had emerged from a regimental dance with two black eyes after a disagreement with him. But he was a splendid loyal man with a caustic humour. A cheerful young lad from Liverpool, 'Buttons' McGrath, sat next to Sam in the co-driver's seat, acting as reserve driver, the hull machine gunner and principal tea-maker.

Together we took part in countless exercises and gunnery camps. We had been doing this for three years now. I was by then in my late twenties and would occasionally reflect what a dreadful waste of time it all was. Nothing ever is, of course, and I deserved no sympathy. Many of my friends were either dead by now, or had lost a limb or worse, or were 'in the bag'. All the same it was frustrating in the extreme to have one's youth drain away in a routine of which we were by now heartily sick, with no certainty that the skills we were acquiring would ever be used.

However we were beginning to realise that the waiting might at last be nearly over, for in early 1944 there came a visit from Monty, the newly appointed commander-in-chief. The performance was well known by now, but it was interesting actually to be on the receiving end – the informal wander round looking intently at the soldiers as he passed and then the summons to form a square round him standing on his jeep for his address. 'I wanted to have a look at you, and you to have a look at me – we have a job to do together – hitting the Boche for six', and so on. The performance was impressive mainly for the remarkable self-confidence and bounce which the little man exuded, though somewhat diminished from having been endlessly reported in the newspapers. Not all the more down-to-earth members of the 23rd Hussars were impressed; Sergeant Don Smith in his deliberate Yorkshire voice was heard to remark disapprovingly that 'the General seemed to have a very good opinion of himself'.

We were still a little suspicious of desert warriors, who had come amongst us with a distinct superiority complex and a certain air of condescension. We had a feeling, a justified one as it turned out, that lessons learnt in the sand might not always apply to Europe, and that after three years of continuous training we were not quite the tyros they thought we were.

The final placings in our team before the big match meant that I lost Chris Seymour, who went to command B Squadron. Peter Walter took his place as my second-in-command. Bunny Jones assumed the rather nebulous role of 'second captain' in squadron headquarters. Only Jock Addison remained of my original troop leaders, and with David King, a solicitor, there were two splendid young men who had arrived two years ago almost straight from school, Mike Pratt and Peter Robson.

Roscoe Harvey presided genially over the 29th Armoured Brigade. He was a fount of wisdom and experience, possessed of the relaxed self-confidence of the highest class of cavalry officer, fortified by years of command in the desert, swapping racing yarns on equal terms with Perry Harding. Behind his glasses twinkled a pair of shrewd eyes which had an alarming way of turning hard if something displeased him. Behind the racing jargon, the geniality and the short-sighted look was a formidable battle commander who bowed his head to no one.

Above him and eight years younger was our divisional commander, Pip Roberts of the Royal Tank Regiment. Short and neat, with a brisk, friendly and engaging manner, a tip-tilted nose which sometimes made him look like a cheeky and cheerful schoolboy, there was nothing intimidating about him at all. Someone with his outstanding record in command cannot fail to be tough, but Pip's strengths were his brilliant tactical sense, his inner confidence which he communicated to others and his ability to impress and charm his subordinate commanders. Most of these were considerably senior to him and men of strong wills and opinions of their own, for by that stage of the war all but the hardest had fallen by the wayside. Pip had them all, however self-willed and bloody-minded, eating out of his hand. He is acknowledged to have been certainly the best armoured divisional commander whom we produced in the war. So 11th Armoured were lucky.

In March 1944 the 23rd Hussars moved to what was to be their last station in England, Aldershot. The whole of the southern counties had by now been transformed into one vast military camp – British, Americans, Canadians, Free French, Poles – with their myriad equipment on a scale, ingenuity and range that were awesome. These were the fruits of years of research, and of trial and error often expensive in lives; the fruits of the inventiveness and the industrial might of the United States and the United Kingdom, all harnessed to this one supreme enterprise, D Day and the liberation of Europe.

The spring of 1944 held the British people, certainly those who lived amongst this mighty concourse, in a thrall of expectation and suspense which lifted them far above their wartime dreariness. Although we were on the threshold of what might be a terrible and for many a terminal experience, we felt uplifted and carried away by the mood of the moment. There had been so much suffering, so much heartbreak, so many tragedies and sacrifices, so much disruption, and now the time was at hand when we were to rise up and strike the blow which could end it all. The British people, for once totally united, held their breath and waited.

Aldershot was handy for London and we were in a party mood. This time 'eat, drink and be merry' was all too appropriate. The dear girl with whom I had walked out for the past year lived nearby, and our final times together provide the happiest of memories, for her, I hope, as well as for me. After I had gone we corresponded until the winter, when she wrote to tell me she was engaged to an RAF pilot – a very distinguished one. I was sad but we were not in love, and I knew she had chosen well.

On 6th June the waiting ended – D Day. The 11th Armoured was not involved in the landings but was to arrive in Normandy immediately after them to help launch the break-out offensive. Just before we packed up finally, we were told to leave behind for a few weeks what was described as the 'Left Out Of Battle' party. This was to be kept safely at home until it was needed as reinforcements. Since Bill Shebbeare was next in line for a squadron command he was the obvious person to be in charge of it and he took the news, predictably, very badly.

Bill was writing a book about the army at this time – another secret – and in his preface he said, 'Although I have been cut off from political life for four-and-a-half years, I have maintained my Socialist faith undimmed. My hatred of Nazism burns even more fiercely than it did in 1939, and my dearest wish is that I shall soon attack it – this time not from a platform in a market place, but from the turret of a tank'. He had been much distressed by Exercise Turnabout and this latest blow almost unhinged him. He was very bitter and far less sensible about it than the rest of his party, whose disappointment was in most cases clearly being mitigated by a slight feeling of relief.

And so on D plus 2 the 23rd Hussars rumbled out of the Cavalry Barracks at Aldershot and at long last went to war.

CHAPTER FIVE

D Day aftermath (June–July 1944)

Four miles inland from the Normandy beaches a burnt-out Sherman tank disfigured the pasture in which we halted for the night, a relic of the battle that had rolled on ahead of us. There was a large hole straight through the armour protecting the driver. Sam English looked thoughtfully at the hulk. 'They don't seem very frightened of these then,' he remarked.

Otherwise the war, passing speedily through the area in which we had harboured, had barely touched the green, rich Norman farmland. We had a few days respite before battle, which would be the first major attempt to break out of the beach-head. Meanwhile the neighbouring town of Bayeux, having enjoyed a trouble-free liberation, was doing a roaring trade with Camembert cheeses and slabs of bright yellow butter, with both of which our tanks were soon filled. We feasted on these forgotten luxuries on lovely June evenings beside our tanks, camouflaged with netting and branches along the thick luxuriant hedges. From now on we lived as crews – eating, sleeping, chatting together like the close friends we had become.

Our waterproof ground-sheets formed a lean-to against the sides of the tanks, and under these we slept. Very soon we would find ourselves digging deep cavities in the ground and running our tanks over them as a protection against

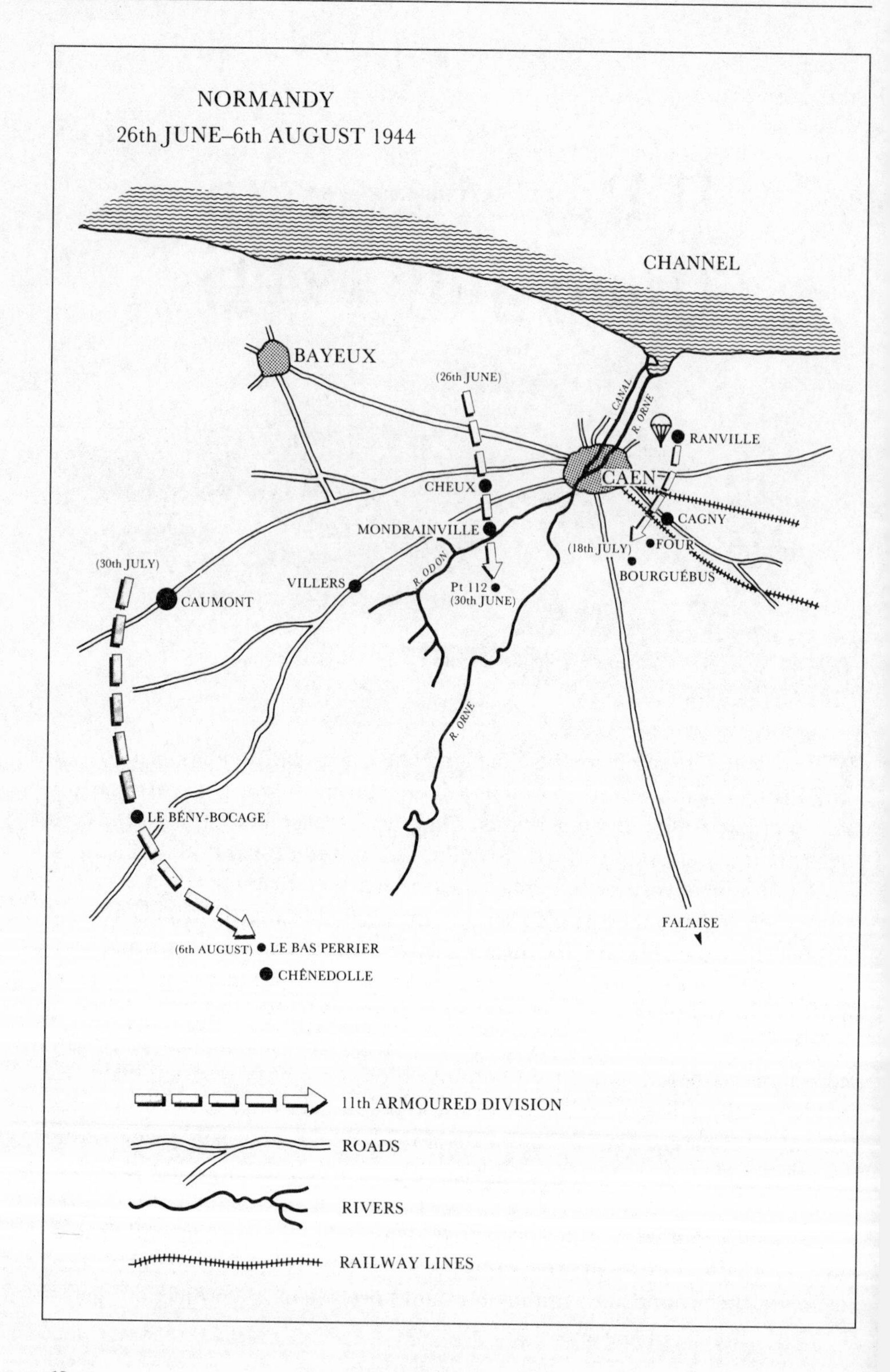
NORMANDY
26th JUNE–6th AUGUST 1944
CHANNEL
BAYEUX
(26th JUNE)
CANAL
R. ORNE
RANVILLE
CAEN
CHEUX
MONDRAINVILLE
CAGNY
(18th JULY)
FOUR
BOURGUÉBUS
(30th JULY)
VILLERS
R. ODON
Pt 112
(30th JUNE)
CAUMONT
R. ORNE
LE BÉNY-BOCAGE
FALAISE
(6th AUGUST)
LE BAS PERRIER
CHÊNEDOLLE
11th ARMOURED DIVISION
ROADS
RIVERS
RAILWAY LINES

shellfire – remembering the cautionary tale of the crew who failed to notice that the ground was soft and that during the night the tank would sink, with consequences we tried not to think about. For the moment we were all above ground, each under his own sheet. Lying awake on the evening before we went into action, the talk was somewhat subdued, and my only memory is of Bert Horrobin saying to Sam English in his slow Lancastrian voice, 'Well, I can't say I'm looking forward to it much, but we've got to get it over with sometime.' Sam's reply was inaudible.

By the third week of June the beachhead had been crammed with reinforcements, with enormous quantities of fuel, ammunition and supplies. Although determined attempts had been made to enlarge the perimeter, they had been costly in lives and had met with only limited success. Now, on 26th June, the first large-scale break-out offensive was to begin, launched by two 'new' divisions, the 15th Scottish Infantry Division and 11th Armoured Division of the VIII Corps*. It was called Operation Epsom.

The 15th Scottish were to break through to a depth of about three miles and establish themselves on the main road running south-west from Caen to Villers. South of this road was a little wooded valley down which ran the River Odon. The 11th Armoured were to seize the crossings over this small stream, advance into the country beyond, where, to use one of Monty's favourite phrases, it was to 'crack about' and aim for the next river, the Orne. This, if achieved, would almost cut off the defenders of Caen from the south-west.

Before day broke on 26th June, the skyline behind us had turned into a flickering, rippling red haze as the 600 guns of the Second Army opened the bombardment. Waiting expectantly in our tanks we heard for the first time the continuous roar of massed heavy and medium artillery, the swish, swish, swish as the shells passed over our heads, and the ker-ump and the ker-ack as they landed a couple of miles ahead of us. No one was under any illusions that the 15th Scottish needed all the help they could get if they were to break the enemy line. The Germans had had three weeks in which to bring reinforcements across France, and it was known that the 12th SS (Hitler-Jugend) Panzer Division – audacious, professional and fanatical – was amongst them.

At first light the Scotsmen rose to their feet and, supported by heavy Churchill tanks with their six-pounder guns and flamethrowers, they walked forward into a savage baptism of fire. We moved up behind them. The 23rd Hussars were the leading regiment of the division, with the Fife and Forfar on our right. The rain that had fallen earlier was clearing, and it was not long before clouds of grey

* The British Second Army at the time consisted of two corps, the VIIIth and the XXXth, and held the eastern end of the bridgehead with the Americans at the western end.

brown dust enveloped each vehicle as it moved, covering everything, penetrating everything – eyes, throats, every crack or aperture, human or mechanical – rendering the vehicle in front invisible, but immediately telling the opposition that inside the haze there was a target.

We reached an unlucky village called Cheux, destined within the next two days to be obliterated. The process had already started and it was here that the war began for the 23rd Hussars. The bombardment in front of us was putting up a wall of earth and dust. It had torn holes in the lush hedgerows and stripped them of their foliage; the stately trees were beginning to asssume the skeletal look with which we were to become all too familiar; the greenery was tarnished by the dust thrown up by the explosions. Around us in the fields lay the pathetic brown and white corpses of the Normandy cattle, once magnificent and their farmer's pride and joy, now spreadeagled on their backs with their legs sticking up stiffly like those of an upturned stool.

A worse sight lay ahead of my squadron as it advanced in the lead. In the field before us lay literally mounds of dead bodies, the bodies of Scotsmen mown down in swathes by machine gun fire as they advanced in their battle formation – a scene that might have been taken from the battle of the Somme. For all too many of these gallant Scotsmen their first battle was their last, and this awful sight was to be repeated many times during the next days. In seventy-two hours the attacking battalions had been cut in half.

Ahead was the crackle of rifle fire and the sudden flare of a flamethrower. The undergrowth was blazing in the thick woodland ahead as were knocked out Churchill tanks. I was then ordered by Perry to bypass this embattled village to the left, or east. We were discovering that the bocage was very different from the Yorkshire Wolds or Moors or indeed anywhere we had trained – very small fields parcelled between steep banks on which grew thick, high hedges; visibility 50 yards at the most. Each tank would rear up until it was nearly vertical, teeter on top of the bank and then crash down on the far side. Luckily for the moment there was no opposition; it was difficult enough to keep four troops of tanks all moving in much the same direction.

In this close country we should of course have been accompanied by infantry. But lessons learnt in the desert still applied, and the 11th Armoured's infantry brigade was five miles away. It took two major Normandy battles to bring armour and infantry together. Until then they fought entirely separately.

We emerged into an open space, and about four hundred yards ahead there was a wooded hamlet called La Byude, suspiciously quiet. I told Peter Robson to manoeuvre his troop towards it, covered by David King's troop. This he did very sensibly and well. Then it happened.

There was an ear-splitting crack and a brilliant intense shower of sparks shot upwards from his leading tank. From it rose a wisp of smoke; then, very quickly, belching smoke tinged with flame against which human figures could be seen crawling out of the turret – a roar and suddenly the tank became a blazing torch. Lance-Corporal Hogg, the driver and one of those who had four years ago trudged up the drive on that first day of the 23rd Hussars existence, never got out but the rest escaped, two badly burnt. This, we discovered in the campaign, was rather better than par for the course. The average was two dead, one badly wounded and the rest intact.

We now learnt that despite the Sherman's many advantages it was what came to be called a 'quick brewer'; it burst very rapidly into flames when hit, much more so than did other types. We never discovered why. We heard later, without amusement, that the Germans dubbed the Sherman the 'Tommy Cooker'.

The hamlet in front of us now came further into life and was obviously well-stocked with anti-tank guns. David King's tank was hit and he was wounded. Peter Walter drove forward to see what was happening to the crew and his tank was disabled with its track knocked off. There was a loud crash and a shower of sparks on the side of my own tank but the shot did not penetrate. This little engagement, in which four tanks had been hit and one man killed, was the 23rd Hussars' first.

We were now withdrawn and the rain returned. Darkness fell at about 11pm and soon after 3am it was light again. During that brief period the supply trucks had to reach us, often after – and certainly on this occasion – a hazardous drive, and refill us; the tanks had to be serviced by us and we had to eat. There was thus only time for a catnap inside the tank but such was the flow of adrenalin that even after three such nights I never felt less than fully awake.

The next morning was spent on the outskirts of Cheux while the 15th Scottish attacked their last objective. The German Tiger tanks now made their first appearance. True to their name they were the kings of the battlefield, huge, heavily armoured and mounting a long and very powerful 88 mm anti-aircraft gun as their main armament. The short and much less effective Sherman 75 mm could not penetrate them, but fortunately we had been provided with one 17 pounder Sherman per troop. These could deal with the Tiger's side armour, though not always the front. The Tiger's younger brother, the Panther, with a long 75 mm gun, was almost as formidable. It had a sloping and very thick frontal armour plate. Even a 17 pounder had difficulty in penetrating it and our 75 mm had no hope at all unless it was lucky enough to hit a weak spot such as the turret ring. Its sides were much more vulnerable. We met the Panthers later, but now a Tiger saw our reconnaissance troop equipped with Honey light tanks resting in some trees and fired a round. It went straight through not one but two Honeys, killing the troop sergeant sitting in one of the turrets.

It was not the 'recce' troop's day. Soon afterwards we advanced with the Honeys in the lead, as the good training manual had directed. Never again. They were massacred by anti-tank guns and Tigers, and it became clear that in a serious battle the one thing not to do was to put them in the lead. Later we took their turrets off and only used them on a flank. C Squadron moved forward, and Sergeant Don McIntosh, directed enthusiastically by the intelligence officer, John Weiner, knocked out a Tiger with his 17 pounder. To level the score another Tiger destroyed Sergeant Craig's tank.

As the afternoon wore on the 15th Scottish were battling inconclusively in the village of Mondrainville, just short of the River Odon, and it was felt time that the 11th Armoured took over the lead. C Squadron was ordered to find a way round the village and capture the bridge. I felt this first called for a personal reconnaissance.

Leaving the squadron behind me, I trundled forward in my tank and entered the thickly wooded village, in which a brisk battle was still in progress, in search of the Scottish commanding officer there. Not surprisingly, in view of what it had been through, the battalion was a bit jumpy, and the sudden appearance of a strange tank in their midst made them more so. I lowered myself out of the turret to find rlfles and sten guns pointing at me in a thoroughly unfriendly fashion. I realised to my horror that I was wearing my Inniskilling green overalls, which the dust had converted into the exact field grey of the German uniform. Then and there I tore off the overalls and never wore them again. In such close-quarter encounters, orthodoxy in dress is best.

I asked about the bridge. They assured me it was still intact but held by the Germans. They felt we could rush it. I therefore told Peter Walter over the radio to bring up the squadron, and entrusted the lead to Mike Pratt. He skilfully worked his way down to the river bank and along it to the bridge. With machine guns spraying furiously right and left he charged across it, followed by the rest of the squadron. We wound our way, still firing frantically, up a twisty little road to emerge, as if by magic, into a lovely quiet, open clear countryside. Bedlam reigned behind us but peace, for the moment, ahead.

As we surveyed the scene a small Volkswagen beetle car drove straight down the road towards us. At a range of twenty yards the leading tank, commanded by Sergeant Hoggins, put an armour-piercing round straight through it. Amazing to relate, the driver got out unscathed and ran – with the sergeant, a Welsh rugby player, pursuing him on foot with a sten gun.

I was then able to take stock. We had emerged from the bocage and the ground rose in a gradual slope, covered in rough grass – no hedgerows, completely open. A mile away the slope ended in a summit on which grew a small, luxuriant wood. It was marked on my map as Point 112. It was obvious that anyone who took Point 112 would command the surrounding country for miles. It was equally clear that no one was in that happy position at the moment. I was tempted to call Perry to suggest that we should occupy it, but by then he seemed to be otherwise engaged.

Regimental headquarters and B Squadron were in the process of descending towards the bridge with a view to joining us, and the Germans had begun to react to our intrusion. Although we had bounced the crossing there were still plenty of Germans around it . Behind us, and on the radio, we could hear crashes and bangs and shouts, tanks were getting ditched, and German Panthers had arrived to augment the confusion. A cry of fury could be heard on the airwaves from Perry directed at his headquarters troop leader, 'Get behind me, you silly bugger, they're shooting me up the dock.' The intelligence officer's tank was hit and John Weiner taken prisoner – by the Hitler Jugend. He escaped and rejoined us some weeks later.

This was clearly not the moment to suggest taking over Point 112. By the next morning it had been occupied by the Hitler Jugend Panzer Battalion. So if we had been sitting there already it would have been an interesting night. It was to prove itself to be a key feature. So important did both sides feel this vantage point to be that it was another month before it was finally captured. By that time the perky little wood on its summit had been reduced to a few splintered spikes stretching up to the sky like thorns. The grassy slope that was looking so peacefully down upon us on that June evening then wore the grim look of another Vimy Ridge. On both sides of the hill scenes of carnage marked probably the grimmest fighting seen anywhere in Normandy. A monument to the 43rd Wessex Division, which finally captured it , now stands on the summit. But all this was in the future. For the moment the little hill was green, peaceful and untouched.

By nightfall most of the regiment had struggled across the Odon, together with the Rifle Brigade company. For the first time we saw German multiple rocket launchers firing, luckily over us, from behind 112. Whilst in no way as effective or terrifying as their modern equivalent, they were frightening enough, with their stream of flaming rockets emitting a weird moaning shriek which earned them the name of 'moaning minnies'. Otherwise in our bridgehead we had a quiet night. As dawn broke we noticed that two German Mark IV tanks – less formidable than the Panther but more than a match for a Sherman – had unwisely bedded down for the night only a 1000 yards ahead of us in full view, with their crews fatally enjoying a late lie-in. Mike Pratt and Sergeant Don McIntosh lost no time in 'brewing them up' – a phrase which now slipped readily off our lips as we became more sophisticated.

Chris Seymour was now ordered to establish B Squadron on Point 112 but by then, of course, it was too late. Tanks and panzer-grenadiers were dug in within the wood, and nothing we tried would dislodge them. After B Squadron had been brought to a halt on the northern slopes, we used medium artillery, self-propelled anti-guns and finally rocket-firing Typhoon fighters. B Squadron had lost some tanks and were now to be reinforced by two troops of what was known as the Forward Delivery Squadron.

This was a brigade reinforcement unit which was immediately available to provide tanks crewed by our own regiment for just such an occasion. The commander of this little force was Bob Clark, who, it will be remembered, had just found a wife 'chez Audrey' at Newmarket. What happened then was tragically all too typical of a keen commander entering his first battle and allowing his natural wish to respond promptly and bravely to conflict with sensible precautions. The ground was strange to him; he was not properly briefed and he had not the self-confidence born of experience to insist on being told where, and where not, to go before committing himself. The result was a fatal misunderstanding.

He motored up the hill as if on an exercise and innocently allowed his tanks to drive too far over the ridge and expose themselves. All were immediately destroyed and casualties were heavy. At about this time I had been told to move C Squadron round B and try to outflank the Tigers on the hill and on the way I diverted my tank to the pathetic group of survivors being tended by George Mitchell and his team. Bob was lying on a blanket and his body seemed much shorter than usual. With a shock I saw that both legs had been chopped off below the knees. He was unconscious and obviously had only a few more moments to live. There was nothing I could do.

We moved round to the far side of 112 and worked our way up to the edge of the wood, which was in fact the hill's summit. Inside it the Rifle Brigade company were having a fight with the panzer-grenadiers, and complained to me that there was a Tiger hidden in the wood making life difficult for them. I got out and went into the wood with them to try and locate it. Having discovered roughly where it was supposed to be, I walked back to a 17 pounder tank commanded by Sergeant Webster and driven by 'Mush' Wright. I stood on its back and we manoeuvred ourselves up to the edge of the wood trying to get a shot. German tanks were very well camouflaged with a kind of muddy matt surface which did not glint in the sun, and the Tiger's position was so much a matter of wishful thinking that for fear of hitting our own infantry I did not dare give the order to fire. Meanwhile the Tiger, very sensibly, sat tight. An exciting but thoroughly abortive interlude.

The whole of the north side of Point 112 was now a milling mass of vehicles, at which the enemy could not fire directly because we had forced them back over the crest line. Poor Bob Clark had shown what happened if we went over the ridge ourselves. Meanwhile we were running out of ammunition because our sole line of supply was the narrow shell torn corridor through Cheux on which the whole Corps was relying. None of our wheeled supply transport had reached us. The 3rd Tanks therefore relieved us.

So ended our first battle and we were able to take stock. For the first time, but certainly not the last, we stood with bare heads round an open grave whilst Geoff Taylor, our padre, conducted a service over the body of Bob Clark, sewn up in a blanket, and later others. The experience, naturally, was emotional and sobering, but when it was over quite another emotion took over – exhilaration.

In these casualty-conscious times this may seem surprising, even shocking. In the past three days the 23rd Hussars had suffered 80 casualties, and nearly half had been killed – nothing of course compared with the 15th Scottish – but even so nearly 20 per cent of our regimental strength. And yet we had a feeling of exhilaration. We found this entirely natural; it was caused partly by relief that we had been spared, but mainly because at last – at long last – we had proved ourselves. Our hard work, our training, our leadership had passed the test of battle. As I walked round the crews to say 'well done' their normal manner of humorous diffidence was touched by an almost arrogant self-confidence. They were real soldiers at last. Their morale positively glowed, and as I moved from crew to crew I warmed myself at it. This was what I had waited for all those dreary years, and it had been worth it. I did, however, retain a sufficient sense of reality to warn them that it wasn't over yet and that much remained to be done.

Soon after this the whole operation was called off and the division was withdrawn into reserve. Operation Epsom's success had been limited – no 'cracking about' this time – but now the high command had to try again, with a bigger, even desperate, offensive, Operation Goodwood.

The element of desperation and the form the operation took were partly caused by the growing shortage of British infantry. Their losses in the landings and in the bocage fighting had been very heavy, and back in the War Office the Adjutant-General was warning that not only was he out of infantry reserves but out of young men available for call-up.

The armour had meanwhile in the bocage inevitably played a secondary role to the infantry, and their casualities had been comparatively light. Moreover there were so many Sherman tanks pouring across the Atlantic that they were piling up in the depots; somewhat unfeelingly the word went round that Shermans were regarded as expendable. This factor, and equally the growing impatience of the Allied chiefs at what they regarded as the slow process of the break-out, meant that all three armoured divisions, the 7th, the Guards, and the 11th were to be used together in one mighty offensive. Its aim was not only to break out into the open tank country south of Caen but to attract all posssible enemy armour to the British front, there to engage it in a decisive tank battle.

While this was being planned I was sitting one afternoon having tea with my crew in a slit trench next to the tank. A despatch rider drew up with a message for me and the bottom of my world fell out. I was to hand over my squadron to Bill Shebbeare, report to regimental headquarters and become second- in-command to Perry. Fond as I was of Perry, I was profoundly depressed. Second-in-command is a thankless role at any time, but in battle almost a non-job; he has to be there in case the colonel becomes a casualty and for little else. But this was no time to feel sorry for oneself.

Bill Shebbeare had wangled himself out from England a week before he was expected, bouncing out of a passing truck one day with a beaming smile and armed to the teeth. Now he was C Squadron leader. Almost the first thing he did was to sit down and write me a note that I received sitting in my strange new surroundings and which I have kept. 'I do indeed believe C Squadron to be,' he wrote, 'the best armoured squadron in the army and everything I have seen of the men's spirit here confirms me in this. It makes me feel such a usurper to have taken over ready-made and without any effort on my part, a squadron that you have taken three years to create. I feel that when we go into action again that I need have no worries except my own ability to give them the leadership they deserve.' He concluded, 'I have always looked forward, and still do, to taking part in this campaign of liberation; but it never occurred to me that I should play a part so responsible and full of opportunity as leading C Squadron. If I have any success I shall owe it all to you and the spirit you have created here.'

East of Caen lay the comparatively flat open area on which the 6th Airborne Division had landed on D Day. Their bridgehead, which had hardly been enlarged since, was well away from the bocage west of the town in which the subsequent fighting had taken place. South and ahead of this eastern end of the bridgehead lay the plain of Caen, open tank country and the obvious objective for any break-out. For this reason the Germans had made it the strongest part of their front, and no serious attempt had been made as yet to attack it.

The forming-up area for our assault, restricted as it was to the landing ground of the Airborne, was going to be extremely cramped. A further complication was that every vehicle in the attack would have to cross the Caen canal and the River Orne, both immediately north-east of Caen, before entering this area; a hideous traffic jam was certain. To pass three armoured divisions over these bridges and fit them into this area before the assault began was impossible. So the leading armoured division, the 11th, was to cross first and form up, the Guards Armoured behind it was to get as far forward as it could before it jammed up against our tail, while the 7th Armoured – the Desert Rats – were to wait behind the canal and the river and cross when it could. All this was to be achieved in 'wireless silence' and at night.

A further complication arose on the day before we were to move forward when it was discovered that the division which had been holding the part of the line south of the Orne had laid a minefield in front of its position. Very belatedly, and secretly, lanes had to be made through it. Only three could be made in time, thus producing a further bottleneck.

The attack was to start on 18th July. On the night of the 16th the 11th Armoured Division was to move to a harbour area just short of the two water obstacles. Special camouflage officers made their appearance and it was impressed on us that the fate of nations depended not only on us arriving before dawn but being completely invisible by then. The night was dark, the dust appalling, the route badly marked and half the regiment nearly motored into the sea, but luckily a thick fog on the morning of the 17th saved the nations from disaster.

On that day we were told the plan. At nightfall we were to cross the river and the canal and form up on the edge of the minefield, where the lanes through it would be clearly marked. The 3rd Tanks were to be on the right, the Fife and Forfar on the left, and we ourselves in reserve.

The responsibility for the launching of this dramatic assault was in the hands of the RAF. The entire British Bomber Command based in England was to' take out' the German defences to a depth of four miles. Then the three armoured divisions were to roar out of the bridgehead, down the lanes through the minefield, fan out and aim for the commanding Bourgebus Ridge, seven miles into enemy country. We were not to manoeuvre. Each regiment, including its halftracks and wheeled armoured vehicles, would move in box formation, 30 yards between tanks. At all costs we were to keep going. Never mind open flanks; these would later be cleared by infantry divisions. The Guards and the 7th Armoured would be charging along behind us in similar fashion.

From our starting point the open cornfields sloped south down to two railway lines, then rose gradually to the Bourgebus Ridge. This feature dominated the corridor along which we were to advance. Tank country certainly, but the villages and hamlets provided ideal and mutually-supporting strongholds for enemy armour and infantry with their anti-tank guns. All was overlooked by the brooding ridge for which we were aiming.

The more we looked at this plan the less we liked it. Minds conditioned by desert battles had clearly been at work. However flat the cornfields looked on the maps and air photos, there would be ditches and potholes, not to mention the bomb craters. The air photos showed that the two railway lines ran through a combination of embankments and cuttings of unpredictable steepness. By the time the queue of vehicles had passed through the minefield lanes, it was hard to see how the prescribed tight formation could possibly be maintained, and how in any case the halftracks and wheeled vehicles could be expected to keep up with the tanks.

Bomber Command were to obliterate the defences to a depth of four miles. 'What support do we get after that?' we asked. 'Oh,' the reply was. 'You'll have broken clean through by then.' Pressed further, it transpired that the medium and heavy artillery, still having to fire from north of the River Orne, would run out of range some three miles short of the objective, and we should only have the light artillery which had travelled with us for support. In the event the German defences were far deeper than four miles and, when we most wanted powerful artillery, there was none that could reach us.

Pip Roberts, our divisional commander, was sufficiently concerned about the plan's shortcomings to protest to the corps commander. All the change he got was, 'Well, if you don't fancy the job, another division can take the lead' – after which of course there was no more to be said.

As darkness fell on the evening of 17th July, the division moved across the bridges and crammed itself into the forming-up area. Grotesque black objects loomed weirdly up around us – derelict gliders lying where they had landed on D Day. The traffic jam became total; we could move no further forward and we slept fitfully in our tanks for what remained of the night.

Dawn broke mistily, promising a gloriously sunny day. As the light grew stronger, it illuminated the whole of 29th Armoured Brigade spread out around us. For a square mile there was a solid mass of armour – tanks, self-propelled artillery, halftracks, scout cars, ambulances... Inside them were the soldiers, lately civilians, of the 11th Armoured Division, waiting to lead the biggest assault ever launched by British armour. The sun rose, the light grew brighter, and there we all were, motionless, sitting in the open and visible for miles.

Before us in the sunshine lay the smiling, calm Normandy countryside. Not a sign of the enemy could be seen in the cornfields ahead, not a sign that the arrival of this enormous mass of British armour had even been noticed, still less resented. The sunlit plain unrolled placidly before us in peace, unknowingly waiting for the executioner.

The approach of Bomber Command was low key. The sky did not suddenly become black with large aeroplanes. Gradually our ears caught a distant drone and every head switched to the horizon behind us. In the dim distance, high over the Channel, hung an almost indistinguishable dot. As if an invisible hand was pulling a thread of dark cotton from a reel hidden below the skyline the great black Lancasters came slowly, one behind the other, into view; hundreds upon hundreds of them streaming ponderously and relentlessly towards us, filling the air with the throb of their engines. High above them in the blue sky escorting Spitfires twisted and rolled like silver fish. This vast armada passed over our awed heads, contemptuous of opposition and apparently unscathed.

For us this was the supreme moment of the war. It was for this that we had suffered the Bull, the years of toil and frustration, the boredom, the disappointments, the endless training, Exercise Turnabout. It was for this moment, the break-through into Nazi Europe, that we had stayed together when it would have been so easy to have sought adventure elsewhere. We stood up in our tanks and waved and cheered.

Before our eyes the quiet panorama over which we had gazed erupted into swirls of grey and brown dust, convulsed as a boiling cauldron. With a drumming thudding roar the bombs obliterated it bit by bit from view until there was nothing left to see except whirling, agitated dust punctuated by violent flashes. After the Lancasters came the medium bombers, an unimaginable number of bombers, continuing to rain destruction down upon the now invisible countryside before us. For an hour or more, growing fainter as more distant targets were demolished, the punishment continued.

The last aircraft turned for home, but the air was still drumming and throbbing with explosions. Six hundred guns had taken over, the prelude to the rolling barrage which would be our cue. All around me crews were settling into their turrets, adjusting their helmets and headsets, commanders shuffling with their mapboards and telling their drivers to start up. Behind regimental headquarters was my late squadron, and my late tank. Bill Shebbeare, unrecognisable beneath helmet and goggles, returned my wave cheerfully; Sam English gave me a parting grin as he disappeared beneath his hatch.

Before us the leading regiments were beginning to move, clouds of blue exhaust and dust were rising as the Shermans revved up their engines, and the medley of assorted accompanying vehicles jolted and jerked forward behind them.

The minefield's lanes were clearly marked, but we had to proceed through the lanes in single file and then fan out into our close formation. As we had foreseen this idea never had a hope of working. The leading tanks were trying to keep up with the barrage and their supporting vehicles had no chance whatever of staying within their regimental boxes. They straggled along behind as best they could. By the time we had emerged from the minefield the leading regiments were at least a mile ahead of us instead of the prescribed 300 yards.

Our flanks were enemy-held, so guns were traversed outwards. For four miles we roared through devastated, reeking, burnt-up cornfields, past smoking villages and wrecked farms. The bombing had reduced the German defenders to zombies – greyfaced, staggering figures making their way back to our lines. Others could be observed shuddering and shaking in their dugouts as we passed.

The first railway line was in a cutting which could be traversed by tanks but not by halftracks and wheels. There was a jammed up gaggle of these vehicles from the leading regiments in front of us waiting for engineers to blow holes for them in the banks of the cutting, while their tanks rumbled on far ahead of them. As we emerged from the country that had been covered by the bombers, it became all too clear that plenty of Germans had not been affected by them. Some Tigers were sitting in the village of Cagny to our left and these knocked out two of A Squadron's tanks. We were ordered to halt and engage them, which we did until we could hand them over to the Guards Division behind us. Regimental headquarters was then summoned forward to meet the brigadier.

Roscoe Harvey peered at us over his spectacles, a very cavalry red hat perched on his head – he scorned a helmet or a beret. 'I can't make out what the Fifes are doin',' he said. 'I can't raise them at all. I want you to take over the lead from them, and get crackin', our masters behind seem to be in the hell of a hurry.'

B Squadron followed by regimental headquarters surged forward across the corn like a battle fleet, with grey dust its wake instead of spray. We reached the second railway line to find an embankment easily passable by tracks. We halted and field glasses glinted from every turret as we scanned the view ahead. Two miles away Bourgebus Ridge frowned down upon us – its lower slopes were littered with tanks, too far away to identify. We motored forward towards them.

We could soon see the tail of the Fife and Forfar, sitting in the middle of an open plain which gave them no more cover than a polo field. But why was there no sign of activity and why in any case were they just sitting there? There was something unreal about their stillness. As we motored closer we realised that they were all dead, burnt-out. The only sign of life came from blackened, dishevelled parties on foot, tending wounded or trickling back. A scout car wound its way through the mêlée towards us, and there was John Gilmour, a squadron leader, begrimed, hatless, but imperturbable. 'I don't think we have more than four tanks left in action,' he said in a matter of fact way. 'Both the 3rd Tanks and ourselves have been stopped by armour and guns up there on the ridge, and as you see there's no cover, so I should watch out.' Almost simultaneously two of B Squadron's tanks blew up. Stationary and exposed in a cup below the ridge, we were sitting ducks.

Oh, for that medium artillery! Without it there was no question of pressing on and meeting the same fate as the Fifes, nor was there any point in staying where we were. Smoke dischargers hard at work we reversed back, firing as we went. A thump, and a fountain of earth flew up a yard in front of Perry's tank, clearly the work of a Panther which had showed itself on top of the ridge. It seemed to be time for the second-in-command to join in the battle. My gunner, no less a personage than the regimental sergeant major, took aim and fired. To our joy the Panther 'brewed up' – presumably we had hit the turret-ring. Well done, the RSM.

As we retreated to the railway line, with B Squadron losing tank after tank, it seemed right to get behind it and make use of the protection it afforded. Perry told Roscoe what he proposed to do and the brigadier was furious. Any mention of retreat always raised his ire and here was his reserve regiment, instead of advancing triumphantly up the ridge ahead as ordered proposing to cower behind an embankment. It took all of Perry's force of character to pacify him.

Back at Corps and Army Headquarters the news that was coming to hand seemed to be beyond belief. It was reported that this mighty mass of armour, supported by the most crushing bomber assault which the RAF could muster, had been brought to a halt two miles short of its objective. Not only was this unbelievable, they refused to believe it. Too much, and too many reputations, were at stake. 'Press on,' they insisted. 'We must get this ridge by nightfall.' The 11th Armoured Division now employed its only armoured reserve, C Squadron of the 23rd Hussars.

Over the air, Bill Shebbeare was ordered to cross the railway line, capture the hamlet of Four some eight hundred yards beyond it, and work his way forward from there towards the ridge. He was made to realise the full urgency and drama of the situation and the need for speed. There was no time for personal meetings, for tactical discussions, for assessment of the risks, for careful planning – time only for rapid instructions by radio as C Squadron bumped forward over the pock-marked ground.

'What would I have done?' I have often since asked myself, if I had been in Bill's shoes. The ground between the railway line and Four was open, with no cover at all. I feel that I should certainly have been wary before I moved across it, probed and prodded until I had found a way. But it is easy to say this now. The mood of the moment was against all caution; it demanded attack – violent, immediate attack. Bill Shebbeare, with the fire so long suppressed within him bursting forth, was certainly in no mood for caution; C Squadron rolled over the railway line with their eyes only on capturing the hamlet of Four. Inside it were Colonel Hans von Luck and his panzer grenadier regiment, bristling with anti-tank guns. Suddenly the colonel saw a whole squadron of Shermans advancing towards him at point blank range.

Peter Walter recalls that they seemed to come under fire from all directions at once. Mike Pratt's troop was the first to be hit; his tank exploded in a ball of fire and he perished with the whole of his crew. Jock Addison saw this happening, fired his smoke dischargers and told his driver to reverse, but he and his troop were easy targets at 200 yards range. He felt a tremendous blow on the thigh, the tank stopped and started to burn. He climbed out and, in a desperate attempt to rescue his driver, opened his hatch – both driver and co-driver were already dead. Jock climbed back into the turret, found the gunner also dead, but managed to drag out his wounded operator.

Through his periscope in the gunner's seat in the squadron leader's tank, 'Oscar' Ward saw tank after tank going up in front of him. 'Our turn next,' he forecast. Surprised at receiving no instructions he looked up at his squadron leader above him in the turret. Bill was transfixed, speechless, frozen, in a horrified stare at the appalling scenes ahead. Seconds later they were hit through the turret.

Bill Shebbeare and Bert Horrobin were both killed instantly and the tank burst into flames. 'Buttons' McGrath flung open his hatch to bail out and his revolver caught in the lip of the opening, holding him back. By now his hands and hair were burning in the intense heat. Sam English was also out and on fire; they both rolled in the grass. As they did so a flaming body fell from the turret, 'Oscar' Ward. He owed his life to the presence of 'Buttons ' and Sam to put out the flames. As it was he was very badly burnt and injured.

The rest of the squadron headquarters were in equally bad trouble. Bunny Jones's tank was knocked out and he was wounded. Peter Walter remembers something coming through one side of the turret and out of the other, and a dull thud on his left hand. His tank burst into flames, burning his face, and he bailed out. After a glance at the tank in front of him he realised he was now in command.

Sergeant Webster, with whom I had chased the Tiger on Point 112, was lying on the ground so badly burnt that he later died. His driver, 'Mush' Wright, remembers nothing of the impact; only the searing heat. If the gun of a 17 pounder happened to be traversed over the driver's hatch the driver was trapped, but Mush's prayer was answered and the hatch opened. Twice he tried to force himself out of his seat and twice his headphones held him back. His face, by now engulfed in flames, was a charred and unrecognisable mess. He joined the ever-growing party of wounded behind a haystack.

Having sent the sole surviving troop back behind the railway, Peter now tried to do what he could for the wounded, administering morphine and fixing shell dressings. His task was not made any easier by a useless left hand, a burnt face and heavy shellfire, but so many were in a worse case that he ignored his own troubles. Then – a most welcome sight – the medical halftrack, with red cross flag fluttering and George Mitchell's determined jaw jutting from it, driving towards him.

George tut-tutted a good deal about the standard of first aid given, re-dressed many of the wounded, attended to Peter's wound and particularly concentrated on the hideously burnt 'Mush' Wright. Jock Addison, himself wounded in the leg, had found 'Mush' lying under the haystack, in acute pain and in danger of swallowing his tongue. For nearly an hour Jock sat with 'Mush', his fingers thrust down his throat to prevent this happening, and almost certainly saved his life.

The memory of 'Mush' Wright's courage and guts have burnt deep into those who observed them; only an outstandingly tough and determined man, mentally and physically, could have survived. Peter had given him a shot of morphine to relieve the pain. 'Don't worry about me, sir' – there even seemed to be a grin on that ravaged face – 'It'll take more than them bastards to finish me off.' George realised that 'Mush' would not survive the journey back unless he then and there was given a hasty tracheotomy, which George performed amongst the blazing corn, the exploding tanks, the shellfire. He then bundled all the wounded into his halftrack and on the back of a disabled tank which was still a runner, and departed for regimental headquarters.

Despite George's urging that Peter's hand wound needed proper treatment and that he should also be evacuated, Peter Walter refused point-blank to leave. He was in command of what was left of the squadron, but had no vehicle to command from, nor was he at all sure what his command consisted of. He then saw a Sherman approaching him. From its turret Sergeant Don McIntosh leaned out, asking how he was. Hardly were the words out of the sergeant's mouth when a shell blew his head off. Inside his turret was his gunner, Corporal Walter Kendall. He had been in my first crew at Whitby and with his pale face and distinctly unmilitary appearance and attitude had not greatly impressed me. Now he coolly, with the operator, lifted his sergeant's decapitated body out and placed it on the engine cover, got back into the turret, picked out the anti-tank gun which had killed his crew commander and proceeded to destroy it. Peter then wrapped Don McIntosh's body in a ground-sheet, with great difficulty as one of his hands by now was useless, and marked it with his name and regiment, hoping that it would be found and properly buried. It was.

At least there was now, although presented to him in a most gruesome fashion, a tank from which to command. Everything inside was in working order, and almost immediately on the air he heard the urgent, enquiring voice of Perry Harding. Cheered by the colonel's words – for Peter admits that by then his morale was pretty shaky – he withdrew the remaining tanks behind the railway line. Suddenly George Mitchell appeared again to dress Peter's wound and see how he was – George had the knack of always being where he was most wanted. Just after he left, a few Tigers moved out into the open through the village of Four. At a range of 500 yards Corporal Kendall scored another hit with his

17 pounder on one Tiger's flank and knocked it out; it sat blazing in the middle of the destroyed Shermans.

Meanwhile a mile away down the railway line and obscured by a low ridge from C Squadron, A and B had been fighting all afternoon against enemy armour. As darkness fell Peter Walter came down the line to see Perry, who reinforced him with four tanks and sent him back. By that time Peter was in a pretty poor way, and Sergeant Don Smith, with quiet authority, appointed himself as minder, insisted that Peter had a few hours sleep and meanwhile took over the squadron himself. As dawn broke the sergeant became convinced that something sinister was afoot in front of him. Sure enough as the light grew stronger a sizeable force of German armour could be seen assembling behind the village of Four. He woke Peter, who realised that this was a job for the artillery.

But he had no unit call codes, which changed daily. All he could do was grab the microphone and violate every known wireless discipline by shouting over the air, 'Hello Gunners, hello Gunners, this is Peter Walter, can I have fire on —.' He remembers that Don Smith buried his head in shame at such abysmal procedure, but it worked. He was given his 'shoot' – luckily by that time some medium guns were in range – and the Tigers dispersed. Soon after this our position was taken over by the 7th Armoured Division, and Peter at last consented to be evacuated.

After Peter had left regimental headquarters on the previous evening, the rest of the regiment assembled in darkness behind the railway line, leaving H Company of the Rifle Brigade battalion to hold the position for the night. Just as we dismounted some very heavy shellfire descended upon us. Several were killed and wounded – amongst the latter was Chris Seymour. He was found lying on his back, quite conscious, but unable to move his legs. It was not until he reached England two days later that a microscopic piece of shell was discovered in his spine. Poor Chris, although he walked again he was never free from pain for the rest of his life.

It was now discovered that there was no chance of evacuating the day's wounded because, for the first and only time in the campaign, the medical services behind were swamped and unable to receive them. George Mitchell and his team therefore had to look after 70 wounded men for the night. His work can be described as heroic. The gallantry of the wounded themselves, with the less serious ministering to those with terrible burns and injuries, fills me with deep emotion to this day.

Two days later, on 20th July, the 11th Armoured Division, which had been reduced to a third of its tank strength, was withdrawn. Soon afterwards Operation Goodwood was brought to a close in a welter of high-level accusations and counter-accusations about what it was meant to have achieved and whether it had been a success or a failure. None of this concerned us. This time we experienced no post-battle exhilaration. Pulled back, we were only given a few days to re-equip before the third of our big Normandy battles, which this time at last did bring the big break-out.

Sitting in the inevitable apple orchard, with an ear cocked for the approach of a shell, I wrote to all the C Squadron bereaved. In due course I received their touching gallant replies, including replies from hospital, from Sam, 'Buttons', Peter, and many more, but not from poor 'Oscar' Ward, who was too ill. 'Mush' Wright spent more than six years undergoing plastic surgery and then returned to his London taxi. He shrugged off sympathy and was wont to comment, 'My wife prefers ugly men.' His unfailing cheerfulness and deep personal dignity marked him out as one of the finest characters I have ever been privileged to meet.

Peter Walter was awarded an immediate Distinguished Service Order. If the full story had been known at the time it should have been the Victoria Cross. It was good to know, anyway, that he was alive and safe. Sitting over my letters I allowed myself to become morbid; I hope not for too long because commanders, even seconds-in-command, on such occasions must play the cheerful optimist. I mourned particularly for my friend Bert Horrobin, a man of real promise, and of course for Bill Shebbeare. Often since, I have wondered about the career that German shell cut short; personally known to Attlee, almost certainly eventually a junior minister in the post-war Labour government, he had a brilliant mind and would have started on level terms with others of his age and with a Service background such as Denis Healey. Too nice, perhaps, for politics, but beneath the charm there was a tough streak. Anyway – it was not to be.

CHAPTER SIX

Normandy break-out (July–Aug. 1944)

The regiment recovered remarkably quickly from the shock it had received. Indeed it went into its third battle sadder and wiser, but all the better for it. It certainly did not approach its next operation, to use a ridiculous expression in vogue at the time, 'with its tails up'. The attitude was rather 'This is all very unpleasant, the chances of being sewn up in a blanket or incinerated in a tank are high, but the job's got to be done and we are going to do it as well as, or probably rather better than, anybody else.' Although there are cases – indeed I experienced two myself – when someone before a battle is convinced, invariably rightly, that he will be killed – a kind of premonition – most have enough built-in optimism to feel subconsciously that 'it won't be me'.

By the end of Goodwood and all those blazing tanks and recumbent bodies, it was natural to conclude that the 23rd Hussars had almost been written off. Indeed we had lost three-quarters of our Shermans but despite the human casualties it was surprising and encouraging to discover that the survivors far outnumbered them and were immediately ready to fight again. We did however require reinforcements, and to provide them other regiments were broken up. We received men from the Gloucester Hussars and from our old friends the 24th

Lancers, who as ex-members of the division had been brought up by the Bull, and were used to our ways. Others arrived straight from England.

I went to select two potential troop leaders from a pool of officer reinforcements. A group of young men, fresh from cadet training after school, presented themselves. I felt as if I was choosing puppies from a litter, and could only adopt much the same principles. I selected two pleasant young men for no better reason than I liked the look of them. They had never heard of the 23rd Hussars, but cheerfully got into my jeep with me; it was obviously a great excitement for them. They had had so little training that they could not be given a troop or even command of a tank, and they were fitted in to learn as ordinary crew members.

The new C Squadron leader was exactly the right man for the job. Len Hagger was an A Squadron man and had no hang-ups about past associations – brisk, tough, and totally unsentimental – exactly what was required. He was a hard man at a time when hardness was needed and he proved to be a brilliant leader.

Chris Seymour was replaced by Pat Wigan – a dear man. He was by profession a stockbroker, open, generous, self-mocking, brave and altogether lovable; one more friend for life. He would be the first to admit to a shortcoming; he was not quick on the uptake. Conversations between him and Perry over the air were not always harmonious. Perry would give him instructions to move to a certain point, and Pat, conscious that the lives of his men would depend on his interpretation of the order, would come back with, 'I understand you wish me to - - . Am I correct?' 'No, you are NOT correct, I told you to - -.' 'I am sorry but I still don't quite understand, you want me to - - .' By this time the air round the commanding officer's tank had turned blue.

Switching from the eastern side of the bridgehead, the next major offensive was to go in on the extreme western end, in the area of Caumont. Here the bocage was at its thickest; denser and far more extensive than any we had encountered before; lush, green, a honeycomb of small fields surrounded by high banks covered with foliage; tiny roads suitable only for farm carts, archways of leafy branches, the worst possible country for tanks, but, it must be said, worse still for the enormous German Tigers and Panthers.

Operation Goodwood had drawn away seven German panzer divisions to the British front and left only two facing the Americans. It had always been Monty's intention to weaken the Germans in front of the Americans west of us. Having achieved this a powerful Allied offensive started on 25th July on the United States sector. Two-and-a-half thousand American bombers unleashed their high explosive on six square miles of the German front. One panzer division was annihilated but unfortunately so were hundreds of American soldiers, the victims of what we have now learnt to call 'friendly fire'.

Immediately two panzer divisions facing our Second Army started to move back to the United States sector, and it became urgently necessary to halt and reverse this process by a breakout offensive by the British. The Second Army was to attack along a ten mile front. The 11th Armoured Division was part of the VIIIth Corps, which had spearheaded the two previous offensives. This time the Corps was to be given a flanking and secondary role to the west of the XXXth Corps, which was to play the lead.

Although we had been given a supporting part in Operation Bluecoat* the VIIIth Corps was still required to break through a powerfully defended line, and the thick bocage meant that at least initially the hard work and the danger would fall upon the poor bloody infantry. Our old colleagues the 15th Scottish were once more charged with opening up a hole through which 11th Armoured would pass. Once that was completed the 23rd Hussars were to team up with the 3rd Monmouths of the 11th Armoured's infantry brigade, a splendidly tough territorial battalion with spirit undimmed despite having already lost 240 men.

On 30th July we were battling through the almost impenetrable bocage – battling with the bocage more than with the Germans – and our attempts to help the infantry were not particularly effective. Mines, too, were a hindrance, and temporarily we lost some tanks – temporarily because a mine would blow a track off and give the driver a headache, but did not usually write the tank off. 'Three Mon', as we called them, splendidly achieved their objective, and then something very strange happened.

Suddenly resistance petered out; no opposition at all. The Monmouths climbed on the backs of our tanks and we actually and unbelievably motored – motored on through a lovely, peaceful forest. We pushed on for several miles in this delightful fashion and came to a small bridge in the woods on which was sitting an armoured car troop of the Household Cavalry.

A mile or two on lay the little town of Le Bény Bocage, situated on a commanding ridge, and we advanced towards it. Sergeant Johnny Sear, the troop sergeant of what had been Jock Addison's troop, commanded the first tank in. The inhabitants were jubilant but restrained. They told him that sitting in the main square was a German Mark IV tank. The sergeant promptly dealt with it and was then able to submit to the first of many subsequent joyous welcomes from the liberated; a photograph of Sergeant Sear, his beaming face emerging from a forest of embracing arms and ecstatic smiles, appears in at least two history books of the campaign.

* Operation Bluecoat. Under the Second Army the XXXth Corps comprised 43rd Wessex Division, 50th Northumbrian Division, 8th Armoured Brigade and 7th Armoured Division. VIIIth Corps had 15th Scottish Division, 6th Guards Tank Brigade, Guards Armoured Division and 11th Armoured Division.

For though we did not realise it, this was an historic moment. Le Bény Bocage – to us just another little town – was in fact the objective of the Second Army's attack, which XXXth Corps were supposed to take. Simultaneously the Americans were breaking out on their front. It was August 1944, described later as the day on which the battle for Normandy was decided. Of course we only heard the full story much later.

The 11th Armoured had attacked, by good fortune, on a boundary between two enemy divisions, and the bridge in the forest which we had crossed had been discovered by armoured cars to be undefended. Pip Roberts immediately realised that this was an unexpected opportunity for a clean break-through and, supported by his corps commander, Dickie O'Connor, had launched his division into the gap to a depth of some six miles behind the German lines.

Meanwhile XXXth Corps, the spearhead, was still stuck back on the start line. General Dempsey, the Second Army commander, now changed his plan; from now on there was to be a new spearhead, and for the third time in four weeks the 11th Armoured Division found itself at the sharp end of a major offensive.

It was not likely that the Germans would take very kindly to all this. With the American offensive gaining pace, Field Marshal von Kluge had a difficult decision to make. If this British break-out had not taken place, the task of the formidable IInd Panzer Corps of 9th and 10th SS Panzer Divisions, recently arrived from Russia, would have been to stop the Americans. Now the Field Marshal considered that the collapse of his front on the British sector posed the greater threat, and the IInd Panzer Corps, plus a Tiger battalion and a heavy mortar regiment, was ordered to take over the 21st Panzer Division already on the spot and eliminate this impudent British advance.

The Guards Armoured on our left were doing their best to come up and cover this flank but had met heavy opposition, and thus for some four miles we had no protection on either flank at all. This did not worry the armour particularly, but behind it there was a long tail of supply vehicles, and they were destined to have an exciting few days.

The 23rd Hussars' next objective was the Bas Perrier ridge some four miles on, another dominating feature. We set off with Pat Wigan's B Squadron in the lead followed by regimental headquarters. After two miles the leading troop met some opposition and our headquarters halted just short of a crossroads. On the far side of the crossroads I saw our medium artillery observation officer, who rode with us in a Sherman, enthusiastically firing his tank gun at the Fife and Forfar on our right.

I walked over the crossroads to remonstrate with him, and on the way back glanced, very fortunately, to my right. There, advancing towards me and only fifty yards away, was a Panther. By the time its commander had recovered from his surprise and let his machine gun off at me I was halfway into my tank, having broken all sprinting records. A high bank was between us and neither could hit the other. I summoned a 17 pounder tank from A Squadron behind us to the rescue, but as it was getting itself into position the Panther fired its main armament and down came a telegraph pole across the 17 pounder gun. The Panther then withdrew.

As we moved forward again, A Squadron was asked to move out on our left flank parallel with us to watch for similar activity. We then pushed on and were established on the Bas Perrier ridge when sounds of battle from the A Squadron direction could be heard. Waiting for them, as they spread out in a field, were a number of Panthers. The squadron had already lost several tanks on mines and now in a few devastating moments all but four of those remaining were hit and blazing. Jimmy Watt, quiet, stocky and ginger-haired, had only recently taken over as squadron commander. His tank was an immediate casualty, and the crew bailed out.

Jimmy, on his feet, realising that this was no place for a commander at this disastrous moment, ran back to his disabled tank and seized the microphone. Instantly a Panther put another shell into it; Jimmy was blown off and badly wounded. The Germans, having lost some tanks themselves, covered the ground with machine gun fire but Jimmy's driver pulled him back into a ditch and stood guard over him with a sten gun.

With great courage the surviving tank crews managed to drag the wounded to safety, and the reconnaissance troop was sent across to evacuate them. Only then would Jimmy allow his wounds to be treated and kept making pathetic and vain attempts to resume command.

On Bas Perrier ridge we could only surmise that something had gone badly wrong. We only heard the full story much later when the survivors had been extricated. As far as the events of the next few days were concerned, A Squadron was thus in effect written off.

On the far side of Bas Perrier ridge lay a village of the same name and beyond it another called Chênedolle. Approaching the second village the leading crews of B Squadron sensed trouble – no flags, no welcoming cheers, just a glimpse of white faces peeping furtively through curtained windows, a sure sign that the enemy was still there. On such occasions the leading tank commander has no choice – however certain he may be that a 50 per cent chance of sudden death awaits him round the corner, round it, however warily, he has to go. And, of course, round that corner in Chênedolle there lay in wait an anti-tank gun, and with a thump and a flash Sergeant Alsopp's tank was destroyed, fortunately without hurt to any of the crew. Indeed I remember the sergeant walking back past us with his crew, wearing the irritated expression of someone whose car had broken down at a tiresome moment.

By now it was getting late and we were told to go back to the ridge and spend the night there. It was covered, fortunately as it turned out, with orchards, large trees, and high leafy hedges, beautiful, unspoilt cherished farmland There we laid ourselves out to expect an attack from any direction, but mainly from the south, where we knew the Germans were only a mile away. We had now exchanged 'Three Mon' for 'Eight RB', the brigade's own rifle battalion who rode in their own halftracks instead of the tops of the tanks as the 'Mons' had done.

Back in Le Bény Bocage the supply vehicles for our advance were building up. The Panthers which had treated A Squadron so roughly had been identified as being the leading elements of the 9th SS Panzer Division. Between them and Le Bény Bocage there was nothing at all. Pip Roberts was understandably apprehensive. As he later said, 'The life blood of the division is in the tail,' and this tail was only two undefended miles from a panzer division.

The Guards were held up behind us by 21st Panzer. Their leading elements were a mile or so short of Le Bény Bocage, and a good five miles short of Bas Perrier ridge. XXXth Corps was still stuck. It was beginning to look all too likely to the British high command that the VIIIth Corps advance might also fizzle out or even be cut off. General Dempsey's patience ran out. He sacked the commander of XXXth Corps, and on the next day the commander of 7th Armoured Division was also sacked. None of this of course had any immediate effect on us.

Dawn broke on our Bas Perrier ridge and we could look for miles northwards across a lovely panorama of Normandy. Southwards we could only see dense foliage. Even the two villages below us were invisible. It would be all too easy for the Germans to work their way up through the trees unseen. Meanwhile the Shermans were in need of mechanical attention from the fitters, and these we called forward from Le Bény Bocage, together with an ambulance for which George Mitchell had asked.

Up on our hill the crews were peacefully washing or writing letters in the sunshine. A slight noise disturbed the peace and a look-out shouted that there were Germans in the valley behind us. Immediately tanks were manned. Across the valley to our north lay a small village, and a lane ran down from it to our hill, only partially visible through the high hedges. On the lane were, incomprehensibly, six khaki figures with their hands held up to their head. My first impression was that they were looking at us, for some reason, through field-glasses. A wisp of smoke was rising behind them.

All became clear when a figure in field grey, obviously armed, stepped into view, and just at that moment the leading jeep, which had evaded the ambush, arrived to tell us the story. The leading fitters' halftrack had been destroyed by a shell, had slewed round and blocked the rest of the convoy. The halftrack belonged to C Squadron and fitter Sergeant George Beresford, ever willing, always the last man out of those Yorkshire bogs, had been killed. Some of the survivors of the column escaped. One of the C Squadron fitters, a young, quiet man, pulled a wounded friend out of the burning halftrack into some cover and played possum. When he saw his opportunity he brought his colleague back to our lines, having shot two Germans with his pistol on the way back and produced a third as prisoner.

A Medical Corps private from the ambulance refused to leave a seriously wounded man, calmly walked past the SS with his patient and pointing to his red cross armlet found his way back to friendly territory.

We could now see large numbers of German infantry walking in open order down the valley behind us and moving into the village which lay across our only supply route. We fired our high explosive shells from the Shermans and the artillery joined in, but the country was thick and the Germans moved cleverly. Meanwhile we had to keep a close watch to our south as well.

Very soon Tigers and Panthers joined their infantry, hiding in sunken lanes and hedges and constantly moving their positions. A tank battle developed at a range of 2000 yards, which discounted our 75 mm guns. By now we had only nine 17 pounders left. The panzers had flashless and smokeless powder. Unless you could spot the tracer arriving and estimate where it came from, the German shell would arrive with no warning and accurate retaliation was difficult. In contrast our guns went off with a big flash and puff of smoke and there was no room on our hill to do much moving about.

A series of resounding cracks and sudden eruptions of dust round our position were our first warning, so cunningly had their armour worked itself into position. C Squadron was on the side of the hill which had plenty of cover, but B Squadron was unavoidably in full view from the north. The crack and whistle of enemy armour-piercing shells became almost continuous, high-pitched against the deep roar of the 17 pounders as they retaliated.

There was soon a crash, a spurt of flame and a cloud of black smoke from a B Squadron tank, then another, then another. Pat Wigan's tank was hit low down and began to smoke threateningly. Typically he felt he should ask the colonel's permission before bailing out, for which he asked over the air. The colonel's operator was not surprisingly busy, and all he got was 'wait – out'. Dutifully Pat waited as the smoke grew thicker, and then tried again. This time he was luckier and a swarm of maps, codes, papers and notebooks preceded the squadron leader's exit. He took command from another tank and twenty minutes later that was destroyed too, but this time there was no chance of asking anyone's permission.

Meanwhile many – too many – of our hopelessly outranged tanks were burning. The Germans then brought in medium artillery to support their panzers. The whole hill began to boil and shake with the gut-wrenching crash of heavy explosive, and the unfortunate riflemen in their slit trenches, unable to take part in this long range battle, suffered grievously. To make matters worse the shells were exploding in the trees with shrapnel whistling down into the trenches.

George Mitchell had his aid post in a sunken lane beside my tank, and one of his halftracks was blown up by a shell. It was proving a most unsuitable place for the many wounded lying in this lane and we decided he must move. At this very moment the Germans spotted regimental headquarters trying to hide behind its hedge. Both the Sherman tanks containing our artillery observers were knocked out. A motor cycle parked next to my tank suddenly jumped five feet into the air. Clearly, not only must the aid post be moved but command headquarters as well. Covered by smoke we retreated amidst a rain of different missiles to the other side of the hill. As we moved a petrol lorry received a direct hit and exploded with a horrific roar and flash. Wounded figures ran to and fro, silhouetted against the swirls of dust and flames. Amidst this chaotic inferno a trail of stretchers, borne by the surviving members of the bailed-out crews, signalled the move of the aid post to a secluded orchard on the other side of the hill.

George claimed this to be the perfect spot, until it was discovered that it was outside our perimeter and undefended. Exasperated, he refused to move again and spreading out his red cross he hoped for the best. As if on cue an American Thunderbolt fighter promptly swooped down upon him and discharged its rockets at the aid post. Another halftrack was destroyed, but no-one was hurt. Regimental headquarters now found itself in the unwelcome situation of being the first troops the enemy would meet if he attacked through the trees to our south. But we covered ourselves with branches and, like George, hoped for the best.

As dusk fell the fire slackened. We were cut off – indeed surrounded – but provided our ammunition lasted out we were not unduly concerned. The wounded, however, were a worry. George had the excellent Rifle Brigade doctor to help him, but they were running out of medical supplies. George was as always magnificent and greatly helped by Geoff Taylor, the padre. This quiet, fair-haired and diffident young man was clearly terrified, but displayed the finest sort of bravery in that wherever the battle was fiercest and the casualties highest, there Geoff Taylor would at once force himself to go. Soothing, comforting, cheering, this slight figure would move amongst the suffering and the dying, utterly and resolutely ignoring his own safety. It was of course a certainty that he would be killed, and later on he was.

News came from Roscoe on 4th August that an infantry battalion was to counter-attack the Germans to our north that night, and on arrival replace the Rifle Brigade. By dawn the 2nd Warwicks had reached the hulks of our fitters' halftracks, and found that the enemy, for the moment, had withdrawn. Soon the road was clear again and 15 ambulances were with us remarkably quickly.

Halfway through the handover between the two battalions – a highly inconvenient moment – we heard the unmistakable screech of 'moaning minnies'. Everyone rapidly went to ground but the next few minutes were unpleasant. The rattle of machine-gun fire confirmed that we were under attack again, this time from the south. There the trees were so thick that none of our tanks could see a target, but the infantry went into action very heavily supported by the corps artillery, their heavy shells bursting effectively in the two villages ahead of us – and in the trees. The Germans did not persevere, though they tried again later in the evening. Again without success.

Next morning it was sad to see how this lovely cherished ridge of rich farmland had been transformed. The trees and hedges had lost most of their leaves, burnt-out tanks smouldered quietly in the churned-up fields, blackened vehicles dotted the hedgerows with, beside them, rough crosses made of two twigs with a pathetic beret or rifleman's helmet resting upon them. Spoil from slit trenches was heaped between the tanks, and below ground crouched the infantry not on duty and the bailed-out crews, together with the drivers of the wheeled vehicles which had all by now been destroyed. The tank crews were tired but unshaken. Most had not spent more than 30 minutes outside their Shermans for the last 48 hours and had at least another 48 before them. No tank could move for fear of giving away its position.

During that day we beat back three further counter-attacks similar to those of the day before. One of them coincided with a visit from our brigadier. Even Roscoe felt it wise to dive in somewhat undignified fashion into a hole under Perry's tank. Indeed the refuge was soon bursting with visitors. We laughed at this when we emerged, but our smiles were soon wiped from our faces when we heard the cry that we knew, and dreaded, that we would hear one day – 'The medical officer's been hit.' George had been badly wounded in the chest. To see him of all people on a stretcher was a shock, for I do not believe that a braver or better doctor served anywhere in the Second Army. His replacement, a very good one, soon arrived and in battle you look forward, not back.

After repelling the last counter-attack the Warwicks managed to enter Bas

Perrier village, together with Ted Harte's troop from B Squadron. They were surrounded by German infantrymen in the village, a situation in which tanks are at a heavy disadvantage. Ted Harte handled his problem coolly and well, though his troop sergeant, Sergeant Pike, found himself having to fire three rounds at point-blank range without effect at a Tiger, which then contemptuously wrote off his Sherman. Despite all this activity the feeling grew that 9th SS Panzer Division might have shot its bolt.

Field Marshal von Kluge would have agreed with this assessment. 21st Panzer had been worn down by Guards Armoured and XXXth Corps, 9th SS by 11th Armoured, and of the IInd Panzer Corps only the 10th SS Panzer Division remained effective. This division was now ordered to wipe out the troublesome British on Bas Perrier ridge.

The British Second Army, meanwhile, confident that the enemy front was about to collapse, decided to start withdrawing the 11th Armoured Division to prepare for its spearhead role in the chase across France. The 23rd Hussars were ordered to pull back from Bas Perrier ridge on the night of the 5th August, and leave one squadron, C, behind temporarily to support the Warwicks. The Fife and Forfar, on another ridge further to our west, was withdrawn altogether.

Regimental headquarters stayed for the morning of the 6th August to watch C Squadron take up its new positions. Suddenly there was heard the unmistakable crack of an 88 mm from the south. For the first time a Tiger had worked its way into a firing position amongst the woods round Bas Perrier village. Although we were much too exposed from that direction, its attention was taken up by C Squadron's response.

It fired back and hit one of the self-propelled guns which had been sent to support us. This gun was surrounded by slit trenches full of men from the Warwicks. Seeing that if the ammunition began to explode it would injure them, the nearest troop leader, Peter Robson, and the Warwicks company commander jumped into the burning vehicle and began to throw out the rounds. The Tiger immediately put another shell into the vehicle and killed them both. So passed the last remaining officer of the C Squadron team with which I had gone into battle five weeks earlier – a fine, brave young man.

Activity then ceased and headquarters withdrew, cheered on our arrival in our new harbour some miles back by the news of a dramatic advance by the Americans into Brittany. We hoped for a restful end to the day, but we were disappointed. 10th SS Panzer had arrived.

At 4 pm on 6th August there descended on Bas Perrier ridge a desperate bombardment launched by every artillery piece the Germans could muster. The first concentration of 'minnies' landed slap on the Warwicks headquarters – not helpful for the immediate task of dealing with the panzer grenadiers who were creeping towards us in large numbers through the trees to the south. The Tiger that had troubled us in the morning reappeared with several friends.

The ridge exploded in a roar of competing artillery and tank fire in chorus with the high-pitched crack and rattle of rifles and machine guns. The Royal Artillery rose magnificently to the occasion, a shattering deluge of powerful shells exploding on the ground, in the trees and in the air.

C Squadron began to lose tanks and the Warwicks' leading company was driven back. Another company of the Warwicks was surrounded in Bas Perrier village, and Sergeant Don Smith's troop was sent to rescue them. By the time they had reached the houses only two tanks survived, Don's and that of Sergeant Fred Jackson, who in civilian life kept a pub near Hull. Fred's tank was a replacement in poor mechanical condition, and just outside the village it refused to go any further. Don continued alone and managed to extricate the infantry, though he found himself at one moment only 30 yards away from a Panther on the other side of a cottage. Machine gun fire was rattling against Don's turret. Neither he nor the Panther fancied moving out into the open; eventually somehow he extricated himself.

He was then called back to squadron headquarters by his squadron leader, Len Hagger, and on his way came across Fred Jackson sitting in his immobile tank surrounded by panzer grenadiers. Len Hagger, hearing that the tank could not move, had ordered Fred to abandon it and return on foot. Fred had indignantly repulsed the German infantry and now his squadron leader was repulsed as well. With the bloody-mindedness that lies not far below the surface of the Yorkshire character he abruptly declined to fall in with Len's order. He was not in the least certain what he was going to do, though he was quite certain about what he was not going to do; no-one would make him abandon his tank until it was blown up under him.

With machine guns blazing from their revolving turrets, the two sergeants dismounted with the rest of their crews, managed, although under fire, to attach a tow rope to the derelict Sherman and to tow it back through the mayhem into the squadron area, where the battle continued unabated.

The enemy infantry grew closer and began to creep round behind the position. The artillery guns must have been almost red-hot by now, but they kept up their incessant and effective drumfire. As the light failed the panzer grenadiers worked their way up close enough to start firing their hand-held bazookas at the tanks. The Tigers and Panthers continued to whack in their shells and one penetrated the turret of the tank in which sat, acting as the gunner, one of the two 'puppies' I had selected only a few days earlier from the reinforcement litter. He was instantly killed.

In our safe area some miles back we listened to the battle over the air with growing apprehension. C Squadron were losing tanks and the Warwicks were in retreat to the top of the hill. The wireless crackled; the urgent voices of the tank commanders were faint as they gave quick orders and information.

The artillery officer went 'off the air'. Len Hagger passed the fire orders back and forth. 'East 200 yards – no, now north 100 yards. That's exactly right, well done.' He was calm, determined, and splendid. The voices on the air grew harder and harder to distinguish through the evening interference on the wireless. The Germans were creeping up the hill in the fading light. The roar of the guns was accompanied by flickering red flashes as they fired. It grew dark. The defenders were withdrawn into a tight ring, infantry and armour together, all very tired. The faint voices now had a slight ring of irritation and strain. But, come what may, they were not going to lose that hill.

Nor did they. By dusk the slaughter in the ranks of 10th SS Panzer had been horrific; the woods were full of their dead. As night fell they called it all off. Now, like 9th SS, 10th SS had shot its bolt. Neither of these divisions appeared again in France. They were sent to recuperate at a town in Holland called Arnhem, where later on they wrote some more pages of history.

Next morning C Squadron were ordered to rejoin us. The column of battered Shermans trundled down the track towards our harbour with dusty, tired, triumphant faces poking out of the turrets. As my old squadron approached me, I walked forward, straightened my back and gave them a salute. Every tank commander rose in his turret, turned to face me, and his hand flew up in response.

Emotional? Sentimental? I don't care if it was.

* * * *

We had much more to do before VE Day in May 1945, but the worst bit was over. Before us were the gruesome shambles of the Falaise Gap, the night march to bounce the Somme bridge at Amiens, the exhilarating swan across France, and the liberation of Antwerp in early September.

There was anti-climax during the early part of the winter amongst the mud and mines of eastern Holland. Christmas Day, amid crackling frost and brilliant sunshine found us sitting round the bridge at Givet on the River Meuse – the seasonal spirit somewhat dampened by the order, which never had to be implemented, to defend the bridge to the last man against the Germans' Ardennes offensive.

The advance across Germany in March and April was frustrating – too many stops and starts. Every morning we heard that General Patton had advanced 50 miles on the previous day while we had advanced ten; our superiors would not let us bypass village strongpoints and push on. They would insist, unnecessarily we thought, that our infantry should clear them, incurring casualties and wasting time while the road lay invitingly open before us. I remember Roscoe Harvey saying, looking grumpily at us over his spectacles, 'I don't think we're bein' very well ridden in this race.'

And so we jerked and jolted across Germany, until one day we were sitting in a field south of Hamburg when a frantic urgency gripped our masters. 'Advance at once, top speed, don't ask why, but go, go at once to Lübeck on the Baltic coast.' At which we took off across the base of the Schleswig-Holstein peninsula and arrived in Lübeck just before the Russians. A few hours later and Denmark would have vanished behind the Iron Curtain.

Instead of the Russians it was the 11th Armoured Division which arrived on the Danish border. It had been a long way from those Yorkshire bogs, and I hope Hobo was pleased with us. At Husum in Schleswig-Holstein the 23rd Hussars reached the end of their road. By then I was commanding, and early in 1946 had the sad duty of presiding over the regiment's disbandment.

When fighting ended the 23rd Hussars had in the space of eleven months incurred just under 400 casualties, 150 of whom had been killed. This total casualty figure exceeded the established strength of the regiment, and meant that we had suffered over 100 per cent killed, wounded or missing. The other two regiments in the brigade were in no different case. The infantry battalions' losses had been far higher; most had turned over their total strength at least three times. Nor was this any worse than the losses sustained by the other infantry divisions which fought in North-West Europe. By the end of the war there were virtually no British reinforcements left. Great Britain had, in manpower terms, given her all.

The personal bereavement, the grief and the loss of talent to the nation had bitten so deeply that ever since there has inevitably been talk of the waste and futility of war. But, as Frankie Festing once said to me, 'The only futile war is a war you had lost.' By the sacrifice of our bravest and best we had just scraped home. If we had not scraped home, if we had lost, our country would have experienced the concentration camp and the gas chamber, and said goodbye to a civilised society. So the loss of so many was certainly not futile. Their sacrifice helped to bar the way to a fate for our country, for ourselves and for our children in which the liberty and the way of life which we now take for granted would have been no more than a pre-war dream. So – 'For our tomorrow, they gave their today.'

All that is left now of the 23rd Hussars is a group of about 100 elderly men who gather together every year, occasionally meeting round the memorial at Bridlington which bears the 150 names of our friends whose faces to us are still young. These old men can be proud of their contribution. It has since been said by senior war-time commanders that no better armoured regiment fought in North-West Europe.

Their record was achieved without the benefit of tradition, or of a regimental history other than the one they wrote themselves. It was achieved by good leadership from top to bottom, by thorough training, by the opportunity to remain together throughout that training and so build up comradeship, friendship, loyalty and regimental pride. These are the essentials, and the hundreds of years of history, the past traditions of a regiment, and the customs deriving from them, are a valuable bonus but no more than that.

And another lesson which I learnt was the depth of courage, initiative and strength lying hidden beneath the placid ordinariness of the British character.

Taken from 11th Armd. Div. History

Foreword by Lieut-General Sir Miles Dempsey
Commander 2nd Army

The 11th Armoured Division proved itself throughout the campaign in North-Western Europe an outstandingly fine division. I have never met a better.

This account of its battles tells what the division did. But it does not tell how great was the confidence which senior commanders placed in it nor does it give the true causes of its great success.

The latter are worth examining. Why was this such an outstanding division? There are several reasons.

At the time of its inception and throughout its early life the technical and minor tactical training of the division was fundamentally sound. It had the best possible start and upbringing, and there is no doubt that, time and again, this proved of inestimable worth in battle. Even after sustaining considerable losses – and 11th Armoured Division had heavier casualties than any other armoured division in Second Army – there was always a sound and well-trained nucleus to fall back on.

The division itself and its component parts were led in the field by experienced commanders, of great skill, character and courage, and the majority of these leaders remained unchanged throughout the campaign.

The division was brim full of that priceless asset – confidence.

True confidence in a military unit or formation means that the men have confidence in themselves – born of a knowledge of their skill and fitness: that they have confidence in their leaders, and that the leaders themselves have complete trust in their men: in each other, and in those above them.

To instil such confidence, as opposed to mere optimism, must be the aim of all comanders: once a unit or formation has acquired it there is nothing that cannot be achieved. The 11th Armoured Division had it in full measure and it was always an inspiration to see the division in battle, resting after some major success, or preparing for fresh ventures.

On more than one occasion I have been privileged to congratulate the formation on its victories: I am grateful for this opportunity to express once again my deep appreciation of the work done by this magnificent division.

M. C. Dempsey

Lieutenant-General,
Commander
SECOND ARMY.

August 5th, 1945.

CHAPTER SEVEN

Ups and downs of a soldier rider (1947–54)

The message read, 'I fear there is no vacancy for you at the Camberley Staff College, but we have managed to get you into the Staff College at Quetta.' Unlike many of my contemporaries I had not been staff trained during the war, and without this cachet an officer's future was limited. Even so ... Quetta!

A really dedicated officer would have jumped at the chance, but I didn't jump at it. Rightly or wrongly, who knows? The only certainty is that my life would have run a completely different course if I had accepted. I would never have met my wife and much of my military service might have been passed east of Suez. By the standards of some of my contemporaries, and from the career point of view, I had not had a particularly 'good' war. During all those years I had spent with C Squadron others had been attending wartime staff courses, occupying wartime staff posts, and returning, often with great distinction, to command in battle. Now I seemed to have missed the boat.

There was only one skill which I possessed – and I was immodest enough to believe to a high degree – an ability to ride a horse. I had longed during the war years to have the thrill of one day testing my skills against others at home, and if I went to India I could say goodbye to all that. No, I would NOT go to Quetta.

Since I did not seem to have much future in the army, I was reduced in rank to major and sent to Suffolk to join what was called the Specialised Armour Development Establishment (SADE). Here were the armoured 'funnies' – vehicles that could could swim, blow up mines, bridge ditches and so forth. Here also were some very serious officers and this was a pity because a good deal of what they were doing was frankly hilarious.

I became involved with the 'jumping tank', a project which was the technical responsibility of a major in the Royal Electrical and Mechanical Engineers, bespectacled, studious, and a thoroughly nice man. Instead of a tank having to trundle over a bridge or swim across a river, it was to be given the ability to jump, to leap across an obstacle.

The test vehicle, an elderly Valentine tank weighing 15 tons, was festooned with rockets considered powerful enough to lift it into the air and propel it across a gap. I personally had my doubts about this, but the experts thought it would work and who was I to argue? The rockets were clamped to the victim. The calculations were made and approved by the authorities. Now we were to test it, and since the outcome was quite unpredictable I need hardly say that the tank was to soar into the air unmanned.

The Valentine was positioned on an eminence in the training area and, as no one was at all certain where it would eventually land, observers were positioned all round it a respectful distance. I drove up in my jeep to see how my technical colleague was getting on with his final preparations. I found him sitting on the Valentine fiddling about with a number of wires; the vehicle from which he would eventually activate the experiment was parked beside him. I encouraged him to make sure that he was well clear himself before he pressed the button, and drove off.

I had gone about 50 yards when there was an appalling, earthshaking roar behind me and I was immediately enveloped in impenetrable clouds of dust. My first reaction should of course have been concern for my REME friend, who must somehow have crossed the wrong wires, but I fear that the knowledge that somewhere in the pea-soup fog above my head was a Valentine tank in free fall claimed my immediate attention. Once reassured I drove anxiously back, expecting to find the major in small pieces. Not at all, he was sitting on the site dazed, deafened and slightly scorched, for fortunately the tank had shed him on take-off. When the dust had cleared it was discovered upside down 30 yards away. Gravely the great men conferred. They decided to abandon the project.

My association with such experiments was not blessed. The next one was a device for extracting bogged vehicles, a cause for which, remembering the North Yorkshire moors, I had sympathy. It was believed that if a vehicle had a powerful rocket fixed to its rear and it became stuck in a bog, the activation of the rocket would – hey presto – blow it forward onto terra firma.

Thus one day a Bren carrier with a large rocket fastened to its rear was driven into a local bog. A bold major volunteered to sit in the driver's seat. A crowd of expectant officers gathered round. The rocket went off with a fearful whoosh; clouds of mud bespattered the spectators. The rocket continued to fart furiously into the morass which by now it had created, and the only part of the experiment which remained entirely motionless throughout was the carrier, except that by the time the clamour had died down it was found to have nestled even deeper into the bog. It was extracted by more old-fashioned methods and this project too was abandoned.

It was not possible, with the best will in the world, to take all this very seriously, and although I am sure much good work was being done by SADE, I did not feel I was cut out for research and development. Luckily however the whole course of my existence was about to be changed for I met the love of my life.

Zulu – her curly hair had given her this nickname in childhood and thus Monkey and Zulu has been the somewhat bizarre linkage of names with which we have faced life since – was a young war widow whose late husband, John Rew, had been killed in North Africa. From the moment I met her I was certain I wanted to marry her, no doubt ever entered my mind. Ever since she has been the rock to which my very happy life has been secured and, quoting from Trollope's *Framley Parsonage*, has been 'One of the pleasantest companions that could be brought near to a man, as the future partner of his home and the owner of his heart – high principles without asperity, female gentleness without weakness, a love of laughter without malice, and a true loving heart'. Particularly the latter.

Her parents, Toby and Phyllis Buxton, lived in lovely old Shelley Hall, near Hadleigh in Suffolk. Toby was tall, fair and goodlooking, the most likeable of men, content to run his farm and sit quietly, alternately chuckling and faintly disapproving, while 'Mumbo', as all and sundry called her, held centre stage.

Charm – what an impossible quality it is to describe. Now that she is gone the effect that Mumbo had on those over whom she cast her spell can still be vividly and affectionately recalled by them but not, sadly, passed on. Her tiny bird-like figure, usually clothed in a curious shapeless garment for which she had paid perhaps ten shillings at the local jumble sale, the beguiling cadences of her voice, the 'bon mots' entirely original to herself and her personality, often designed to provoke or shock and always funny, her concerned sympathy, her calm good sense – no description begins to describe the indefinable being who was Mumbo.

Children fell hopeless victims and remained enchanted by her in adulthood. Shelley seemed permanently full of family and friends in the same state of mind.

The house and garden staff adored her – the staff particularly because she seemed to do all the work herself. A common sight was Mumbo toiling at a task watched by a crowd of admiring domestics.

She was a member of a somewhat eccentric branch of the Barclay family in Norfolk. Her mother had died young and her father had the unenviable task of bringing up a large family which in temperament ranged from the unusual to the definitely peculiar. I like the story of the occasion on which he took five daughters stalking in Scotland and, on sighting a stag, told them to get down and crawl along behind him for the stalk. Suddenly well out of shot the stag bolted and the hot and testy stalker looked back through the heather to share his disappointment with his recumbent fellow-sportswomen. It was at once clear to him why the stag had vanished, for behind him, long since fed up with crawling, marched a fully upright crocodile of young ladies. Looking down on their infuriated father they squealed in their family language, 'Ee, Dadda, you DO look 'riche'!' Poor man.

Mumbo was not eccentric but she was certainly unusual. I was luckily never a target for her rage, which could be formidable, and she delighted in taking a view which she knew to be unconventional. Her likes and dislikes were strong but unpredictable. For some reason, for he was not personally known to her, she conceived a hatred of the Dr Beeching who was appointed by the government in the early 1960s to close down a number of railway lines. To mention his name to her would provoke a Mumbo 'tour de force'.

My in-laws were at the centre of the East Anglian family network comprising Buxtons, Barclays, Birkbecks, Gurneys, Backhouses ...The network was close-knit, and ever since my marriage the word 'relations' has loomed large in my life. They were naturally interested to hear of and get a sight of Zulu's fiancé and hit upon the idea of asking me to judge the hunter classes at the Swaffham Show.

This would enable them to achieve a number of objects. They could observe the new man in her life and, what was better, they would have a ringside opportunity of criticising his riding; if that more or less passed muster there was always the hope that he would display his ignorance of horseflesh by selecting the wrong prizewinners. They were too polite to communicate their verdict to me, but I cannot believe I escaped scot-free.

We were married at the peak of what was known at the time as the 'Shinwell shivers', so named after the Minister for Fuel in the post-war Labour government who ran out of coal during the arctic winter of early 1947. The church could not be heated, the organ was silent, and candles provided the light. Currency restrictions prevented us from going abroad and we honeymooned for some reason at Pulborough. After that we moved to a village near Andover named Ragged Appleshaw, handy for Tidworth, where SADE was now located.

Our house was also handy for Alec Kilpatrick's racing stable at Herridge near Collingbourne Ducis, and I had already got to know him. He possessed the kindest of hearts, heavily camouflaged beneath a Scottish dourness which only occasionally relaxed into a twinkle and a joke, usually of the 'put-down' variety. Like other stables his was building up its string after the war, but nevertheless Alec was still prepared to help and encourage the ignorant amateur rider, usually a soldier, a policy which was greatly appreciated by those whom he helped but must often have been a sore trial to him.

I was by now past 30 and did not have the time to work my way up through point-to-points. It was the deep end for me. I had saved a few hundred pounds during the war in order to buy a steeplechaser, and this task I entrusted to Alec. At least then I would have one horse to ride, and I hoped that the modest animal which I could afford would provide me with enough success to encourage other owners to put me up in due course. Happily this hope was realised.

Alec did not do what many other trainers would have done and buy me an elderly 'schoolmaster' on its way downhill. Instead with my delighted agreement he took a chance and found a young horse almost as ignorant as I was but not without promise, called September Air. Every morning, before my not very exacting military duties began, my trusty two-stroke motor bike would trundle me to Herridge, down the drive and into the stables for 'first lot'. There followed an exhilarating ride across Salibury Plain, some plain speaking from the trainer about the shortcomings of his amateur jockeys, and then coffee provided by dear Mary, his wife, in Alec's small study.

Here we would discuss plans, in some ways the most enjoyable part of racing. 'Hope springs eternal', and if it didn't there would be few racehorse owners. Sitting in a comfortable chair discussing entries and plans over coffee, ambition soars magnificently unchecked by minor problems like the quality of possible opponents and the limitations of your mount. Caution is restricted to 'Well, anyway, let's enter him and see what the others are like'. Already you are riding into the winner's enclosure at Aintree.

For Liverpool was the Mecca of the post-war steeplechasing world, far more than it is now. To have a runner in the Grand National, or to be invited to ride in the race, was every amateur's ambition. Actually to win it would be a peerless summit, no achievement anywhere could match it. There were two Aintree meetings in the season, one in November and the Grand National meeting in March. This was of course long before the Mildmay course, with its smaller fences, was built and every steeplechase was run over the Grand National circuit.

My first venture with September Air was at Nottingham and I discovered that he was a quick but somewhat flippant jumper. I came unstuck two fences out but otherwise would have been concerned with the finish. Delighted, I rode him again at Fontwell Park and this time was fourth. Then came a big freeze and all racing stopped.

That cold spell remains the worst I have experienced, for the ground froze solid early in January 1947 and remained solid continuously over the whole country until late March. It happened that the Grand National meeting provided the first opportunity for racing to resume. Since there were no all-weather gallops in those days horses, particularly novices, had by then become distinctly out of practice.

In the euphoria of one of those coffee sessions at Herridge, we had talked of qualifying September Air for the Grand National. Much the most likely way of achieving this was to be placed in a race round Aintree, and the Stanley Chase, over one circuit of the National course, was for novice horses. September Air was duly entered, and as we emerged from the deep freeze we welcomed this opportunity of returning to the fray, only slightly deterred by the prospect of tackling the Aintree fences on an inexperienced horse after only two races together and after such a long lay-off. Mad, of course, but hope springs eternal.

I had never been to Aintree before and walking the course was sobering. It was long before the authorities decided to slope the fences and above a small slanting 'apron' of some two feet high they reared up almost perpendicular – like towering cliffs and almost as solid. The thaw had caused such a thick fog that the effect was to make the obstacles look even bigger than they were.

Sixteen jockeys all mounted on novices contested the 1947 Stanley Chase. September Air bounded happily over over the early fences including the Chair, and we turned away down the long stretch which leads eventually to Bechers Brook.

The race then became all too exciting as the 'drops ' on these fences caught out the inexperienced novices. All around me were crashes and thumps and horses' legs waving in the air, and the company began to dwindle. Our survival was too good to last and sure enough at the fence before Bechers we seemed to collide with a brick wall and hit the ground hard.

I rose crossly to my feet and September Air vanished into the fog. I was beginning my gloomy trudge back when I heard a shout behind me. There was my horse being led by someone whom I recognised as one of the lesser known professionals called Tommy Cross, who had not been riding in the race himself.

I started to thank him but he interrupted excitedly, 'Well, come on, don't you want to win?' I gaped. 'Come on, everyone else has fallen, all you have to do is finish the course and you've won it.' Tommy was prone to exaggeration and I did not believe him – in fact I was not sure that I wanted to. How could anyone tell in this fog anyway? And yet … A small group of spectators gathered round and joined in the debate. Their attitude was like that of a boxing crowd who from their comfortable seats and behind their cigars urge their man to go in and fight. I decided to play the reluctant hero.

The real hero was September Air. He had just experienced the solidity of the Aintree fences, and now his rider was urging him from a trot to a canter to a gallop in the direction of Bechers Brook. He was a brave horse, if not very bright, and he took it well. As we rose in the air above the jump I saw that below me on the landing side was a group of spectators gazing with morbid satisfaction at the corpse of a horse stretched out upon the ground. I swooped upon them with a loud yell; they shrieked and scattered as I sped on.

Over the Canal Turn we sailed, over Valentines. I soon found that negotiating these enormous fences at hunting speed was not all that difficult. Onlookers, in the belief that there was now an interval between races, were walking about examining the fences and gaped in astonishment at this wild and muddy apparition careering past them out of the gloom. The stands were empty, but here and there groups of racegoers raised a rather bewildered cheer.

Tommy Cross, beside himself with excitement, met me and led me into the winner's enclosure. It was a slightly hollow triumph for no one was there; they had gone to watch the preliminaries for the next race. Soon however its normal guardians received news of an intruder and sped back, bearing with them disillusion. Apparently minutes earlier it had already been occupied. Tim Molony, then at the start of his career, had done the same as I had but somewhat faster. At least they could not deny that I was second, and this meant £200 and a qualification for the Grand National. Once Zulu and Alec had been retrieved from the foggy murk into which they had disappeared in anxious search, out came the champagne.

This not particularly distinguished achievement brought the offer of a few rides from other owners, and with September Air winning a couple of small races I found myself reasonably well launched. It was far easier then than it is now for part-time amateurs to find rides, for National Hunt racing was still recovering from the war. The pre-war Army riders had all retired and at that time there were only two soldiers who rode regularly, Robin Hastings and myself.

Robin was then an instructor at the Staff College, having achieved almost certainly the best war-time record of anyone of his seniority. Appointed to the command of a battalion in Sicily at the age of 24, he was one of the first ashore on D Day and had held a high staff position as well. Although he was not an outstanding horseman, his courage and intelligence made him an excellent tactical race-rider. It was not long before he gave up the army and joined the British Bloodstock Agency, of which eventually he became a most able head; a great loss to the military. I have always since felt that he chose a path, however interesting, which did not enable him to reach his full potential. Not that he had any regrets, as far as I know.

A distinguished survivor from the pre-war days was John Hislop. He was in a class of his own as an amateur riding on the flat and one of the best in National Hunt racing – polished and knowledgeable as a jockey, articulate, and fluent with his pen. The army had ceased to be the chief breeding ground for amateurs, and replacements were coming from other walks of life; some were farmers' sons such as Dick Francis and Tim Brookshaw; there was Dickie Black, who won the Cheltenham Gold Cup on Fortina as an amateur, and of course there was Lord Mildmay of Flete. He was already renowned for his near-miss in the pre-war Grand National when his reins broke on Davy Jones, and had since matured into an extremely competent jockey. He accumulated a powerful string of steeplechasers trained by his friend Peter Cazalet.

I have always retained an admiration for Anthony Mildmay, and not just as a jockey. He was a natural leader, with the assurance and poise of the aristocrat combined with a down to earth, first hand knowledge of the sharp end of racing and of the jockeys' changing room. Whilst no intellectual, he was wise, thoughtful and forward-looking. His early death by drowning was an immeasurable loss to racing; his counsel as a Jockey Club member during the difficult times ahead would have brought informed and practical authority to the Club's discussions which no-one else could have begun to rival. He was unique, and a racing personality of the first order. But at the time of which I am writing the roar of 'Come on, Milord' would be heard on racecourses for a few seasons yet.

A new generation of professional jockeys was making the headlines. Many of these were Irish, who had been able to keep their hands in during the war, although the Irishman who became the most distinguished of them all had, as has been seen, fought in action with the British Army. I had seen Bryan Marshall just before he was demobilised riding in a show-jumping competition in Germany at a trim, fit twelve stone seven excluding the saddle. A month later he was riding in a steeplechase in England at ten stone nine including the saddle. At the end of that season he was second in the jockey's table and the following year he was champion. As in that motor-bike race at Northampton five years earlier he achieved miracles by going the shortest way, and his power and horsemanship made him unrivalled in a finish.

He has been described as the most accomplished horseman-jockey of this or any other era. There are other strong contenders for this title – Fred Winter and John Francome are two – but none of them had to overcome the interruption of six wartime years. In 1946 Bryan was 30 years old and had barely started his career. Neither did the others have to struggle as he did with his weight problem, for he was a powerful, broad-shouldered man. Eleven years later he had to retire because he could no longer ride at 12 stone, having been champion jockey several times and counted two Grand Nationals amongst his many wins. After a long life during which I have been privileged to watch the finest horsemen in the world in all equestrian sports I still rate Bryan Marshall as the strongest and most effective rider of them all.

Then there were the Molony brothers, Tim and Martin. Tim was what he looked, a strong, fearless jockey with a fine tactical sense. Martin, whose career was cut short by injury, was more than this – he was a genius. Without apparently exerting any pressure on his mounts, horses with Martin in the saddle simply went better, jumped better and won more often than with anyone else. For one period in 1951 he had the remarkable average of one winner in every three rides.

I was carried along very happily on this wave of resurgent National Hunt racing. The professional jockeys were condescending but kind to the amateurs. At that time there was no question of them feeling that we were taking the bread from their mouths; there was quite enough bread for everyone. They were certainly however not above trying it on. An amateur clamped firmly to the inside rail turning into the finishing straight would sometimes hear an urgent, dramatic shout from the jockey immediately behind him, 'Move over, sir, move over, sir.' If, fearing that some catastrophe impended, one was fool enough to fall for this ploy and move away from the rail, quick as a flash he would have pinched the 'inner' off one and stolen the race. I soon learnt that the attitude of an officer and a gentleman was not always the most effective in this professional world.

My military duties at this time were not, luckily, exacting, but now and then we began to wonder about my future. I had been told by a staff officer at the War Office that I was now too old for the Staff College, but at the end of the steeplechasing season we decided to check whether this advice was correct. Indeed, it was not correct. I had one last chance, though this meant, horror of horrors, actually taking and passing an examination only a few months ahead. I embarked on a correspondence course and worked far into the night.

In this, the first post-war Staff College examination, candidates had to achieve an average of 50 per cent marks on the overall test, and not less than 40 per cent on each individual paper. Failure to get this 40 per cent on every paper meant outright failure.

All went well until the Military Law paper. In this the candidate brought with him the *Manual of Military Law* and each question described a different form of military misdemeanour. You then had to search the *Manual* until you found the appropriate section, quote it, and write down the answer. There were seven questions. I dealt with number one, but spent a fruitless hour over two, three and four, each of which totally defeated me. I looked at my watch; there were only 20 minutes left. Unless I answered the remaining three questions in that time and got them all right, I could not achieve the necessary 40 per cent and would fail the whole examination. On the next 20 minutes hung my military future, for this was my last chance.

The Almighty then took a hand. Miraculously – for it really was a miracle – he guided my fingers to the right sections of the *Manual.* The answers flowed smoothly from my pen, all correct. I achieved the 40 per cent and passed the whole examination. Why the Almighty took all this trouble has always defeated me; I have since given him a pretty moderate return for his pains. Soon afterwards came my nomination for the Staff College course of 1949 at Camberley.

My second racing season got off to a disappointing start with hardly any winners. My plans for the Grand National centred round September Air and although he was far from being a top-class horse he would not, with a light weight, have been disgraced in the big race. We decided however that he required further experience of the Aintree fences and ran him in November in the Valentine Chase. I still have a vivid recollection of the fall I took at Bechers, horse and rider completely upside down in the air with on the way down the thought crossing my mind that this must really be one of Liverpool's most spectacular. I was carried off with a cracked pelvis, and Zulu, who had not enjoyed her two visits to Aintree, firmly vetoed any further attempts round the course on September Air. For by no means the last time I had to admit she was right.

This was all very disappointing, and time was short because I was due to return to my regiment in Germany for a few months before going to Camberley. Then Fortune turned to me with a charming smile. Alec's stable jockey was Johnny Gilbert. As his small figure indicated he had graduated to jumping from the flat and was a brilliant racerider. His legs were however too short to wrap themselves round a big steeplechaser and, whilst he won many top hurdle races, over the bigger fences he was not so successful. Alec decided to restrict his rides to hurdle races and that left the stable star, Sir John, without a jockey. He was a lovely horse of whom great things were expected.

One day Alec rang me up and asked me to ride Sir John early in January in the big race at Manchester, then one of the leading courses but since closed down. This was a real honour. The horse had cost a fortune to buy, but luck had not run his way and since coming over from Ireland he had failed to win a race. His elderly owner was becoming restive, for his eyes were firmly fixed on the 1948 Grand National. Advised by Alec, he was prepared to take a chance with the stable amateur, inexperienced and out of luck as he was.

We won convincingly from a high-grade field at Manchester, and it was at once obvious to me that Sir John was a class horse. Although I had the feeling that this young star was being asked for too much too soon – in which I was right – in the euphoria of the racecourse bar his participation in the Grand National was announced, as was my engagement to ride him. For an all too brief but blissful period I found myself the stable jockey for the Kilpatrick steeplechasers. All too brief, because I was due to go back to Germany.

It was good to be reunited with my regiment, but the British Army then was in transition between demobilisation and the beginning of peacetime National Service. There were few men, hardly any equipment with which to train them and nothing much to train them for. We concentrated on sport, in particular trying to produce – with reasonable success – the best athletics, football and boxing teams in what was soon to be called the British Army of the Rhine (BAOR).

I now had to play the part of the Kilpatrick stable jockey while situated several hundred miles away across the North Sea. The nearest airport was Amsterdam and the only way of getting there was to use the leave train to and from the Hook of Holland, jumping off and on – illegally – at Utrecht, and then board the Dutch train connected with the airport. I was temporarily in command of the regiment at the time as the then commanding officer, Alec Scott, had gone off to train for the Wembley Olympics, and sometimes a military contretemps was only narrowly averted.

The commander-in-chief of BAOR announced that he would visit the regiment on the day after I had two rides in England, and the return journey, always dependent on connections between unpredictable trains and planes, did not go to plan. Hence the acting commanding officer, sweating slightly, eventually drove into the barracks only an hour before the great man's arrival. In the event all went smoothly. Once General Dick McCreery, a pre-war amateur jockey himself, had discovered that I was to ride in the Grand National in a few weeks time, military matters were barely discussed. But although my duties were not heavy, my absences in England had to be kept short. Indeed their frequency depended largely on how generous owners were with travelling expenses.

I achieved a nice double at the Grand Military meeting at Sandown and had several other good rides apart from Sir John. He ran in two National Trials, was third in one and fell in the other. I realised that apart from his inexperience he had two short-comings. He hated firm going – and the ground was getting firmer every day – and he seemed invariably to make one bad jumping mistake in his races. Neither were a good omen for Aintree. From being one of the favourites after the Manchester race he slipped in the betting and eventually started at 40 to one.

On the morning of the race all the horses are out exercising in front of the empty stands, with only a few knots of people to watch. Here on this occasion were Anthony Mildmay, looking very wasted and ill, on Cromwell; John Hislop on Cloncarrig; Bryan Marshall on Rowland Roy. Lord Bicester's pair, Roimond and Silver Fame, with Dickie Black and Martin Molony riding, cantered past together, with Arthur Thompson on Sheila's Cottage and Ron Smyth on Klaxton. Sir John moved smoothly and well, but the ground was firmer than he liked and the sweeping, effortless stride through the Manchester mud was not being reproduced here.

Memories crowd in – 45 jockeys in two very small changing rooms pulling each others' legs; weighing out with the newsreel cameras clicking and flashlights exploding; good luck telegrams, some from wartime comrades in the 23rd Hussars; the shout of 'Jockeys please'; the long walk to the paddock; once there the strained conversation as the horses circled round us. Then, the leg-up; the parade, and the stable lad's hand relinquishing the bridle; the knowledge that all that can be done for you by others has now been done – the same feeling that you experience as you ride into the arena for a big show-jumping competition, or on the athletics track as you walk to the start of a race, or up the steps into a boxing ring. Now it is up to you and, in a riding event, your horse in partnership. No one else can help.

Soon we were thundering down to the first fence, a sight now familiar to the television viewer. The size of the field, and the number of loose horses that soon materialise, make the jockeys anxious to achieve a good start, and by the time the horses have covered the 400 yards to the first fence they are really travelling. By now I was familiar with this fence and knew how easy it was to be caught out by the drop. I steadied Sir John as much as I could. Impressed by the size of the fence he rose high above it and plummetted innocently down. He touched ground with a gasp of dismay about a foot lower than he expected, fell on his nose and recovered, much the wiser. All around me were cracks and thuds; on the ground crouching figures bunched tensely till the storm had passed.

As the field grew smaller over the next three fences the loose horses began to appear. Always unpredictable, one of them that has jumped two fences soberly and well may suddenly decide to veer off through the wing of the next, taking you with it. At the fence before Bechers I was baulked by a loose horse but survived. Bechers loomed up and Sir John, meeting it in his stride, jumped it brilliantly. This is, I believe, the most thrilling sensation that riding a horse has to offer. To sail through the air at that speed from that height, with your horse perfectly balanced, and to be confident that all will be well when you land is a joy one does not forget.

We galloped on to the Canal Turn. This left-handed bend is extremely sharp.

In the National you seem to be jumping straight towards a solid phalanx of people not many yards away, and you have to jump it on the turn. As we landed over Valentines and began to approach the end of the first circuit there were about 20 of us left. I was well placed and could see that John Hislop and Cloncarrig were in the lead. But just as I had identified him that distinguished amateur's heels and his horse's tail flew up in the air and they disappeared from view.

Over the Anchor Bridge fence we rejoined the racecourse and galloped down the long stretch of open leading towards the stands and the end of the first circuit. At this point there is a plain fence before the Chair and we rode into it hopelessly out of stride and bound to hit it. A moment of agonised effort, a crackling and splintering of wood, a frantic effort by Sir John to regain his feet, a thud as we hit the ground and we were out of it.

I walked back to watch the finish with John Eustace-Smith who had fallen at the same fence. As the survivors came onto the racecourse for the second time there were only four in it, First of the Dandies and two mares, Sheila's Cottage and Zahia, with Cromwell and Anthony Mildmay a few lengths behind. In Reynoldstown's Grand National before the war, Anthony's reins had broken at the penultimate fence when victory seemed certain and his horse had run out at the last fence. Now, with Cromwell apparently still full of running, fate played an equally cruel trick. Three fences from home Anthony Mildmay's backbone, as a result of a racing injury sustained some time earlier, seized up in a position which left him helpless, head and shoulders rigidly trapped and bowed. It was almost certainly a recurrence of this spasm which led to his death by drowning off the Devon coast not long afterwards. Temporarily almost paralysed and unable to help his horse, he was carried past the winning post third.

Meanwhile there was a more obvious drama. The mare Zahia, in the lead at the last fence but one, looked a very likely winner. Suddenly she left the course. In those days the line to the finish was not so clearly marked as it is now, and it is all too probable that the unfortunate Eddie Reavey, her jockey, mistook the way. The dismounted jockeys standing at that point waved and shouted frantically in warning but too late. A very real chance of winning the 1948 Grand National had gone beyond recall – another of Aintree's 'might have beens'.

Sheila's Cottage won it, with First of the Dandies second and Cromwell third. At long intervals the survivors trickled in. One of these was Klaxton, later to be a tiresome thorn in my side in my efforts to win the Grand Military at Sandown. I recall that he did not seem particularly distressed; certain courses did not earn his full cooperation and Liverpool was obviously one. Meanwhile the victor was in the unsaddling enclosure. Surrounded by crowds of cheering people stood Arthur Thompson, the hero of the hour. A small, utterly miserable figure slipped quietly into the weighing room – Eddie Reavey, the rider of Zahia. As I followed him in I reflected, not for the first time, that racing was a chancy game.

I had been surprised at how easily I had made the weight of ten stone three pounds in the big race, and annoyed by friends on the day who said how white I looked, implying that I was scared out of my wits. Two days after returning to Germany the reason – I like to think the only reason – was made clear. I was stricken by an agonising stomach pain one night and rushed to hospital with appendicitis. This of course finished my racing season, and my rides including Sir John – sadly killed not long afterwards in a race – went elsewhere, mostly for ever. With the Staff College immediately ahead of me prospects for the following season looked and were bleak.

Now that I had actually reached the Staff College the top priority was to make the most of my time there and emerge with an interesting appointment at the end of the year. Some of the possibilities were depressing and the song then popular 'I want to get you on a slow boat to China' was all too apt. Avoidance of such a fate was all-important and retaining the rides which I had so painstakingly acquired was a losing battle. Jockeys who can only appear on Saturdays are not much in demand. But one day the Brackley trainer, Bobby Norris, rang up and wanted me to ride a good horse of his at Kempton on the following Tuesday, in February, during the early, intense part of the course.

I looked at the programme. On that Tuesday we were due to write our first operation order, starting at 10.30 a.m. and handing in the complete exercise before five. We could however write it unsupervised, though we would not receive the question paper before 10.30. The race at Kempton was at 2.30, which meant leaving Camberley before one o'clock. That implied finishing an exercise for which six hours had been allotted in two hours and a half. To hand in the exercise uncompleted would make me most unpopular at best – I should be lucky to avoid the slow boat to China – with disastrous consequences at worst. On the other hand I could not let Bobby and the owner down at the last moment. I accepted the ride.

We were always being told to use our initiative and to plan ahead, and this seemed an opportunity to follow such excellent advice. Luckily the Staff College instructors on the preceding day so played their hand that the observant could glimpse some of the cards which were meant to be hidden. Our work on that day consisted of discussing the plan for an attack and on completion we were handed the 'school solution'. My heart leapt. It was more than a good bet that this plan would be the subject of the operation order which was to prove so crucial to my Kempton commitment. I could now do most of the work in anticipation.

Into the night I laboured with this premature birth but as I sat down at my desk at 10.30 on the following morning I knew that if I had backed a loser I was in for an awkward day. The question paper was handed out and, joy, I was on a winner. Shortly after midday, to the astonishment of my fellow students, I smugly rose, dropped the completed exercise into my instructor's box, and left.

I had a good ride at Kempton and was third, much where Bobby and the owner expected the horse to finish. I drove back refreshed and rejuvenated. Meanwhile the Staff College instructors had been watching the racing on television and were somewhat intrigued to see one of their students riding a finish at Kempton Park. My instructor, having visited the lecture room to see if I had a double, found my exercise reposing in his box. Luckily it found favour, though in fact it was not luck at all for I had worked on it for rather longer than the six hours allocated – an unauthorised change of schedule on which I kept quiet. On the whole, though, I felt that I had better not push my luck too far and that this escapade should not be repeated.

Not surprisingly my rides evaporated and I found myself looking for a sporting challenge other than racing. One day I happened to meet Percy Legard, a member of the pre-war British Modern Pentathlon team. 'Why don't you have a go at it?' he suggested. 'You can ride and run, and you'll soon learn the other three.'

Knowing nothing about the sport I looked at the official history which read 'The athlete is required to ride a horse across country, fence with an epée, shoot a pistol with the greatest precision, swim 330 yards and conclude by running two-and-a-half miles across country – all this in the space of five days. Each competitor receives a certain number of points according to the standard of his performance in each event, and victory goes to the man with the highest total.'

I could run and ride. I had often fired a pistol. I had never fenced. I could swim, but only after a fashion. I soon realised that, since most people have a 'weak' event, swimming would be mine. A stroke resembling that of a shrimp, achieving little forward movement with maximum effort, earned me a time over the required lengths that I was too ashamed to reveal. I realised I must learn the 'crawl'. I rode my two-stroke motor bike to the Aldershot baths during the Staff College luncheon interval. The only person there at such a moment was the swimming pool attendant, Mr Dixon, and he told me roughly how to achieve a 'crawl', shouting advice or rebukes as he hung up towels or stoked the boiler. After much toil I achieved times which were just acceptable for international competition then, but would be greeted by roars of laughter now.

Pistol shooting is not too difficult once you have overcome your nerves. At each exposure of the target you have to hit it, the more centrally the better, with five shots in a very short time, then reload and wait for the next exposure. Tension builds up, particularly on a big occasion, expressed sometimes by a disastrous twitch in the pistol hand just as you press the trigger. It is all too easy to 'put one off', or even two. I am told that since my day there was a period when some of the international firers would 'tranquillise' themselves before the shooting. The story of a Bulgarian competitor slowly keeling over and passing out in mid-firing is probably apocryphal, and in any case modern dope-testing has ruled the practice out.

I learned fencing by invading a gym and dragooning one of the instructors into teaching me. I never enjoyed it much, but my reasonably quick eye and reactions made me an adequate performer. Riding was no problem. Indeed to be seriously immodest I never met another pentathlon competitor of my standard and although I was past my best as a runner, not many could beat me at that either. These events had however to pull me up from a pretty disastrous swimming time and mediocre results in the fencing and shooting.

Whilst at the Staff College I joined the regimental Pentathlon team of three which won the team event in the British Pentathlon Championships three years running. Peter Duckworth was the British champion and far the best of the three. Our third member was Lance Corporal Ron Bright. For many years now he has been Mr Ron Bright, the manager of the Olympic medal-winning British team, and a leading figure in the sport. He will forgive me, I hope, looking down from his eminence, if I remind him that in those days in the shooting he was by no means above 'putting one off'.

When my Staff College year ended I was gratified to be posted to the Joint Planning Staff in the Ministry of Defence. As a member of a tri-Service team I would sit day after day, writing, writing, writing, occasionally visiting the War Office to obtain advice from the appropriate expert on subjects ranging from the nuclear deterrent to the strategic importance of the Falkland Islands – concluding in the latter case that it was non-existent. As I commented at the time, if I had been made President of the Board of Trade I could hardly have known less about my new job, but I was soon much enjoying doing something so completely different. London, too, was convenient for Pentathlon training.

I swam at lunchtime in the RAC baths, joined the London Fencing Club, shot my pistol and ran round the running track at the Duke of York's Barracks. I rose up the ranking table and at the end of 1951 was selected for the British team of four to compete in the World Championships in Sweden. Considering the amateur way in which we had prepared we were pleased to finish fourth out of the nine competing teams, though the Swedes, Finns and Brasilians, all far more professional in their attitude, beat us easily.

On our return we maintained that the British would never win any Pentathlon medals until we copied other countries and devised a system in which a competitor trained whole-time and did not need to earn his living. This was clearly a step which the strictly amateur and law-abiding British would never dream of taking, for it meant, in the case of a soldier, striking him off his normal duties but continuing to pay him as if he were still performing them. This was of course out of the question, unheard of, immoral, unsporting. Nevertheless this is exactly what was eventually done. For years Sergeant Jim Fox never moved from his barracks at Arborfield, never did any serious soldiering and practising for the Pentathlon became his sole duty. Result, a gold medal for the British team in the Montreal Olympics and fame, if not fortune – for there is no money in the sport – for Sergeant Jim Fox. Soon afterwards he became Captain Fox, for although before the Olympics when he had applied for a commission the Commissioning Board found him unsuitable, when he applied again after the gold medal and the headlines they suddenly found he was suitable after all.

The World Championships marked the end of my Modern Pentathlon activity, and although I could well have made the British team for the Helsinki Olympics of 1952, my next army move made this impossible. I was to go back to the Staff College as an instructor, a move which opened up the possibility, as Robin Hastings had shown, of a limited return to the racing scene but quite ruled out the training time necessary for the Olympic Pentathlon.

Instructors at Camberley had to work hard, but had a good deal of independence. We spent three thoroughly enjoyable years there. I was by then in my middle 30s, an age at which your brain is apt to be at its most active and enterprising. You have had enough experience to have developed strong opinions and, not being senior enough to make policies, are not weighed down by the need to justify them. Your brain – at least in my experience – flicks here and there, flirting and experimenting. Greatly daring, I submitted a light-hearted piece to the *Spectator* and the then editor, Walter Taplin, not only accepted it but was kind about it. I contributed on a fairly regular basis until the journal changed hands. My oil paints were splashed about with enthusiasm – sadly the swans of the period when they come to light in the attic are unmistakably geese.

We lived in Number 18 Bungalow. Water ran down the sides of the walls and left mildewed patches. It was heated by one coke stove situated in the long passage down which the family – for by now Terence and Philip had made their appearance – and guests clattered to use the solitary bathroom and lavatory. If a modern lieutenant-colonel was offered a residence like this he would at once hand in his papers, but we were very happy there.

My colleagues and their wives inhabiting similar bungalows in the 'patch' nearly all became friends for life. Standards of tidiness and orderliness were much more relaxed then; I suppose it was the effect of the war years. Now when I drive past the neat gardens in front of impeccable, immaculate little red brick houses which have replaced the bungalows, I thank my stars that we lived as we did and not as instructors do now.

The craze for gardening had not caught on then, and if the bungalow children had ponies, where better to graze them than the garden? Animals abounded; when Pat and Susan Hobart came to stay they brought eight cats with them. Another fellow-instructor's garden had long since abandoned a decorative role, and the nibblings of successive ponies had reduced it to a dustbowl. After tossing a bundle of hay to the tethered livestock, the colonel's lady, often 'en déshabillée', would relax, cigarette in mouth, in a tattered deck-chair, waving languidly to passers-by. On one occasion when we found ourselves with one more horse than the stables could accommodate, it had to reside in our wooden garage. Minutes after it was installed there was a splintering of glass and a well-bred head was poking out of the garage window. Later it demolished its residence altogether. No one seemed to mind.

As I resumed my racing after this interval we were determined to replace September Air, now sold, with a top-notcher, even if it meant waiting for years. Meanwhile I found I had not been completely forgotten.

Alec Kilpatrick had bought for Colonel Freddie Noble, a patron of his stable, a promising young chaser from Ireland. It was certainly the oddest animal I have ever ridden. Despite being a mare, she had been christened Ronnie Cronin. She was kindness itself, quiet and placid until she suddenly 'flipped her lid'. A series of prodigious fly-jumps would launch her into a flat-out gallop, almost regardless of the direction she was facing, and no arms, however strong, could make the slightest impression on her. She stopped when she felt like it, not before. She was a nut-case.

Bert Morrow, the stable jockey, had several hair-raising experiences between leaving the paddock and arriving at the start of a race. At Worcester she only decided at the last moment not to take on the River Severn against which Bert had desperately tried to stop her, and at Fontwell she completed an unauthorised circuit before the race had started. At this stage someone had the idea of putting up the stable's amateur.

I was delighted, for she had real potential and was a superb and safe jumper. The only way to arrive at the start of a race without disaster was to allow her to perform her fly-jumps and embark on her mad gallop, to throw the reins at her when she saw the other horses circling round the starting gate and shout 'whoa'. She would then consent to cooperate and, amazingly, would line up with the others as good as gold. Once in the race of course she would go off like a rocket and, unless I could 'kid' her into a slower speed while in front, she was liable to run herself out before the finish.

Her jumping ability made her a 'natural' for Liverpool, but first I had to try and win the Grand Military Gold Cup for Freddie Noble on her. Since winning the substitute race on September Air in 1948, I had been second once and third once for other owners. At that time the regular winner was David Gibson's Klaxton, one of the best horses in the country but unpredictable. He hated Liverpool, disliked Cheltenham, but unfortunately for the soldier owners loved Sandown. David would let him lob along at the back and, just as you were hoping that something had gone wrong with the combination, this powerful apparition would loom up over the last fence and it was all over. He had now won the race twice and was bidding for a hat-trick in 1952. Although the bookmakers made Ronnie Cronin a strong second favourite I had a nasty feeling that for the third consecutive year I would find myself watching the bottoms of David Gibson and Klaxton pass the winning post.

So it proved. My attempt to settle the mare in front were wrecked when a no-hoper came rocketting past us. That set her off and although we were still leading at the last fence we were rapidly slowing down. Second again.

Our next engagement was what used to be called the Topham Trophy at Liverpool, the big race on the Thursday before the Grand National and over two and a half miles of the National course. A high-class field had turned out and we were not given much chance by the bookmakers or the Press. Ronnie Cronin proceeded to give me the best ride I have had on any horse in my life. She made not the semblance of a mistake and sailed at least six inches over every one of these huge fences. Her jump at Bechers was sensational – she must have cleared it by a foot.

Better still, she was so impressed by the fences that she settled in docilely behind the leading bunch. As we came onto the racecourse proper, with three fences to jump, I found myself gaining on the leaders. In a desperate finish I was beaten into third place, but since she was only defeated, at level weights and by a short head, by the horse that started favourite for next year's Grand National we had every reason to be delighted. We wired joyfully to Freddie Noble, steaming back from the Middle East, that he would have a fancied runner for the great Aintree race next year. For the first and only time in her turbulent life Ronnie Cronin probably gave her true running and showed what a good mare she could have been.

But then, as sometimes happens in the best of establishments, there was a cock-up. Ronnie Cronin did herself much too well out at grass during the summer, and was allowed to run before she had shed her fat. Result, broken blood-vessels in her nose during a race. The blood then runs back down the horse's windpipe and half-chokes it – it must be a frightening experience. Certainly it made her madder than ever.

Before a race at Doncaster she for once ignored my tactics on the way to the start. On the television screen viewers, whch included my family at Camberley, were soon watching me galloping, totally out of control, the wrong way round the course and crashing through a hurdle which, since we had to jump it backwards, tripped Ronnie Cronin up. I remounted and took part in the race but remember nothing about it, only regaining my senses in the weighing room afterwards. I had badly dislocated my neck, for the third time, and most reluctantly had to agree with my doctor's very firm advice not to ride in any more races.

This was all the more depressing because we had just found our star, the best steeplechaser we were ever to own. Alec produced for us a gangling brown four-year-old which had only just been broken in, but which after our first look at him we had no hesitation in buying. We called him Pointsman.

He was so big and backward that we should have taken him home and allowed him to mature by riding him about. But we had paid so much for him that we did not dare. The Staff College stables were far from ideal for a horse like this, and then there was the Camberley traffic. There was also Alec, who would not hear of his pride and joy leaving his stable.

So there was really no argument about this but it was a pity all the same. I rode Pointsman in a novice hurdle race at Newbury for his debut. He was far too immature for such a race and ran without troubling the leaders, but I knew at once that we had something special. He ran a couple of times more, again without distinction, and then I had my bad fall. He ran once more that season and showed promising form, but I still believe he should have been taken more slowly.

The chief result of his hurdling experience was to instill in him a hit or miss style of jumping for which afterwards he became notorious. He had an immensely long stride, was not a natural jumper, and was never properly educated. Pointsman had difficulty in adjusting when he met a fence wrong and during his peak years was never a confident jumper. He seldom fell but his errors either dislodged his rider, despite Bert Morrow's remarkable adhesive powers, or lost him several lengths.

Even so, by February in his second season during which he graduated to fences, he had won four races and was being hailed as a coming star. The Grand Military Gold Cup was in March and Pointsman was of course entered. This presented a problem because it was one thing to watch a professional rider on our horse and quite another to put up an amateur soldier of whose ability I might not be confident. There was only one answer to this, and after some brainwashing Zulu and Alec agreed that I should defy doctors orders and ride him myself.

Klaxton had by now retired but the 1954 Grand Military was none the less a vintage race. Pointsman was one of the best young steeplechasers in the country, and another young horse, Roughan, ridden by Philip Fielden, later won the Topham Trophy at Liverpool and many other good races. Point of Law, ridden by Michael Gordon Watson, was more mature and had been a regular winner in Ireland.

I suppose I was by some way the most experienced rider in the field but I had not ridden in a race for 15 months, and had never been on Pointsman's back in a steeplechase. He was looking light after a hard season and had obviously passed his best for the year. It was dismaying therefore to find us the hot favourite. I let my stirrups down to a most unjockey-like length, determined that whatever else I did I would not fall off.

There were eleven runners and we surged over the first fence uneventfully. Down the back straight we settled into our new partnership. He was jumping perfectly and as we turned back past the stands to complete the first circuit his devouring stride had taken us up into third place. No horse of any consequence, however, was in front of us and our two dangers were close behind and waiting. We turned away from the stands and took advantage of the slight downhill gradient to start racing in earnest.

A mile from home we were still in third place and then came crisis number one. We galloped into a fence right out of stride. First Pointsman decided to stand off it and reach for it. Then he changed his mind, diving through the fence about two feet from the bottom. For a split second there was no horse in front of me at all; the grass lurched past me below, and one long brown leg appeared from nowhere to save us. I clutched everything – reins, saddle, neck – and miraculously recovered my seat. By then we were last. Although the wind must have been knocked out of him he gave two stupendous leaps and with that formidable stride in full working order he pulled the leaders back. As we began the turn into the final straight we hit the front. Then Roughan, with Philip Fielden sitting ominously still, galloped easily past us and took a two length lead. Point of Law loomed up alongside. I began to feel uneasy.

Coming into the Pond fence – the third from home – the three horses were well clear of the rest and Pointsman was closing on Roughan. I drove him into the fence and there he made the worst mistake I ever experienced. There was a thudding jolt and a crackle of birch. Again I seemed to be tumbling into an abyss yawning below me; the reins tore through my hands. Frantically I clung. Once more, when all seemed lost disaster was averted by that long brown leg appearing from nowhere. As he recovered Pointsman's nose, according to several spectators, actually touched the ground. By the time we had staggered upright again we were nearly stationary. Several lengths ahead Roughan and Point of Law were galloping into the penultimate fence. We could hardly be better than third.

Amid my despair a violent spasm of determination possessed me. I was NOT going to lose this benighted race yet one more time. I gathered Pointsman together and hurled him forward in pursuit. It looked quite hopeless until I began to realise what a tremendous horse I was riding.

At that time Pointsman was a comparatively undeveloped six year old and had had a hard season. In this race he had made two mistakes, either of which would have been disastrous to a normal horse and which had lost him a conservative 20 lengths. In a quarter of a mile, starting from almost a stand-still, he had to overtake two good horses which had a lead of six lengths over him or more. He lowered his head and dourly extended his stride as he battled up the Sandown hill.

Coming into the penultimate fence, which he jumped superbly, he had cut the distance to four lengths and, ridiculously, I began to hope. I thought I could detect signs of the well-known Sandown gradient beginning to have its effect on the two leaders. They began to weaken very slightly and they both came away from the rails into the centre of the course. Pointsman and I, ravenous for every inch of ground, hugged the rails. As we rode into the last fence we were only a length behind.

Everything depended on this last fence. But I could feel that he was hopelessly out of stride and all set for another ghastly error. The only chance we had was for him to stand off nearly from outside the wings and reach for it. If he tried to take another stride, as he had done twice before, we were finished. I asked him to perform this nearly impossible stand-off and he rose magnificently to the occasion. Few people can have appreciated what it cost this young horse, by now very tired, to put everything to the touch as he now did. Our two wills fused and exploded, and he did the only thing that could have won us the race, a decision welling up instinctively from the fighting intelligence which only top-class thoroughbreds have. He unleashed a rocketting bound which carried us past the two leaders, and after a desperate struggle up the straight, past the post – by a neck.

So at last I had the honour of receiving the Grand Military Gold Cup from the Queen Mother. I received another honour too. In the bar afterwards we were toasting with champagne not only my first win of the race but Alec's as well, when the trainer's stern, impassive features cracked into a smile and he paid me the only compliment I ever received from him. 'Monkey, that last fence was a real good effort.'

Over this glass of champagne my active racing life ended. I have deliberately not called it a career because it does not merit the word. I started too late and there had been too many interruptions, but I would not have missed it for anything. All the trouble, the time, the worry, the disappointments, the expense

– each succumbs to the all-powerful infection which is called the racing bug. And, of course, hope springs eternal.

Soon after this I went north to command my regiment and, our finances being in an even worse state than usual, we were forced to sell Pointsman. Although the main point of owning him had gone because I could no longer ride him, Alec was furious and never really forgave me, but it had to be done. We made sure that the horse stayed in his stable by selling him to Sir Percy and Lady Orde, the owners of Alec's other star, Galloway Braes.

In a career marred by his jumping errors Pointsman remained for years one of the best two or three steeplechasers in England or Ireland. The newspaper headlines of the time tell the story. Here are a typical couple, Press cuttings from long ago. *The Times* 'Fine riding by Morrow – Pointsman survives uneasy fencing'. The *Daily Telegraph* 'Pointsman the Gay Cavalier – just about the best three mile chaser in England'. And so on over the seasons, until he strained a tendon, when the Ordes generously gave him back to us.

There were many years left of my association with this magnificent horse. We patched up his leg, sent him back to Alec and now he was ridden by Tim Brookshaw. That fearless and powerful horseman never had the slightest trouble with Pointsman's jumping. For the first time in the horse's life he was confident and relaxed in his races and hardly ever made an error. On his second appearance he took on the top three miler of the day, Mandarin, at Worcester at level weights and beat him by three lengths, so earning one of his last headlines – Hotspur in the *Daily Telegraph*: 'Enigmatic Pointsman in the Limelight Again. Pensioned off chaser used as a hack beats Mandarin'. This form encouraged us to enter him in the King George VI Steeplechase at Kempton on Boxing Day, the eve of his 12th birthday, in 1959.

As usual all the best chasers in England and Ireland had been entered, and we were desolated to hear on Christmas Eve that Tim Brookshaw had hurt himself and could not ride on Boxing Day. Alec put up a comparative newcomer, Tony Keen, who was soon afterwards killed in a motor smash.

Over the last three fences Mandarin and Pointsman had drawn several lengths clear of a field which included Pas Seul and Lochroe, the first and second in the Cheltenham Gold Cup three months later, and had the race to themselves. They fought it out in a desperate finish, neck and neck to the winning post, where Mandarin gained the verdict by a short head.

Tony Keen had ridden an excellent race but I remain convinced that Tim Brookshaw, with his strength, experience and knowledge of the horse, would have won the King George VI Steeplechase for us by a length or more. The finish had been so fiercely fought that both horses were drained and exhausted. Pointsman had to come out of training and ran but once more, many years later;

that battle signalled the virtual end of Mandarin's career too. I like to feel that this final 'tour de force' showed the true measure of Pointsman, then approaching the veteran stage. His reputation in racing history is that of a talented horse but a clumsy and careless jumper. If he had been properly educated in his youth this last race showed that he had the ability to have been a really great steeplechaser.

After the race he came home, and being then at Sandhurst I hunted the Staff College Draghounds off his back, with my two sons sometimes acting as whippers-in on their ponies. Having earned his hunter's certificate he won the Grand Military Hunter Steeplechase at Sandown by 15 lengths, admirably ridden by Nick Ansell, without the semblance of a mistake and aged 14. To prove further there was nothing wrong with his jumping he won several show-jumping competitions and later, when we were stationed in Northern Ireland, he carried me magnificently over the stone walls of the Galway Blazers.

I had first mounted Pointsman when I was a major and my last win on him was as a major-general. Back on Salisbury Plain we achieved the feat which, although totally unsung, still gives me more pleasure and pride than any other I have achieved on a horse. In an important Open Hunter Trial across country there were entered several leading three day event horses and at least one top show-jumper. The fences were high and flimsy and had to be jumped against the clock. Our veteran partnership scorched round, clearing all the fences and won the event by completing the course a full minute faster than anyone else. Nothing careless or clumsy about his jumping that day. By then he was rising 17 and soon afterwards his gallant life was over.

To have owned, if only for part of his racing career, and ridden a horse like Pointsman was a privilege for which I, as a professional soldier, am truly grateful. My thanks must mainly be laid at the feet of Alec Kilpatrick, for he could so easily have sold this promising young horse to a rich and established owner rather than to me and have had him ridden by a professional. I hope he felt that I had perhaps earned the honour.

Meanwhile chance – and Alec – opened another door.

CHAPTER EIGHT

Double life (1955–61)

Catterick Camp in North Yorkshire in the 1950s was the perfect background for the plays which have since appeared on television about the horrors of National Service and the iniquities of the army generally. The writers had usually failed as soldiers and become embittered; many had tried for commissions and had been found wanting. The icy Nissen huts with their stone floors and coke stoves, the bleak east wind or driving rain which whistled round them, the brown-grey monotony of the landscape and the general ghastliness of the camp in those days must have been manna from heaven to these authors as, many years later, they dipped their pens in bile and began to write.

I took command of my regiment in 1955 after it had begun its stint as a training unit for recruits, the vast majority of whom were National Servicemen. Our regular soldiers, trained to fight in tanks, had willy-nilly and temporarily to become instructors; not all found it easy but the good humour and practical intelligence of the cavalry soldier soon mastered the problem. They got on with the job and made a success of it, as they always do.

We tried to ensure that the regimental friendliness, compassion and professionalism percolated down to the teenage civilian shivering in his Nissen hut.

On the whole I believe we succeeded. A minority of recruits were determined to hate their National Service and did; the majority were neutral, in our camp benevolently neutral. These were the 'nig-nogs' who kept calendars beside their beds on which they crossed off each day's march nearer home. A sizeable minority actually enjoyed their two years in the army and a good many of these went so far as to stay on as regular soldiers.

The wing for potential officers was run by Ian Manning, who after his retirement in later years was to be found presiding as clerk of the scales over racecourse weighing rooms throughout the land. Jockeys and trainers can be temperamental and unpredictable, and Ian's potential officers must have helped to get his eye in for his future role. As might be expected, they were an entertaining and varied lot. Some have since become prominent – a well-known comedian, one of the present leaders of the television industry, some who have now qualified as 'great and good' – all passed through Ian's hands with varying degrees of military success.

The regimental signal sergeant of the day was heard expressing in later years at a regimental reunion his fears concerning the country's economic recovery. Evidently he had just learned from a newspaper the names of some of those connected with it. 'I took these people line-laying,' he said scornfully, 'and whatever I said I could not make them understand that a ladder must be placed against the trunk of a tree, not a branch. Usually they would place the ladder against a bough. All four would struggle up the ladder until they passed the point of balance. They are now high positions. God help us all.'

Some of the sons of the nation's then leaders came under our wing, and did not all appear to have inherited the qualities of their fathers. This could cause problems. The son of one particularly important Minister was considered by Ian to be a certain failure for a commission and should under no circumstances damage the regiment's reputation by being allowed to appear before a War Office Selection Board. Whilst agreeing with Ian's assessment of the lad I felt it would be wise to send him and, lo, he passed.

Every five weeks a batch of recruits would pass off the square, and the parade provided an opportunity to meet and entertain – and perhaps impress – their parents. In the short address which I gave at the end of these parades, I was fully aware that I was not only talking to the recruits. In the make-shift stand behind me might be sitting captains of industry, prominent figures in the TUC, senior civil servants, headmasters, members of the 'media', the distinguished together with the less distinguished, many of whom, in their genuine pleasure at what they were seeing, were a joy to meet.

The eventual passing of National Service was certainly not lamented within the army, but the loss of the contact which the Forces had to maintain with the

Frankie Festing (right) on tour in the USA 1959 in usual garb.

ABOVE: *Gerald Templer (left), Frankie Festing (looking unusually dressy). Two Chiefs of the Imperial General Staff on handover day 1959.*

LEFT: *1935, Sandhurst winning the mile in the triangular athletics match against Woolwich and Cranwell.*

ABOVE: *August 1936, my troop at camp near Lewes.*

BELOW: *Big Ben (centre) coming through to win his race at Aldershot 1939.*

ABOVE: *The Mark VI B 5-ton tank with which the BEF Divisional Cavalry regiments were equipped in 1939/40.* (With permission from the Tank Museum)

BELOW: *Our infantry (the 3rd Monmouths) take a rest beside one of our tanks on the road to Le Bény Bocage, August 1944.*

ABOVE: *Sgt Sear, first tank commander into Le Bény Bocage is thanked by the populace, August 1944.*

RIGHT: *Major-General Pip Roberts, GOC 11th Armoured Division.*

ABOVE: *Peter Walter DSO (left), Fred Jackson MM (right). Two gallant 23rd Hussars in later years.*

MAJOR W. G. SHEBBEARE

Former President of Oxford Union Society Missing

Major W. G. Shebbeare.

LEFT: *Newspaper cutting about Bill Shebbeare. Originally reported missing he was in fact killed in action.*

RIGHT: *Brigadier Roscoe Harvey (left), Lieutenant-Colonel Perry Harding (right), 1945.*

LEFT: *With Alec Kilpatrick.*

ABOVE: *The Chair, Aintree 1952.*

BELOW: *Receiving the 1954 Grand Military Gold Cup from Queen Elizabeth the Queen Mother after Pointsman's win. My father watching on my immediate right.*

ABOVE: *Over the last fence, The George VI Steeple Chase, Kempton Park, 1959, Pointsman v. Mandarin.*

RIGHT: *With Pat Smythe 1959.*

ABOVE: *The Queen, with the prize winners of the Rome Grand Prix 1961, meets Workboy and rider.*

BELOW LEFT: *Off to Ascot races.*

BELOW RIGHT: *Visiting a stud with Zulu on tour in New Zealand.*

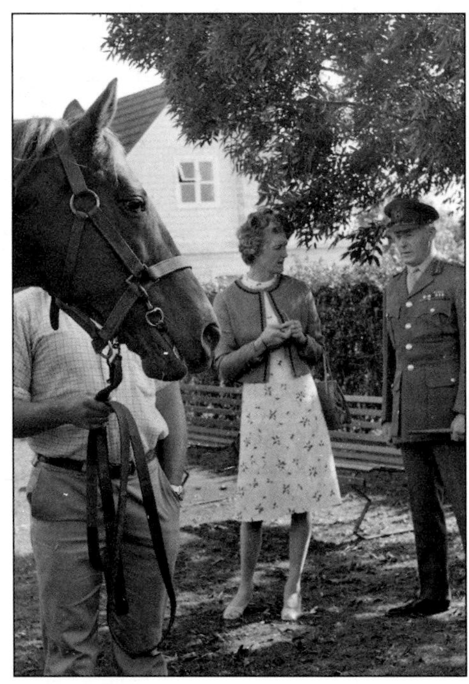

Workboy in the Hickstead Derby.

LEFT: *A helicopter view of Arnold's Spur, with the Wadi Dhubsan off the picture below right.*

BELOW: *From the left: Jack Dye, Denis Healey, Charles Harington (C in C), self, in the Radfan.*

ABOVE: *The para gunners see something. Denis Healey (left), Charles Harington (centre), and self in the Radfan.*

BELOW: *Watching a TA para company preparing for their jump in the Strategic Reserve exercise at El Aden 1965, and looking cross because my C in C had forbidden me to jump with them. Brigadier Glyn Gilbert in the background.*

ABOVE: *The Adjutant-General meets some Chelsea Pensioners.*

LEFT: *Phil Bull.* (By the courtesy of Timeform Ltd)

RIGHT: *Paul Maze at work.*

BELOW: *My impression in oils of a local view.*

ABOVE LEFT: *Philip, who was a professional steeplechase jockey but now sculpts.*

ABOVE RIGHT: *Terence, who writes.*

BELOW: *With our last racehorse, Proud Pilgrim, winner of seven races, and Perry.*

British public is certainly a matter for lament. Nearly every member of that public had a relative in the Services and had to take an interest in what was happening to him. A kind of love-hate relationship grew up between the civilian and military worlds and much misapprehension was thereby avoided. Now the regulars have withdrawn to their camps and live their own introverted lives; the military world is a closed book and, except in emergencies, an irrelevant one to the great majority of the British public. This is sad, but is a price that had to be paid.

The National Serviceman soldiered, often with distinction, through the overseas emergencies of the time, and I would never criticise the contribution which he made. Small as the modern regular army is – and now getting smaller still – without doubt the present system is far more professional, far more effective and far more economical than the National Service system it succeeded. Indeed, having been a participant in the 1970s of the emergency in Northern Ireland, I believe that the political and psychological pressures on our soldiers might well have been too heavy for the National Serviceman. I know I was always glad that it was a professional soldier who was standing in those streets enduring, from both sexes and from children, the missiles and the abuse.

The command of a regiment – and no doubt of a battalion, or of a ship, or of an RAF station – is a responsibility so consuming of thought, time, energy and compassion that I cannot believe that a comparable role exists outside the Services. For the only time in my life, the buck really did stop here. The brigadier above played no part in the day-to-day life of the regiment; the squadron leaders below were only responsible for their squadrons. The regiment's performance, outlook and character reflect that of its commanding officer. This is no surprise for almost every decision and policy change is made personally by him; he is involved in its work, sport and family life totally. To avoid becoming ridiculously overworked, one's conscience has to be kept in check and a sensible system of priorities operated. Once this is done the life of a commanding officer was, and doubtless still is, immensely rewarding, satisfying and enjoyable.

The role of a training unit was demanding but smacked too much of the production line. For thrills we had to rely on sport. We soon found that the only way of avoiding sporting ignominy in the highly competitive garrison of Catterick was to take a leaf out of our opponents' books. Our football officer was soon visiting Manchester United and Liverpool and our boxing officer the northern boxing clubs to recruit prospective stars whose National Service was imminent. I had no scruples about doing this at all, and it worked. Soon our football, boxing and athletic teams had made their mark in circles wider than the Catterick garrison, and this was good for morale.

Although I personally participated in the athletics and the boxing, we had been willingly reclaimed by the hunting field, and memories of days with the Zetland and the Bedale hounds are very happy. The hunting families of North Yorkshire were welcoming and kind, and those who still survive – alas, few – remain in contact to this day. For more competitive equestrian sport I turned my eyes to the three day event, and we bought a tough little horse called Bellman.

He was a first-class buy except that he hated dressage, and being a horse of character would only perform a test under protest which he made all too clear. Very soon I began to feel the same as my horse. I submitted myself to the guidance of the leading dressage trainer, Edy Goldman, but even his explosive talent could not conjure a relaxed test out of us.

My eventing career was brief. We entered in a one day event and trailed up to Northumberland for it. The dressage test with which Bellman and I opened our campaign earned such wounding written comments from the judge that I felt like bursting into tears. A brilliant cross-country restored my morale, but then, for the first and only time in my life, I entered the show-jumping arena, started before the bell had rung and was eliminated. A subsequent venture elsewhere provided further evidence that without a horse which would consent to perform its dressage test with more abandon, I was wasting my time – too much time in any case. As a reasonably conscientious commanding officer I could ill afford the long and tedious hours needed to make my horse fit enough and in circling endlessly to improve the dressage.

It was now summer and Bellman showed that he infinitely preferred the sport of show-jumping. In the local shows we were reasonably successful and although he did not have the spring to jump a really big course, he excelled at the 'speed' competitions over the smaller obstacles. Indeed two years later we sold him to no less a personage than Hans-Gunter Winkler, the Olympic champion. Meanwhile I found show-jumping at local level an adequate way of keeping the adrenalin flowing but entertained no great ambitions in the sport.

Show-jumping since the war had found its Messiah in my old regimental friend, Mike Ansell. Blinded in France in 1940, repatriated from a POW camp later in the war and awarded the DS0, this remarkable man found an outlet for his drive and energy in putting show-jumping, and later other equestrian sports, on the sporting map. I deliberately do not say 'back on the sporting map' because in truth show-jumping in this country had never been there. The pre-war horse shows at Olympia and Dublin were restricted to army officers, and at the local country shows the sport existed in an altogether humbler scenario. Two fences would be erected along one side of the ring, two alongside the other and a water jump in the middle. The rider, having cleared the four fences, would pause at the top of the ring to undo his tight martingale which restricted the horse's head, would then hurtle down over the water and disappear out of the ring. The sport generated no interest amongst the British public.

Mike soon changed all that. The world of the horse has never appreciated the good fortune which came its way through the tragic ending of Mike's army career. Had he emerged intact from France as a young commanding officer, his leadership qualities, given ordinary luck, could well in my judgement have taken him to command of an army corps as a lieutenant-general by the war's end – given ordinary luck, quite a big proviso, knowing Mike's character. His father had been killed in command of his regiment in 1914 in the first few weeks of the war, leading from the front; his son would have led in the same way. Again, his autocratic temperament and towering personality would sooner or later have led to personality clashes; had one of these been with, say, Monty, his career might have withered on the vine. But all this is irrelevant conjecture. The reality was that fate had contrived to place this outstanding leader, still in his early 40s, in charge of a sport in which he had himself reached international standing before the war.

As far as was possible he acted as if he was not blind at all, and talked quite naturally about 'seeing' people, or 'watching' a competition. He developed a formidable memory and an uncanny way of sensing what was going on around him. He grasped every opportunity to promote equestrian sport, and shrewdly realised that show-jumping was a 'natural' for television. He also realised that the way to public recognition and applause was through international success. For all this he needed money, and to attract financial help he had to have at his elbow a personality from the business world. He found his man in the advertising firm of Pearl and Dean.

Bob Dean was a master-negotiator and you could see why. His charm and wit were overwhelming, but underneath you sensed the shrewd financial and business brain which long experience in a tough environment had developed in him. Mike and Bob made a perfect partnership, the one decisive, forward-looking and commanding, the other flexible, engaging and with a clear eye for the main chance. Jack Webber, Mike's secretary-general, ran the office and the day-to-day routine – the ideal foil, calmly absorbing the rough with the smooth, and skilled at pouring oil on waters that could become distinctly troubled. This exceptionally able team of three worked whole-time at promoting and directing the competitive horse world. It is hardly surprising that this world prospered exceedingly.

Show-jumping was also lucky in the late 1940s that two individuals appeared who in their different ways appealed to the public. Harry Llewellyn was one of nature's winners. He had ridden prominently in the Grand National before the war and had reached the rank of lieutenant-colonel during it. He was already a successful businessman and now he had the time and the money to deploy on the stage of show-jumping his skill as a horseman and his will to win. His acquisition of the famous Foxhunter was not luck. It was the result of a thorough and intelligent search for a horse to take him to the top. Being Harry, he succeeded, and the bronze medal Olympic team in 1948 and the gold medal team in 1952 were not only led by him but largely mounted on his horses.

The other personality was Dorian Williams, the commentator in the television programmes. He was the fortunate owner of a voice which people liked listening to; it made them relax and feel comfortable. I expect now that he would be considered too 'la-di-da', but he maintained his popularity over 30 years. His style was that of the best sort of schoolmaster – which he once was – informative, humorous, knowledgeable, enthusiastic, allowing occasionally just a hint of his erudition to show through. No one since, in my view, has come near to casting the spell that Dorian could, and he played a crucial role in the 'selling' of equestrian sport to the public in those early days.

I viewed all this with detachment and from the sidelines. Then in late summer a casual and unpremeditated act of mine opened a door into a land of which I had only dreamed. I picked up the *Horse and Hound* magazine and my eye fell idly on the list of horses due to be sold at Ascot sales on the following day. I saw one name on the list and was wafted back through the mists of memory to an August morning six years ago on the gallops at Herridge. I was standing next to Alec Kilpatrick and looking with wistful longing at a little black four-year-old horse called Workboy.

It was during the period when we were still searching for our star chaser and on this sunny morning Alec had put me up on this new acquisition for a school over hurdles. My mount was young, undeveloped and not particularly impressive, still rather undersized but cheerful and wiry. It was when we turned to advance upon the hurdles that my eyes were opened. He pricked his ears, obviously viewing with delight the prospect of jumping, and flew over the obstacles in a manner which took my breath away. Never had I ridden a youngster that could jump like that.

Consumed with longing, I asked, 'How much would he be, Alec?' The trainer looked at me sadly, 'Two thousand, I'm afraid.' In those days this was a lot of money and as far as I was concerned that was definitely that. It was indeed his jumping ability that made him so expensive; in Ireland he had already acquired an outstanding reputation, having been hunted over banks and thoroughly schooled. He was soon snapped up by one of Alec's owners and over the years I watched with interest his career as a two mile steeplechaser. His courage and speed matched his jumping, and he was soon perhaps the best two miler in the country, with wins at Cheltenham, Newbury and other leading tracks.

In all he won 13 steeplechases, but by then the strain began to tell. He pulled a tendon badly and no longer was of any use as a racehorse. His owner, like, alas, so many, had no more use for him and sent this faithful servant, whose gallant struggles had enabled him so often to preen himself in the winner's enclosure, to be sold, to anyone, anywhere. What did it matter now? The horse was no good.

We did not hesitate to try and buy him despite having no idea of what we would do with him. The possibility of show-jumping him never crossed our minds. We telephoned Alec and he kindly went to the sales. For the sum of 137 guineas Workboy was ours. He arrived bearing his ten years lightly, but the tendon looked terrible. Obviously it would have to be fired and this was done so well by our vet that the leg never gave any more trouble during the seven years of work that lay ahead of him. It is worth remembering that if the present ban on firing had existed then Workboy could only have gone to a knackers yard.

Once recovered he became Zulu's hunter and his excitable nature made this at first a doubtful pleasure. When the season ended we decided she and Workboy should accompany Bellman and myself to the local shows. The more experienced combination was given little time to be condescending for, on his second appearance, Workboy was placed in a novice class, and then, in only his third time in the ring, gave a magnificent performance to finish runner-up in the novice Championship of the North. Following this we had to fend off the professionals who approached us with fancy offers, and, realising that we had on our hands a potential star, Zulu with typical generosity handed him over to me. This was a real sacrifice; much of Workboy's subsequent success was due to the love, sympathy and understanding which she had lavished on this far from easy horse during his early training.

So, in August 1956, began my partnership with Workboy. I was almost as inexperienced as he was, and it was lucky that his ability as a jumper was matched by his courage, for some of the troubles into which we, sometimes literally, fell, were spectacular. These troubles did not manifest themselves until I got ideas above my station and entered him in open classes against all comers. In his racing days he was accustomed to launching himself into space and relying on his spring. These tactics worked well enough over comparatively small novice fences because he was able to bound over them like a stag from wherever he decided to take off. In such classes we usually jumped several clear rounds and won.

Emulating the top jumpers I would take him round the course slowly and deliberately. When we first competed in open classes with far bigger fences, wider spreads and tricky combination fences this method proved disastrous. Poles crashed, splintered, flew up in the air and I had to retire, extremely crestfallen. Bryan Marshall, the jockey, had watched in horror. 'For God's sake, Monkey, take him faster, these old racehorses are lost without speed.' Wise advice, which I followed. We now galloped round and, as my eye for measuring strides improved, our disasters became less frequent.

The season ended, leaving me with a clear idea of the gulf that separated us from the leading jumpers. We watched on television the Olympic teams in Stockholm battling it out over fences far more imposing than any I had ever dreamed of. But ambition was astir. I realised that fate had, again but in a different sport, presented me with the horse of a lifetime. He was certainly good enough to jump that gulf and I hoped I was too.

Early in 1957 my regiment left Catterick and returned to the British Army of the Rhine. The military tempo became a good deal brisker there and I had little time for horses. But there were just enough spare moments to visit some German shows, and Workboy could not have had a better education than jumping round the German courses. They were vastly superior than any to be found at the British county shows, even after some years of Mike's influence – far better built and more encouraging for the horse.

Show-jumping is more deeply rooted in Germany than it is in England. The passion for fox-hunting in the British Isles had diverted much of our natural talent away from competitive equitation, while continental talent had no other outlet. In any case the relaxed 'make it up as you go along and never mind the finer points of riding' attitude of the hunting field was anathema to the Teutonic temperament. The Germans abhorred the deliberate amateurism and, in their eyes, the ignorance, of the British horseman. They practised meticulous and orderly control learnt in the dressage arena leading, when the horse graduated to jumping, to the rider's domination of the horse's every movement and to the elimination of any initiative on the part of the horse. Applied to the unpredictable demands of the English or Irish hunting field this method would soon have left most of its practitioners upside down in a ditch. In a show-jumping arena it was a different matter. The leading British show-jumpers of today – the Whitakers and Nick Skelton – have managed to combine the accuracy of the Germans with the dash and initiative of the British and so are in my opinion the three best show-jumping riders in the world. But in the 1950s the difference was still marked.

After reasonable success in German shows I was bold enough to enter Workboy, though still technically a novice, in the Hamburg 'Spring' Derby. This competition was at that time unique, though it has since been copied almost fence by fence at Hickstead. The high steep bank with the rail at the bottom so familiar to British television viewers is an imitation of that at Hamburg, and the Hickstead Devil's Dyke was in Hamburg called Pulverman's Grave. The course contained several other banks, no combination fences and was a kilometre long. Every leading horse and rider in Germany were competing, and Jean and Guy Wathen from my regiment and myself had inserted ourselves as an unofficial British team, parading behind a Union Jack without any permission from the British Show-Jumping Association.

The competition began before an enormous crowd and beneath black and ominous clouds, which soon delivered themselves of intermittent showers. The first into the ring was Winkler, the Olympic champion, with his second-best horse. He went round with twenty faults. For a long time this was the best score. Horses were having trouble on the high bank; they either refused to go down it at all, or tried to jump down and collapsed, or slithered down sideways. Very few arrived at the bottom and were capable of then jumping the five feet high rail there. In those days a good many of the German horses were heavy and common; these became tired and careless towards the end of the kilometre course.

I entered the ring on Workboy after 60 competitors had gone. Someone had just done a round with eight faults and was in the lead. As we cantered round waiting for the starting bell to ring a heavy shower began; as the bell rang and launched us, the rain suddenly became much heavier. By the time we had jumped two fences it had become a tropical downpour and I was soaked to the skin. I was much too casual about my equipment in those days and had not even provided myself with a pair of string gloves. The reins became like two slippery eels in my hands.

I guided my horse as best I could and left the rest to him. We were soon going a good gallop and he made light of the first five fences. Then came the open water, wide and with no fence in front of it – strange to him and he put a foot in it – four faults. The rain lashed down with furious intensity as we turned towards the big bank. Workboy pulled the reins straight through my hands and galloped determinedly up the two steps, charged over the rail at the top, and there immediately below us yawned the 14 feet drop. We seemed to be going much too fast and the crowd thought so too, for they gave a yell of expectant apprehension. I shut my eyes. I expect I should have prayed, but in fact all I said was, 'You can sort this one out, chum.' He did. We slithered effortlessly over the cliff and with a quick heave of his hindquarters Workboy propelled us neatly over the rail at the bottom.

Fifteen more fences passed unscathed below us. I still fought frantically to hold the reins. There loomed up a pair of very wide parallel bars with a deep ditch between them. My steeplechasing instinct took over and I asked for far too big a stand-off. He gave a gigantic bound in response but his hindlegs came down on the far bar. Eight faults. Three fences to go but they included one which

I well knew Workboy much disliked, Pulverman's Grave. He jumped it but not well enough. 'Bump, went the first bar, 'bonk' went the second. Two fences later we finished with 16 faults, to an astonishing ovation from the crowd. Evidently our battle in the teeming rain had impressed them, for they yelled their heads off as we left the ring.

We were only just out of the prize money, and I was consoled for this by the knowledge that Winkler and Halla, the Olympic gold medallists and the best combination in the world, had also incurred 16 faults. I have never had a more exciting ride show-jumping.

We jumped at several more German shows before the season ended. With the Wathens we ensured that the Germans could no longer ignore the Rhine Army competitors, though their stars continued to twinkle undisturbed above our heads. Then I returned to England and the CIGS's office, as has been related.

I experienced a good many testing times during the 15 years which I spent in Whitehall during my army service, but the first nine months of 1958 remain in a class of their own. Working for Gerald Templer, considerate as he was, during a summer packed with international and national crises, was in itself draining enough without trying to show-jump. Workboy was lodged in Knightsbridge Barracks, and somehow I had to exercise him as well as to take him occasionally to the shows. Each day provided a different conundrum of when and how. Our sporting summer was not particularly successful, but the office tempo eased in the autumn. We went to Brighton Show, where most of the show-jumping talent was assembled, and crowned a good week by coming third, against all the top stars, in the South of England Championship. We were nearly there.

On my return I spread out all the entry forms for the Horse of the Year Show in October, then held at Harringay, on my Whitehall desk, and wrote the name of Workboy against all the big competitions. This time I had not aimed too high. Workboy thoroughly enjoyed himself at Harringay. He loved crowds and the chance to show off; the bigger the occasion the better he jumped. He went brilliantly and won or was placed in every competition in which he jumped, including the puissance, and concluded the week by taking third place in the championship of the show on the final night. As I rode out of the ring I found that my old warrior had won many friends, and several rushed up to enquire if he was the same Workboy that they used to admire on the racecourse. I thought with pleasure of Alec and the staff at Herridge, doubtless watching with excitement on television the flowering of their old favourite's second career.

Shortly afterwards Workboy and I were asked to join the party of horses and riders selected to train for the British team. We had arrived.

I settled back in the Whitehall routine and forgot about show-jumping. 1959 opened comparatively quietly with a trip with Frankie Festing to the latest trouble spot, Cyprus, the only incident of note. On our return I received a letter from Mike Ansell asking me if I would accompany Pat Smythe to Chile and jump for Great Britain there. Having assured myself that the letter was not a leg-pull I read on and discovered that each of the leading show-jumping nations had agreed to send two riders to compete on borrowed horses produced locally in what was to be called the Inter-Continental Championships, to be held in February in Vina Del Mar. Frankie Festing was mildly surprised when his Military Assistant asked if he could go to South America at short notice, but Whitehall was fairly quiet at the time and he raised no objection. In the few days before my departure I enjoyed observing the expressions on the faces of my fellow Whitehall warriors when I told them that what they proposed for me next week would not be feasible because I would be in Chile.

South America is not on the list of places normally visited by the British military. To look down from an aircraft before landing at Rio de Janeiro, with the enormous statue of Christ presiding from a high hill over the wide sweep of the bay and Copabacana beach, to fly down the endless, sandy, palm-tree-studded east coast of South America and over the magnificent brown grandeur of the Andes, was deeply enjoyable. I was met by my team-mate, Pat Smythe, and formed a friendship which lasts to this day.

Pat at this time was at the height of her fame, at the point in her life during which if she came into a restaurant or bar the conversation would cease and the silence would be broken by hushed murmurs of, 'It's Pat Smythe, Pat Smythe.' She had in the early 1950s made a perfect foil for Harry Llewellyn as a competitor – Harry the dominant, wealthy and all-conquering male; Pat the demure, perky, attractive girl rider who had made the grade all on her own. The rivalry between them was good news for show-jumping publicity. Rather like Julie Andrews on the screen (whom she slightly resembled) Pat was the fresh, unspoilt English girl who won through in the end. She was showman enough to wear a red coat instead of the normal black for lady riders, and she made an attractive but resolute picture as she battled against all those hefty men. And she was, like Harry, a winner.

She is also an exceptional lady, far beyond her flair for show-jumping. That in itself places her on a sporting pedestal higher than that of any lady show-jumper, for she was unquestionably the best ever. Others – very few – may have equalled her skill as a horsewoman but none have had the same indomitable will to win, the nerveless reaction to the big occasion and the amazing ability to snatch victory in a jump-off by a fraction of a second against opponents who seemed unbeatable.

I could have had no more entertaining companion. She was, as always, determined to extract as much fun as possible from the trip, and her fame opened the doors of the large British colony who lived in Chile in the happier days than those which came later. Self-taught, she spoke several languages and was liable to burst into Spanish-American songs accompanied by her guitar. In her few spare moments, inexhaustible, she went on writing her latest book. She was, admittedly, going through her 'anything you can do I can do better' period. If, for example, you happened to say that you were thinking of learning to fly an aeroplane, she would be sure to tell you that she had already been allowed to pilot an airliner over most of the Atlantic. Competition was so much a part of her nature that a riposte like this was irresistible to her. Underneath all the fun and laughter, however, was a tough and very intelligent lady, of a staunchness which she was to need later in her life.

A constellation of international stars had assembled in Vina del Mar, but of course they all had to ride South American horses which they did not know and which had all been schooled in the South American way. This was a great leveller and a help to me because I had no fixed technique. I merely got on a horse and asked it to perform. I was well accustomed to mounting racehorses strange to me, whereas the Olympic champion, Winkler, cut a far less impressive figure when his mount ignored his signals instead of instantly obeying as a German horse would have done.

Besides Winkler and his wife from West Germany, the caste included Piero D'Inzeo, with his clown's face and classic seat, from Italy. Brother Raimondo fell out at the last moment, reducing our number to 15 and depriving us of the simultaneous presence of the reigning Olympic gold, silver and bronze medallists.

Spain sent Paco Goyoaga, a former world champion, and Commandante Espinosa de los Monteros, possessor of a memorable clanking French accent and 11 children. From France came Capitaine de Fombelle, a prickly and determined character, permanently smouldering. He took against South America from the first day and from then on everything, in his view, was expressly arranged to annoy him. His team mate, Pierre d'Oriola and former Olympic gold medallist, was in contrast calm and relaxed – a great man for a party, and he and Paco Goyoaga rarely got home before breakfast. To all these varied Europeans were added the best two riders from the Argentine, Chile and Colombia.

All depended on the standard of the jumper that each competitor pulled out of the hat and I drew a good one. Pat was not so lucky. We all had to ride our allotted mount in three competitions and the best four went through to the final in which they rode the other three horses in turn as well as their own. I managed to overcome my apprehension on entering the ring for my first international competition, and to my surprise I found that at the end of the three competitions

I was one of the four to qualify for the final. I was not sorry to find that neither Winkler nor Piero d'Inzeo had – one past Olympic gold-medallist, the Frenchman d'Oriola, was quite enough to be going on with. The other two were both South Americans.

The final developed into a battle between d'Oriola and myself, which experience narrowly won, and I had to settle for the runner-up. A brief celebration and I rushed to the airport, for the CIGS was due shortly to start on a visit to the Middle East and Africa.

When we returned from this trip, the 1959 season was about to start – the year in which Workboy and I made our bow upon the international stage. Our partnership was in its fourth season and he was still not the easiest of rides. He was excitable and preferred to gallop round a course as if he was still racing. Timing his stride into very large spread fences and tricky combinations still sometimes defeated my 'eye'. Despite all the knocks and vicissitudes of two careers, Workboy still loved jumping. He possessed the three necessary qualities for an international show-jumper – the ability, the courage and the instinctive carefulness which caused him to do all in his power to avoid knocking a fence.

In 1959 the Rome Olympics were only a year away, and with the leading riders short of adequate horses there were no certainties for the team. The field was wide open.

As I found many years later when I was chairman of the selectors, it is very easy to criticise. Even so, it soon became clear to me that the methods adopted to prepare and train the team were not going to end in success, and nor did they. Bernard and Lavinia Norfolk had had most generously allowed the potential team to use Arundel Park as a training area; their daughter Sarah was beginning to distinguish herself as a competitive rider and they were at the time benevolently disposed towards show-jumping. It was decided that these magnificent facilities should provide the base for a deliberate attempt at centralised training.

It did not work. It never has worked with the individual-minded and pig-headed British. The Americans, the Germans, other nations regularly and successfully practise it. Here it has always been a failure. The trainer and Olympic 'chef d'équipe' was Lieutenant-Colonel Jack Talbot-Ponsonby, saturnine, smoothly elegant and a highly successful cavalry rider before the war. He had made a study of the sport and was then chiefly occupied in building show-jumping courses, a task on which he had become an expert. If he was accused of sometimes devising a course which would suit the horses which he wanted to win or would not suit those which he did not want to win, at least the accusation was a tribute to his skill.

The potential members of the team ranged from stars like Pat Smythe, Wilf

White, Peter Robeson and Dawn Palethorpe, through the inexperienced but veteran combination of myself and Workboy to the young hopes for the future, David Barker, Ann Townsend, Sarah Fitzalan Howard – and a young brick-layer from Yorkshire called Harvey Smith. Harvey, a year or so previously when visiting a local horse show, had concluded that he could do just as well as the riders there and had found a horse of similar character to himself called Farmer's Boy. Neither cared anything for the orthodox, in appearance or technique, but they were winners. Quite how they achieved this was not easy to see, but win they did. The smooth and conventional show-jumping ladies and gentlemen of the day were scornful and inclined to jeer at this humble combination; in their myopic way they quite failed to appreciate the size of the fish which show-jumping had hooked.

He and I soon became friends and, despite ups and downs over the years, have remained so. Harvey's horsebox was usually parked next to my trailer, and it often became my duty to push this ramshackle machine down a slope to encourage it to start. This it accomplished with earsplitting cracks and jolts, accompanied by crashes from within as the petrol stove, the cooking utensils, the food, the dishes, the dog and the brave young lady who had agreed to become Mrs Harvey Smith, all fell about together.

Jack Talbot-Ponsonby was successful in training the young who were starting more or less from scratch, but he persisted in believing that similar methods would work with those who were more set in their ways. We were not allowed to train our mounts in the way which we had proved to be successful in the past; we had to scrap all that and abide by the gospel according to Jack T-P. This all too often consisted of being launched round a course of enormous practice fences in cold blood and, since Workboy was by now elderly and only jumped his best when the adrenalin was flowing, this was courting disaster. Others much more distinguished than I but equally set in their ways felt the same as I did. Pat Smythe remained there under protest, but Wilf White was soon on his way back to Cheshire and Peter Robeson left too.

I could anyway only make sporadic appearances because I had other matters to attend to, but somehow I avoided the sack. I could always tell when I was out of favour with the trainer – which was most of the time – because although he was personally suave and inscrutable, his wife Daphne was never able to hide her feelings. When I greeted her on the training ground in the morning and her eyes transmitted a laser beam of furious dislike in reply, I knew where I stood.

Luckily we were able to jump in true competition away from Arundel, and Workboy's courage enabled him to shake off his training experiences, which had included one spectacular fall. We performed well enough to ensure our selection for the British team to travel to Lisbon and Madrid. In Lisbon Workboy won his first international competition and in Madrid helped to win the Nations Cup for Great Britain.

The 1959 International Horse Show took place soon afterwards at the White City. This big outdoor stadium, now demolished, was not easy to fill with spectators and when half-empty could seem cavernous and depressing. On the Wednesday night, however, the King George V Cup was decided and every seat was taken. Nothing in equestrian sport has since equalled the glamour of this occasion, then the pinnacle of the show-jumping year. Every foreign rider especially wished to win the King's Cup, a truly international event. The acres of stone steps and serried enclosures were packed with spectators. The ring glowed golden, shot with colour. Round it, towering back into the darkness and seeming all the vaster for being half-concealed, the crowd muttered and hummed with anticipation. Soon it would be see-sawing in excitement between cheers and groans, building up in intensity until a roof-raising yell hailed the winner. Nowadays, with few foreign riders and until recently held indoors, the King George V Cup is a faint shadow of its great days at the White City.

It was the particular competition in which I had always longed to compete. In that year I had one pole down and failed to reach the jump-off, though in the following year I was equal second. In 1959, however, we won one big competition, the Imperial Cup, and as we stood in the spotlight with the crowd rising to God Save The Queen my thoughts ranged back to that school over hurdles on a little black four-year-old ten years ago.

We qualified for the Daily Mail Cup, the championship of the show, on the last afternoon. By that time my double life had left me so jaded that on my way round that enormous course in front of the packed crowd and the television cameras I twice, unbelievably, caught myself thinking about the arrangements I had made for the CIGS's trip to Australia – a very long way from the job in hand. I was riding deplorably, but Workboy was now able to look after himself, took complete charge and jumped round clear. With my mental processes better focussed we went clear again, but in the second jump-off against the clock were just beaten. Later that evening I was escorting the Field Marshal into his aeroplane for Australia.

By the time the 1960 show-jumping season had begun I was at Sandhurst as Assistant Commandant. The remaining 'possibles' for the Olympic team reassembled at Arundel, and again I joined them when I could. But not for long. The prospective team horses were examined by a vet who crushed my hopes by declaring that Workboy's heart was so badly strained that he might drop dead at any moment. Daphne Talbot-Ponsonby no longer needed to flash her laser beams at me for obviously I was no longer in contention.

Finding this hard to believe I asked our own vet, Peter Scott-Dunn, for a second opinion. 'Well, Monkey, it's bad, and there's no doubt you are taking a chance in riding him. It's up to you. I personally believe that he could well last for another two seasons yet.' An accurate prediction, as it turned out. The heart condition was obviously the result of those battles through the mud during six very tough years of racing, but the old warrior had never shown any outward sign and was clearly in perfect health. So I went on riding him but not for that year in the British team.

Nevertheless he was still jumping brilliantly and we won several big prizes at home. Observing this the selectors in 1961 had a change of heart, and for that season we were not only back in the team for Rome, the White City and Dublin but I acted as 'chef d'équipe'.

Meanwhile the team for the 1960 Olympics had been short of horses that were good enough. Pat had Bob Hanson's Flanagan, and it was only because Pat was riding him that he was considered; his scope was too limited to be that of a true Olympic horse. Dawn Palethorpe no longer had Earlsrath Rambler and was restricted to the 17-year-old Hollandia, well past his best. The young David Barker on the inexperienced Franco was a protégé of the trainer and a brilliant horseman. The fourth horse and rider, both then virtually unknown, proved to be the stuff of legend.

Sunsalve still remains in my memory after 30 years as the most extraordinary show-jumper I have ever seen, though not the best for he was too unreliable. His spring was so prodigious that he seemed to be flying, but he was headstrong, wild and appeared sometimes almost to go off his head. His owner, Elizabeth Anderson, had battled nobly with him, but he was far too much for her and she made him available to the British team. He was a far better jumper than Flanagan and so was offered to Pat Smythe.

She at once removed the complicated collection of ironmongery which the Andersons had in desperation inserted into Sunsalve's mouth and rode him in a plain snaffle, the simplest bit of all. Being Pat, she was soon able to canter him about calmly and controllably, and when she rode him in competitions all went comparatively well until she had to go fast against the clock. Then the usual dementia took over and the famous lady rider had for once to admit defeat.

The selectors played their last card. There was a 19-year-old lad in Wales who had been winning many prizes on an ex-army horse called Wildfire. His name – David Broome. His father, Fred, was a master in training difficult horses. So, more in hope than confidence, Sunsalve was sent to his stable. Fred replaced most of the Anderson ironmongery in the horse's mouth, and his son took him to the Rome Olympics. He promptly won the bronze medal in the individual event and jumped the best round of anyone in the team event. Sunsalve was as crazy as ever and David had many difficult moments with him, but then, like Lester Piggott in racing, David is a genius.

The rest of the Olympic story of 1960 is sad. Only three riders were then allowed in the team event, and all three had to complete the course or the whole team was eliminated. By 8 am on the appointed day our team was out. David Barker and Franco had refused three times, been eliminated and that was that. Two years of preparation had gone down the drain in two minutes. I have no doubt that the selectors were right not to risk jumping Workboy after the vet's verdict but all the same I know that we would at least have completed the course.

In 1961, although the old horse continued to jump with distinction in the British team in its tours abroad and was a regular member, he was rising 17 and his winnings were well down on the previous year. I decided that this must be his last international season. It was also time I finished. Many army officers only heard of me when they saw me riding on the television, and some were beginning to wonder if I ever did any soldiering. When a general met me in London and said breezily, 'Well, how's Sandhurst? Oh, I forgot, you're never there', the words struck home. Henceforth Workboy and I would only jump at local shows, when and where we liked.

Before our first appearance in 1962, I gave him a final school over a practice course at home. It was a joy to be on my old friend's back, to revel in his elegant flashing stride and to feel in his turns and responses the result of years of training and experience together. No longer did he make wild leaps into space; all was now timed, regulated and controlled – quick brain and wiry body in harmony. We soared over the line of fences, turned sharp and flicked perfectly over a five feet rail. That was enough. He was ready again. Tomorrow an exercise with his groom, and the next day back into the firing line. I walked him home quietly.

Next morning I passed his box as he was being made ready for exercise. His coat gleamed black and, with arched neck and ferocious mien, he made his usual pretence of savaging me. I laughed at him, commented on how well he looked and went indoors for my breakfast. Twenty minutes later there was a thunderous knocking on the door and there, panting, was one of the stablemen. He pointed to a distant wood. 'Workboy's collapsed, over there.' We got the land-rover and drove off. With the Olympic vet's prophesy surfacing in my mind, I knew what we would see. As we approached, his groom's distraught face told us all we needed to know. The black coat was dull and lifeless; his body seemed to have shrunk. Just an old, dead horse stretched out upon the ground.

CHAPTER NINE

Foot soldier (1962–66)

I was due after Sandhurst in 1962 for command of a brigade and an officer in the army posting department very civilly asked me where I would like it to be. 'Oh, please,' I replied, 'let me go off to Africa or the Far East and command a local brigade there.' There was a shocked pause. 'Oh, no,' he said, 'you can't possibly do that, you won't earn enough 'marks', not nearly as many as a brigade in BAOR.' 'But why?' I asked. 'I've already soldiered in Germany and in tanks and I'd like to do something different. Surely I'd get more marks for that, not less?' 'Oh well, it won't be easy, but I'll see what we can do.' So they sent me to command 39th Infantry Brigade in Northern Ireland.

It was certainly different, but at the time – the early 1960s – it was also a rest cure. The regular army garrison in the Province then consisted of two infantry battalions and an armoured car regiment. Since the brigade had no operational role as a brigade, I was provided with only four staff officers and a very small clerical and signals staff; none of us was overworked. Each of the three army units happily carried out its own training and pursued its regimental life; the brigadier took a benevolent interest in all this and occasionally tried to justify his existence by organising military or sporting contests between them.

When asked what our role in Northern Ireland was I used to say that we were a 'political presence'; available to act in an unspecified way against unspecified potential trouble in the Province. My predecessor had had to deal with some comparatively minor IRA activity on the border but by the time I arrived this had ceased altogether. The RUC occasionally produced reports, which we felt were unduly alarmist, about what might be brewing, but until the unhappy events of 1969 Northern Ireland remained a peaceful military backwater.

The general officer commanding, then as now a lieutenant-general, was Shan Hackett. He too was not overworked, and was enjoying what was virtually a sabbatical between the important posts he had recently filled and the even more demanding roles he was to occupy in the future. It seemed to me that he struck exactly the right note in the Province; he impressed the influential personages there with his formidable intelligence and character; he made his mark in all the different fields of activity and put in some useful practice on Ulster TV – where he was constantly in demand – for his future as a television personality. He had the knack of knowing what was going on in the military world without apparently trying; he left me to get on with my job and I enjoyed working under him. I found him extremely agreeable and stimulating but alarming. He was so clever and erudite that in conversation I was never quite sure if, ill-read as I was, I had missed some abstruse allusion or if I was just having my leg pulled.

My political boss was the Home Affairs Minister, Brian Faulkner. He was also master of the Iveagh Harriers, so we met in two fields of activity. He was an enthusiast in all he did and this certainly applied in the hunting field. Indeed he was fearless to the point of recklessness, and would gallop, reins flopping, flat out down the middle of a slippery road, eyes and attention fixed on the hounds. The last time I saw this brave little man was in much less happy days across a conference table at No 10 Downing Street in his concluding months as Prime Minister of Northern Ireland. Not long after that I was desolated, but not at all surprised, to hear that he had been killed out hunting.

Brian Faulkner in those days was politically very highly regarded but a somewhat isolated figure. Northern Ireland was then run by the 'gents' and they did not consider him to be 'one of us'. He was acknowledged to be the ablest politician on the scene, but the ruling class did not exactly clasp him to their bosom. One of them once muttered to me that of course Brian had not 'gone to the war' – a cardinal sin in such circles even though in Brian's case there was probably a perfectly good explanation. In the end, of course, in its hour of need the Province had to turn to him, and across the water I was then in a position to watch with admiration and concern his handling of what had by then become an impossible task.

In the early 1960s the Prime Minister was Lord Brookeborough, then in the concluding stages of his 20 years in power. He and his wife Cynthia were extremely kind to us, and lent us one of their houses on the Colebrooke estate as a second home. He is now in retrospect much criticised for not taking action to loosen and make more acceptable the Protestant grip on life in Northern Ireland, and there is surprise that in 20 years no one had managed appreciably to change his policy of leaving matters as they were.

As so often, looking back, the factor of personality is apt to be forgotten. Basil Brookeborough in force of character, presence and poise stood head and shoulders above anyone else in Ulster. His urbane and relaxed charm masked a formidable determination and strong prejudices, and towards the end of his long premiership no doubt the comfortable routine of the job added its own weight against any pressure for change. History will probably condemn much of what he stood for, but at the time there was no-one strong enough to take him on, and no-one, certainly not the British government, ever effectively did so.

Thirty years ago, too, Northern Ireland in its attitude to its ruling class – the gentry – was a good many years behind comparable attitudes across the Irish Sea. Ulstermen and women in general were much more respectful, less critical of authority and much more inclined to resign themselves to life, with all its injustices, as it was. It was not until a more liberal hand than Brookeborough's eased the lid off the cauldron that this attitude changed and the religious divide was brought savagely into the open.

The Ulster people are – a small minority apart – likeable, friendly, true and intensely loyal. To my mind it is inconceivable that we could ever leave these faithful people to the fate of civil war by pulling our troops out. Having said that, one is left with the depressing opinion that, however many political initatives there are, there is no solution to the basic problem of Northern Ireland. It is something that we have to live with, to make the best of and to hope that the more extreme manifestations will be softened by time. To try with rational argument to mollify the bitterness between the two sides simply provokes friendly, normal, easygoing people into becoming altogether different beings, passionately deaf to logic and reason. At times the antagonism seems instinctive.

Many years later, when visiting Belfast I met a Protestant on a line which by then had been drawn between the two religious communities, and he was uttering blood-curdling threats about what he would do to any Catholic who walked past him. I enquired, 'But how would you know that he was a Catholic?' 'I can smell 'um,' was the reply. And yet – and yet – sometimes the signals point in the opposite direction. A few weeks after this episode I visited my regiment, the Inniskilling Dragoon Guards, in Germany. The commanding officer's driver was a staunch Protestant and the batman, working closely and happily with the driver, came from the Bogside. It is no good trying to apply logic to this.

Back in the 1960s these problems were ever-present and indeed profoundly affected life in Ulster, but they were largely submerged. The main manifestation was the seasonal marches. We would watch these proceeding down the lanes of Fermanagh, for the military were encouraged to disappear during such occasions and we would be at our country retreat. Familiar now to television viewers, to us these marches were something new and revealing. Crammed into their bowler hats, swathed in 'the sash my father wore', the Orangemen marched in endless columns with an almost religious intensity and like a battering ram down the roads – beneath highly coloured banners and pictures of King Billy, drums thudding, pipes skirling, brass blaring, a cross-section of the whole countryside headed by their gentry. The processions would roll relentlessly and deafeningly over hill and dale, a defiant aggressive swagger masking a deep feeling of insecurity.

There was little to detain us in the headquarters at Lisburn, and we spent much time in Fermanagh. John and Rosemary Brooke became great friends. They opened the doors to fun and sport, much of which took place across the border. We crossed back and forth without a thought, and the Dublin Horse Show authorities were even persuaded to permit me, the British brigadier from the North, to ride the Brooke's show-jumper, Tyrenny, in their spring show as a civilian.

We fished for trout in two little lochs above Fivemiletown with the moors rolling down to the border a couple of miles away. Along the border we could glimpse some of the delightful houses that were situated there, and John and Rosemary suggested that we should buy one and eventually become permanent Fermanagh residents. Even on a heavenly evening with trout rods in our hands and with the lush green of the peaceful Fivemiletown countryside behind us, we had enough sense to realise that this was not really a very good idea. Now the little lochs are deserted because it is too risky to fish them, the houses along the border empty, the familiar villages of Lisnaskea and Belleek beleaguered, and Fermanagh a wary front line. Perhaps, God willing, it will one day recapture the peaceful charm which we were so lucky to know.

Meanwhile in the world outside Northern Ireland the dissolution of Empire proceeded apace and brigades, regiments and battalions were rotating feverishly on operational tours in the various trouble spots. The newspapers constantly told us that the British Army was overstretched, overstrained, and running out of soldiers to meet its commitments. We in Ulster knew that the British Army had not yet run out of soldiers; the brigade sitting there was far from being overstretched or overstrained. I pointed this out to the London authorities, but in vain. Northern Ireland was sacrosanct; none of us would be moved, whatever I said. I was considerably mollified by the splendid news that I was to be promoted to major-general and to command the 3rd Infantry Division, the strategic reserve, on Salisbury Plain, but that was nearly a year away. Meanwhile we seemed firmly stuck on the sidelines.

There was so little to occupy us at Lisburn that I could see no reason why, during the following winter, I need be there at all. We decided to take the whole family to County Limerick and spend the winter hunting with the top Irish packs. Six hours drive and I could be back in Lisburn if wanted, and there was always the telephone. In Croom House, County Limerick, there lived Audrey King, late Balding, of the Newmarket wartime days, two husbands later, residing in considerably more spacious surroundings, but otherwise still the same Audrey and still giving parties.

Croom House was the usual rambling, austere-looking Irish mansion, though there was nothing austere about what went on inside. Audrey warned that her dogs in the yard would kill anything smaller than a horse, but we could leave neither our dog nor our cat in Lisburn so they had to take their chance. Heavily chaperoned the Dalmatian, Pongo, survived but chaperoning our cat, Marie Louise, was impossible. She had a sand tray indoors, and after dark she was furtively let out for what we hoped would only be a brief exposure to danger. She did not always cooperate, and returned one morning agitated and with a much distorted tail. At least seven of her lives must have been lost on that night alone, but then she saw sense and kept miraculously within her nine.

The post-war Labour government, and the restrictive regime it introduced, had caused a mass exodus of the hunting gentry and their ladies from high Leicestershire in search of a more genial and relaxed sporting milieu. They had risen like flocks of migrating birds and had descended on the Irish counties which covered the Limerick Hunt, the Duhallow and the Black and Tans. Very soon, certainly in Limerick, they had effectively taken over the hunting and social life. The combination of Irish gas and Leicestershire glitz made a potent brew – horse and hound with the best Irish packs by day, and wine, glamorous women and song by night. The only news considered to be worth reading were the racing results; events in the outside world were a deadly bore. The hot news were more on the lines of, 'My dear, would you *believe* it, Jeremy's shacking up with Veronica and Freddie is *simply* furious but as he's been going to bed with Jane for months I can't imagine why he's so cross. Anyway why don't you come with the Tans on Monday – Thady says it's a good meet.

They were nearly all good meets. As the fox left the gorse covert there stretched before you a rolling green vista of little fields separated by high bushy banks. Crossing these obstacles provided none of the floating exhilaration of the English fly fence; this was a battle, each bank demanding different tactics. Most were precipitous and had bushes and undergrowth on the top; it was impossible to look over them and see what hazard awaited on the far side. You had to trot your horse at the bank; it would clamber vertically upwards and, provided it had not meanwhile entangled its feet in a concealed piece of rusty barbed wire, arrive at the top. If you were not in control your horse might well launch itself straight off again, often into a huge chasm or a wire fence. Better to stop and decide what to do. Usually it was wise to proceed along the top of the bank until a suitable exit on the far side presented itself. A safe descent with another imposing bank behind you was exhilaration in itself, always heightened by the soul-stirring cry of the hounds ahead.

Another and trickier variety of bank had nowhere on top on which to pause; the horse had to kick back and propel us into the next field regardless of the prospect on the far side. Only Irish hunters had the necessary knack and luckily all ours possessed it except for poor Pointsman, my old steeplechaser. He would bravely fight his way up to the summit of a broad bank, but the narrow banks were quite beyond him. When for the third time we picked ourselves up after collapsing into the next field I looked at Pointsman's reproachful face and decided we must make a different plan for him. After that I would drive him every week to Galway. There he was happy and so was I. Striding together across those wild fields, with the occasional glimpse of the Atlantic and a series of stone walls stretching out into the distance, riding a Rolls-Royce like Pointsman and with the Galway Blazers screaming along two fields ahead in full view – what an unforgettable joy.

Back in Limerick I sometimes wondered how the local Irish were reacting to our presence and to that of the all-conquering emigrés. As far as we were concerned, since the emigrés accepted us as one of themselves, the shopkeepers, farmers, grooms and staff did so too. But I could sense that amongst some of the Irish hunting men the British Army brigadier from the North was not an entirely welcome guest. Not that they ever openly showed it. The Leicestershire invaders were, unlike us, by now part of the countryside, spending a great deal of very welcome money, and the natural good manners of the Irish hardly ever slipped. But anyone sensitive to atmosphere could feel something in the air which made me glad – immensely though we enjoyed our winter - that we did not live there. Now, 30 years later, the surviving emigrés have almost all re-emigrated. The party's over.

One day my headquarters telephoned to tell me that the Chief of the Imperial General Staff, Field Marshal Dick Hull, was coming shortly to inspect my brigade. Leaving the family behind to continue hunting I drove north. The Field Marshal, whom I knew quite well, was his usual intelligent and friendly self, and at the end of the visit I ventured to tell him that he was not deploying the British Army to its fullest effect if he continued to ignore the existence of my brigade, all of which, as he had just seen for himself, were well capable of helping him solve his problems. He smiled enigmatically and went away; I drove back to Limerick.

In due course we said goodbye to Audrey and Croom House, and in the spring resumed our fishing along the Colebrooke river. Suddenly an urgent signal arrived from London – the headquarters of the 39th Infantry Brigade was instantly to be despatched to Aden to take charge of the operations in the Radfan region north of the port. I discovered later that the CIGS had made this decision in the absence of the major general in charge of army deployment, who had planned to send another headquarters. When this officer returned from leave he was furious, particularly that the CIGS had responded to my lobbying. Nothing infuriates the middle man more than to discover that some tiresome junior has gone straight to the top and missed him out, especially if the junior gets away with it. Failing to change the plan, he tried the ploy of proposing that, since I was only a few months away from my divisional command, the officer appointed as my successor as brigade commander should go instead of me. He failed again. But such is the vindictiveness of a certain type of staff officer that he had another try two years later, in quite a different context, to put a spoke in my wheel. Again he was out of luck.

Within two days of the message's arrival I was in an aircraft with my advance party bound for Aden, followed two days later by the main body. Zulu suddenly found herself with two children, several horses, two houses, minimal military backing, and scores of abandoned wives to look after. Military families in those days by no means all resided in a compact married patch; most of these were scattered about in lodgings all over Belfast. Soon she was to find herself popping in and out of houses in such areas as the Falls Road and the Shankhill. 'I did think that once or twice people looked at me a bit oddly,' she was later to remark, but only as an afterthought.

We landed in Aden on 4th May and walked down from the aircraft into a temperature of 115 degrees. The soldiers who followed me out suggested that we should move away from the heat of the jet engines to somewhere cooler, and were dismayed to discover that their discomfort was not caused by the jets but by the normal heat of Aden; there was nowhere cooler. Soon I was being briefed by Major-General John Cubbon, who was to be my immediate boss, with above him the Commander-in-Chief Middle East Land Forces, General Sir Charles Harington.

What was the problem which we had come all this way to help solve? After the operations were over the headquarters of Middle East Land Forces produced a thick tome – described by Charles Harington as 'a big book about a little war' – which was inevitably a somewhat turgid read. The author, however, before

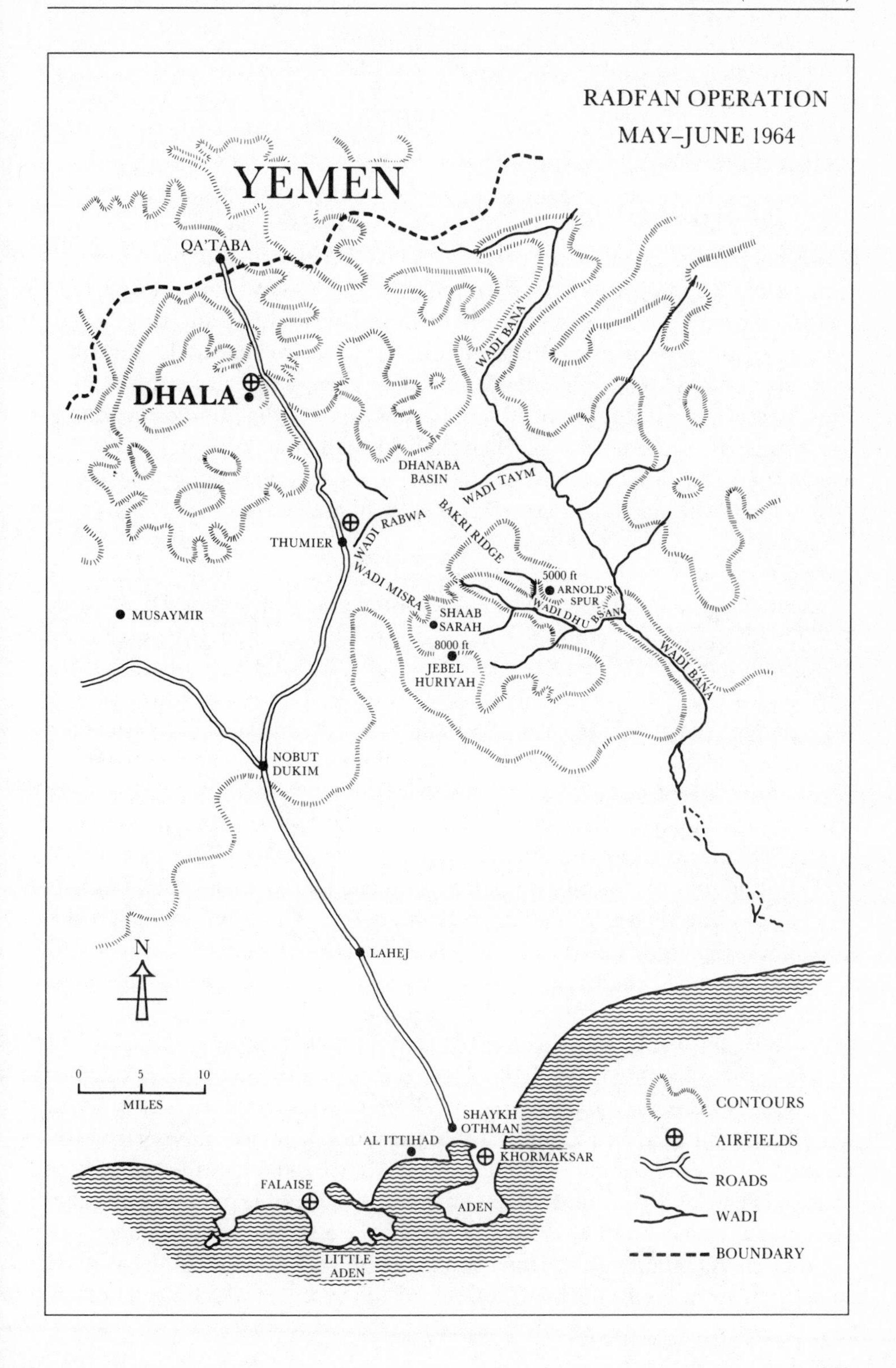
RADFAN OPERATION
MAY–JUNE 1964
YEMEN
QA'TABA
DHALA
DHANABA BASIN
WADI TAYM
WADI BANA
WADI RABWA
BAKRI RIDGE
THUMIER
WADI MISRA
5000 ft
ARNOLD'S SPUR
WADI DHU BSAN
SHAAB SARAH
8000 ft
JEBEL HURIYAH
MUSAYMIR
NOBUT DUKIM
LAHEJ
N
0 5 10
MILES
SHAYKH OTHMAN
AL ITTIHAD
KHORMAKSAR
FALAISE
ADEN
LITTLE ADEN
CONTOURS
AIRFIELDS
ROADS
WADI
BOUNDARY

plunging into the army abbreviations and Staff College prose, opened by waxing positively lyrical.

> Many years before the birth of Christ, trade started to move north from Aden into the Yemen and on into Palestine and Europe. From Zanzibar, Socotra and India came perfumes, frankincense, myrrh and many spices which were carried on camel caravans to Petra, Damascus and from there they were taken on to Rome, Paris and London. Caravans moved out of Aden through the forest and fertile basin of Lahej and wound their way through the mountains to Dhala and on to Qataba, well inside the Yemen border. Throughout Mohammedan history, pilgrims have used this road to Mecca and it is therefore sacred. However this has not prevented tribesmen from menacing this route from the high mountains on its flanks, and for centuries they have swept down on travellers, pilgrims and merchants with their camel trains and held them to ransom.

It was a good start but he could not keep this up.

The mountains of the Radfan lie to the east of the all-important Dhala road, and though nominally under the Federal government in Aden they were in fact not administered at all. Nor were they controlled. The turbulent tribesmen who inhabited the region ignored all authority. They had however in the past few years started to make their way to the Yemen and there sold their services for arms. The Yemenis, then hostile to the Aden administration, encouraged them to return in order to attack the forces of law and order in South Arabia, a task which the Radfanis greatly welcomed. The Dhala road became their main target.

The Radfan massif lies some 60 miles north of Aden and resembles the North-West frontier of India. If you were painting a scene in hot, steamy Aden, with its terraces of white houses dotted about on rocky slopes, shimmering under the glaring sun, you would have to use a lot of yellow ochre. In the Radfan you would also use raw umber, alazarin crimson, cobalt blue, just to start with – and even then only the greatest of artists could capture the majestic, many-hued grandeur of those jagged peaks and sheer cliffs rising to 6000 feet. The heat was 115 degrees by day and the reflection off the rocks made the temperature higher still, but it was much cooler by night. There was no water, except in small quantities in the two comparatively fertile areas, in villages ingeniously terraced on the hillsides and containing wells and cisterns carved out of the rock. Every tribesman carried a rifle, and there were look-outs, invisible, on every hill. The Radfan, magnificent as it was to behold, conveyed a strange air of menace.

The task of defending the Dhala road was the responsibility of the Federal Regular Army of South Arabia (FRA), the senior posts of which were held by

British officers, but by January 1964 the situation had begun to get out of hand. Several hundred Radfanis had returned from the Yemen and were operating in formed bodies, much too successfully. The FRA mounted an operation to deal with them, but since their main role was to guard the long Yemeni frontier and they only possessed four battalions, the numbers available to deal with the Radfanis proved inadequate. They were withdrawn, and soon reports began to come in of a build-up of forces crossing from the Yemen, of mines, sniping and armed hold-ups. The Federal government requested the aid of British troops and in mid-April Radfan Force had been formed.

The commander of Aden garrison was Brigadier Louis Hargroves. He was directed to form an operational headquarters and take command of the 45 Marine Commando, two FRA battalions, a company of the 3rd Battalion of the Parachute Regiment which happened to be on a visit from Bahrein, the armoured cars of the 4th Royal Tank Regiment and a battery of the 3rd Royal Horse Artillery. There was a very dusty airstrip along the Dhala road at the western end of the Radfan massif, near a village called Thumeir, and here Louis Hargroves and his 'ad hoc' headquarters were deposited by helicopter. The airstrip was too small for transport aircraft and the road from Aden was 60 miles of very hot, very bumpy and very dusty sand-track.

Radfan Force carried out some successful operations against the tribesmen, but after a week it became clear that the task would need a full operational brigade headquarters. (Since 39 Brigade Headquarters consisted of myself and but four staff officers, I must have briefed the CIGS all too convincingly.) On 2nd May we had received our orders to move, and by the time, six days later, we had assembled in Aden we were indeed a full operational headquarters, additional staff, clerks and signals having miraculously materialised from far and wide, all very excited and enthusiastic.

A week later I flew up to Thumeir and took over from Louis, who had obviously done splendidly against opposition rather more formidable than had been expected. He had established British and Arab soldiers in the 'fertile' areas of the Dhanaba Basin and the Wadi Taym, and had captured an important crag after a brisk operation which had cost the parachute company two killed and two wounded. But looking around me through the heat and haze of Thumeir, I very soon realised that there was no chance whatever of the new broom sweeping aside all opposition and advancing relentlessly into the mountains until a great deal of sorting out had first been done.

Operations in the Radfan had much in common with the traditional North-West frontier tactics, of which 'picquetting the heights' was the cardinal principle. This principle still held good but there was one fundamental difference between then and now – the helicopter, for moving troops, for reconnaissance and, above all, for supply. The whole pace, impetus and success of any operation would depend on the 'chopper' – and its availability when most wanted.

Louis Hargroves had had at his disposal four medium-sized Belvedere helicopters throughout. These were the only means he had of supplying, chiefly with water, the equivalent of two battalions which had advanced through the rocky foot-hills into the areas they now controlled. Even though they needed little ammunition re-supply and their food took up comparatively little space in the helicopter, large and heavy loads of water were vital. In the brief battle which had taken place the parachute company had had to carry out a two-hour climb up a cliff in the mid-day heat, and this had represented the consumption of two water bottles per man.

Now the Belvederes were due for a refit and the crews for some rest, and the first decision that had to be made was how to keep the two forward battalions supplied. The answer was a compromise, a drastic reduction in Belvedere numbers but not their complete disappearance, a reduction in the numbers of soldiers forward, construction of strips for light aircraft and the energetic pressing ahead with a road from Thumeir into the Dhanaba Basin and the Wadi Taym. I spent my first few days encouraging cheerful and hard-working sappers, with their supplies brought forward by camels, battling their way through the rock and shale of the lower slopes of the Radfan mountains.

The base at Thumeir grew daily bigger, and so did the force under my command. By the time we could start operations again I had four British battalions, two FRA battalions, an armoured car regiment, a gunner battery, an engineer squadron and a squadron from 22 SAS. Martin Jones, my highly competent and imperturbable brigade major, was assisted by my old friend Charles Taylor, who had been my regimental adjutant in days gone by, and whom I knew to be first-class. Barry Lane, my 30-year-old administrative major, had no hesitation in telling full colonels at Middle East headquarters that their immediate compliance with his requests was expected, and they all obediently fell into line. In just over a week the headquarters had blossomed into full operational competence, and out of confusion had materialised an effective administrative machine – all the result of my young staff's hard work and ability and very little to do with their commander, who had usually just flown away in his helicopter when they wanted him.

An unexpected problem arose immediately I arrived in Thumeir. The Secretary of State for Commonwealth Relations, Mr Duncan Sandys, proposed to visit my headquarters on the following day to tour the area and expected to be fully briefed by me. I knew from my previous experience of this Minister that it would be pointless to ask him to make allowance for the fact that I had only set foot in the place 24 hours before. If I could not brief him competently, I would soon be on a flight back to Belfast. Clearly I had to do some rapid reconnaissance.

The lieutenant-colonel commanding the Army Air Corps squadron of four-seater Scout helicopters and small fixed-wing aircraft, Francis Graham-Bell, chose to be my personal pilot and soon became an invaluable – and highly entertaining – companion. Together we now made the first of countless flights together, and I learnt as much from him as we flew over those jagged peaks as I did from the troops on the ground. At that time of year the Radfan was prone to patchy low cloud which descended over the peaks and rendered them only fleetingly visible. We needed to land on top of some of them. It was not always easy, as we approached a cloud, to know whether we could fly straight through it or if it was what Francis called 'a cloud with a hard centre'. He was a brilliant pilot and needed to be. Even then I had to hold my breath more frequently than I liked. On this first day of my command my brain and memory were working in over-drive, and by the evening I believed I had a good chance of satisfying the Minister on the following day.

I now profited greatly from having observed Mr Sandys in action when I had been in Whitehall. I knew that the only technique which worked with him was to answer his questions briefly and to the point and then shut up. A fatal error, which I had observed others make, was to volunteer a comment of their own to supplement their answer. This would immediately spark an inquisition. 'Why do you say that? Give me your reasons' ... 'Well that is not at all what I had been led to believe and I don't find it convincing.' Members of his staff would then intervene, the commander-in-chief would be asked for his views, the temperature might rise, and certainly the thread and the harmony of the briefing would be lost.

So, after I had formally briefed him from a map, I played all his questions with an entirely straight bat and it worked – my bails were left undisturbed. In what passed with the Minister for a good mood we then set off on our travels round by helicopter; there were no clouds with 'hard centres' and all went well. One company commander made the error mentioned above and gave Mr Sandys his views. Predictably he was chewed up and spat out again, but no harm was done and soon the Ministerial concourse was winging its way back to Aden carrying none of our scalps on their belts.

I now had to decide what to do next. Once the sappers had driven their road through to the forward troops, all the Belvederes were to return to Aden for at least a week. That meant – or appeared to mean – that no major operation could start until they returned and that we would be restricted to patrolling sufficiently actively from the areas which we held already to keep the Radfanis on their toes.

This delay was badly timed, for some of the battalions could only remain for a short while before being needed elsewhere. One or two were due to leave only a few days after the Belvederes reappeared, and this applied to the squadron from 22 SAS. They had been sent here to train in desert conditions for a month on their way to the campaign then proceeding in Borneo. They had already been in the sand for half of their stay, but had found that the training plan had quickly been jettisoned in favour of active operations.

Their regimental second-in-command, Mike Wingate-Gray, had accompanied the squadron and soon became a close confidante. He had a pronounced twinkle and a solid confidence-giving personality, but I soon realised that, in true SAS style, he was telling me all I needed to know and nothing more. The young squadron commander, Captain Peter de la Billière, was fair, fresh-faced and much like any other high-class junior officer until you looked at his eyes. These at once gave the game away; they told you why he was the most resourceful and battle-experienced officer of his generation.

The Radfanis had given the SAS an unpleasant welcome. Before I arrived there had been an assault on an enemy-held peak for which part of the plan had required a parachute drop by the 3 Para company – subsequently cancelled. An SAS troop of nine men had been told to secure the dropping zone some six miles behind enemy lines. The troop lay up some two miles from its objective, unfortunately in an area which was an enemy base. At dawn a shepherd wandered into their position and soon afterwards the Radfanis proceeded to surround it and snipe at it. Artillery fire and aircraft called in by the troop held the enemy off till late afternoon, but meanwhile the rebels had discovered that they were faced by only nine British soldiers. They assembled a force of some 90 men and at dusk they launched an attack. The troop was surrounded but fought its way out, losing two men killed. A few days later in the main square of the Yemeni capital, Sana'a, two severed heads were being displayed on poles. This news found its way into the columns of the Press, and a 'frisson' of disgust swept through the Western world. From then on the Radfan operation was regarded as a worthwhile target for the Press and we soon had to endure a permanently manned Press camp at Thumeir.

After this unhappy affair the SAS deployed their troops so that they could support each other. They were highly effective; their night operations causing a general withdrawal of the rebels from the areas in which the SAS were operating. Unfortunately before I could start full-scale operations again they had left for Borneo – much missed.

It was clear that our slippery but courageous foe was not going to give us the opportunity of securing victory in the orthodox way by facing us in open battle. Before deciding to launch a serious advance into the maze of cliffs, wadis and rocky peaks – an advance certain to be costly and difficult to supply, and likely to result in casualties and losses of expensive equipment – it was necessary to be sure about what I wanted to achieve. It was all too likely that, after enormous effort, our arrival on a peak would simply cause the Radfanis to slip away to the next peak and wait for us to get bored and leave.

I did not believe it to be very sensible simply to blast away at them with artillery and rocket-firing aircraft. Nor would it for long have been politically acceptable. A way had to be found to make them realise that opposition to us was pointless; we had to impress them psychologically that there was no stronghold of theirs into which we could not penetrate if we wanted to. Their two most inaccessible and and most-prized places in the massif were first, the Wadi Dhubsan, down a steep ravine in the heart of their wildest country and reputed to be their main stronghold. They would fight for this, I was told. The second was the highest peak in the Radfan, the 8000-feet Jebel Huriyah, situated at the end of the strongly-held Wadi Misra and dominating the whole of the Radfan. I resolved that if we reached its summit we would stay there. No Western foot had ever trodden either of these two strongholds.

The Wadi Dhubsan lay at the heart of the Radfan, and the only feasible route there was along the summit of a high and craggy feature called the Bakri Ridge. Our position in the Wadi Taym already gave us access to the lower slopes of this ridge, which rose steadily for some ten miles to a peak towering over the Wadi Dhubsan. It was ten miles if you drew a straight line on the map, but we soon discovered that each mile became three if you walked, or rather scrambled, struggled, tripped, slid or climbed through the razor-sharp rocks, the boulders and the shale in the searing heat. The escarpment harboured several large parties of the enemy. I decided that we should fight our way along this ridge until we could look down into the Wadi Dhubsan and then think again.

But this would have to wait for a week until the supply helicopters were available again. Meanwhile the RAF would keep up the pressure by strafing the enemy positions along the more distant half of the Bakri Ridge. That was the plan, until the arrival of the 3rd Battalion the Parachute Regiment minus the original company which had gone back to Bahrein.

From the areas of the Wadi Taym which we had already taken over, the 1st East Anglian, the SAS squadron and the FRA, combined with artillery and rocket attacks on known enemy positions, had by the 17th May so softened up the opposition on the lower slopes of the Bakri Ridge that patrols were meeting nothing. The RAF were to 'control' the more distant half of the ridge from 21st May and our main advance up it was due to start on the 25th. Meanwhile why not use 3 Para to patrol forward from our end of the ridge? They could not be expected to get very far without supply helicopters but it would be better than sitting still and waiting for the Belvederes to return.

I had reckoned without the commanding officer of 3 Para, Tony Farrar-Hockley. I had known him two years earlier when he had been instructing at Sandhurst, and he was obviously a remarkable character. How remarkable I was now to find out. I told him to take his battalion to our end of the Bakri Ridge and start to patrol forward along it. The depth of his patrolling would be governed by supply, and without Belvederes the assumption was that his advance would be local and limited.

On the night of 18th May Tony turned one of his companies into porters and advanced with the other. At first light his two Scout helicopters lifted the portered supplies further forward to the leading troops. He had evidently abandoned the patrolling idea in favour of a general advance along the ridge – not what he had been told to do but welcome nevertheless. I agreed that he should do the same on the following night and see how far he could get. By the night of 20th May, having had one brush with the enemy, 3 Para had made a spectacular advance and were established half-way along the ten mile – as the crow flies – Bakri Ridge.

I was amazed and delighted to receive this news from Tony at first light on 21st May. But there was a snag. 3 Para were now sitting in an area which the RAF were due to bomb in a few hours time. I contacted the RAF in Aden and asked them to avoid the position which the battalion had so enterprisingly captured. No problem, I thought, but there was. The RAF were highly displeased. The officer to whom I was speaking even, unbelievably, suggested that 3 Para should retreat off the ground they had captured so that the RAF could bomb it as planned. On this I cut short our conversation and, John Cubbon being ill, got straight on to the commander-in-chief. Charles Harington was as always understanding and helpful, and the bombing was shifted further along the ridge. But the RAF remained huffy. They sent a group captain, a welcome and delightful man, to sit at my elbow and prevent these wild army types from acting in such an unorthodox and unpredictable way. This was a happy arrangement and there was no more trouble.

Tony's enterprise had in effect advanced my plans by a week. I told him to continue up the Bakri Ridge and then launched two other operations. One was a sweep by the armoured cars of the 4th Tanks, commanded by Brian Watkins, round the south of the Radfan massif to put pressure on the enemy from that direction, and to stop the camel trains which were allegedly bringing supplies in from the Yemen. The other was a slow and methodical advance by 45 Commando up the Wadi Misra, with the Jebel Huriyah as their ultimate objective.

The 4th Tanks advance was admirably conducted and, according to our intelligence, had the effect of virtually stopping the camel trains from using this supply route from then on. The advance by the marines, due to start on 25th May, was partly to be supplied by the newly-arrived naval air squadron with their Wessex helicopters. The sailors provided a complete contrast to the airmen. Most were dark, bearded and piratical; they took terrifying risks with their helicopters and obviously delighted in doing so; miraculously they got away with it nearly, but not quite, always. This is no criticism of the RAF, who were first-class, reliable, steady and never let us down, but they played by the rules, while the sailors, at least to my untutored eye, thoroughly enjoyed bending them.

Just as the 45 Commando advance was due to begin – and I was soon to be heartily thankful that it had not already begun – the heavens opened and let fall a prodigious deluge. The rain seemed to pour out of the sky in solid sheets, and the Wadi Misra, up which the marines were to advance, became a torrent of swirling water. A naval helicopter pilot flying down the wadi was able to winch two soldiers off the roof of a fast-submerging scout car; he had to do this to another pair a few minutes later and then a couple of marines standing forlornly on a rock above the torrent. The rain continued and, since 45 Commando were soon due to leave me and return to Aden, I called the advance off until I could make a new plan.

Meanwhile 3 Para had had a sharp battle with 40 rebels determined to stop this impertinent advance into their heartland. The Radfanis had five machine guns and fought bravely. They were becoming accustomed to attacks from rocket-firing Hunters and when they saw one lining up on them they would dive behind their stone sangars, bobbing up again after the rockets had exploded. Crouching behind the rocks they were safe from anything but a direct hit from the artillery. This battle was the first occasion on which we had provoked the Radfani hard core to come out and fight. 3 Para – and this is a tribute to their tactical skill – took no casualties but picked up three enemy dead.

As darkness fell the Radfanis disappeared, and during the night 3 Para were able to reach the final summit of the Bakri Ridge. Sergeant-Major Arnold was the first man to set foot on it, and at dawn Francis Graham-Bell flew me to join 3 Para on what was now called Arnold's Spur. Foremost in my reception party was the large, tough figure of the sergeant-major, another Sandhurst instructor friend, and with Tony Farrar-Hockley we looked down into the Wadi Dhubsan.

It lived up to its reputation. Arnold's Spur was like a high diving board, about 5000 feet high, with drops of 1000 feet on either side and 2000 feet almost sheer in front. The Wadi Dhubsan lay at the bottom of what was in effect a ravine. Steep jagged cliffs on either side stretched as far as we could see, and it was immediately clear that there was no chance at all of a large supply helicopter easing its way down between them; the space was far too narrow. Indeed, even our smallest helicopter, the Scout, would find the descent difficult enough though Francis was confident it could be done. There was therefore no question of anything heavy, such as a vehicle, being lowered into the wadi, and the only – and difficult – way of supplying a force there would be by airdrop from a light aircraft. Casualties could only be evacuated by Scout helicopter.

There was however one helpful feature. On the right-hand side of the ravine as we looked at it was a flat-topped hill, a good deal lower than Arnold's Spur. This was the anchor on which we could lay hold in a crisis. Picquets from this feature could cover the descent into the wadi from Arnold's Spur and provide a base for a covering force through which 3 Para could retire.

I thought hard before sending them down there. From the supply angle alone there was no question of remaining in the wadi for longer than two or three days. The operation must therefore take the form of a large-scale raid. Was it going to be worth it? Nothing heavier than a load liftable by a Scout helicopter, once down, would get out again. Casualties could only be brought up by Scouts, vulnerable to fire as they lifted them out. The weather was breaking, with thick clouds round the hills until about 10 a.m. after which a strong wind got up.

Suppose there was heavy fighting and the weather closed down so badly that we could not evacuate the casualties? Local opinion held that the Radfanis would violently oppose an invasion of the Wadi Dhubsan, hitherto unentered by Europeans and regarded in the Radfan as an impregnable stronghold. It was this last factor which made me decide to risk it and press ahead. But I was very clear that I was taking a big chance.

Before making the descent into the wadi, 3 Para were to rest for a couple of days and a company of 45 Commando were lifted by naval Wessex helicopters to Arnold's Spur as reinforcements. Then Tony was to take his battalion down into the Wadi Dhubsan, fight off the enemy, search for arms and documents in the houses and, above all, clearly dominate the whole area before retiring after two days.

3 Para reached the bottom without much difficulty, and at first light Francis and I descended in our Scout to join them. There was certainly no chat between us on the way down; even Francis looked rather strained as we lurched to and fro between the cliffs on either side, but it was a relief on landing to know that it could be done. Another Scout followed us down for Tony's use. Then the weather closed in above us and I was there for three hours, chatting to Tony and the paratroopers who were cleaning their weapons and having a meal before starting their advance along the wadi bed. There was an eerie and sinister feeling about the place. All of us were aware that from a series of look-outs on the cliffs ahead of us hostile eyes would be watching our every move.

The battalion began its advance down the valley and, as the weather cleared, Francis and I were able to prove that as well as getting down it was possible to get up. Just after I had left, Tony took his helicopter and went forward to contact his leading company. For some reason he overflew it, ran into a fusillade of enemy fire and was shot down. His intelligence officer was wounded in the arm and they scuttled rapidly and otherwise unscathed back to safety, leaving the helicopter sitting in enemy territory. All very unfortunate.

A fierce battle, at least by Radfan standards, then ensued, for there lay ahead a strong and determined party. They caught the marine company as it advanced down the middle of the wadi, covered by the para companies working along the base of the cliffs on either side. One marine was killed and two others badly wounded, and later four paratroopers were also hit. Fighting went on for four hours, for the Radfanis overlooked us and were hard to locate. Hunter rocket-firing aircraft performed some remarkable feats of flying and accurate aiming, and by the late afternoon the enemy had faded away, leaving six dead behind them. From then on we were in complete control of the Wadi Dhubsan.

There was still the problem of the damaged helicopter, which if not solved promised to wreck the effect of the whole operation. The prospect of having to leave this hostage behind us when we withdrew set off an unpleasant train of thought. Within days the Arab Press would be gloating that the British had been put to flight and had fled leaving valuable helicopters in victorious Radfani hands; the world Press would embellish the story with wounding comments and we should be left looking very silly indeed. 'For God's sake, Francis,' I said, 'somehow this bloody thing has got to be made to fly.' He went up to examine it and saw that we had been unbelievably lucky – the Radfanis had not continued to fire at it and finish it off while it was sitting on the ground in front of them. Even luckier, one component – and one only – was damaged; a replacement was available in Aden and would be flown up at once with two fitters.

There arrived as darkness fell Corporals Carcary and Hustwith of the REME, armed with the component, canvas screens and torches. Through an uneasy night, with rifle fire ricochetting off the cliffs around them, they worked, a glow amid the darkness. I was back in the wadi at first light. A silence, full of suspense. Then, joy, the sound of a helicopter's engine starting. Moments later the machine rose triumphantly off the ground, a mass of red berets was thrown in the air, cheers echoed from the rocky cliffs, and the brigade commander was filled with a profound sense of relief. If I could have done so I would at that moment willingly have elevated those two corporals to the peerage. But as it was they have had to be content with a picture now hanging in the REME officers mess at Arborfield, in which their brave and skilful feat is graphically portrayed for posterity.

3 Para took over the Wadi Dhubsan, destroyed arms and foodstuffs, found a great many documents in the houses and met no opposition. Then they climbed back onto Arnold's Spur.

Two days later they returned to Bahrein, but not before I had assembled the battalion and congratulated them on a very fine feat of arms. Tony Farrar-Hockley was awarded the DSO, and in later years became Commander-in-Chief Northern Europe, a leading military historian and television pundit. His two company commanders, Tony Ward-Booth and Mike Walsh, both became major-generals. Mike was afterwards appointed Chief Scout. So this was a good team, and its quality was reflected all the way down the battalion. I discovered many years afterwards that one of the junior paratroopers was one Tom McClean, who later rowed the Atlantic and earned a spot on 'This Is Your Life'. So ... farewell to 3 Para.

I had asked myself before the operation whether it was going to be worth the risks and had decided that it would. After it I asked myself if I still thought so. We had clearly shown the Radfanis that we had the power, if we so wished, to enter their most cherished stronghold and take it over. I believed there was a good chance that this demonstration would affect their enthusiasm for continuing the rebellion – not decisively but appreciably so. On the whole I concluded that we had certainly been lucky but that it had been worth it – just. The Jebel Huriyah, however, should be the decisive one.

But there had to be a pause while battalions changed over. Meanwhile the base at Thumeir continued to grow. The airstrip had been almost upgraded to an airport and enormous transport aircraft were regularly using it. The Press had by now become very interested in our doings though mercifully television had not in those days spread its tentacles into field operations. The climate of opinion in 1964 was ambivalent about the kind of operations that we were conducting, and there was certainly not the whole-hearted support enjoyed in recent years by the Falklands and Gulf campaigns. The Conservative government appeared to be in its death-throes and the Opposition were in full cry after policies which smacked of 'colonialism'. This was reflected in the newspapers which supported them.

I spent a good deal of time briefing the Press and, as is apt to be the way at the sharp end, they were friendly and understanding. But criticism was never far below the surface, partly because they could not actually witness what was going on at the front. The harsh terrain and the helicopter situation made this inevitable. One or two managed to hitch a lift in a Wessex to the top of Arnold's Spur while the Wadi Dhubsan raid was going on, but all they could do was peer forlornly over the precipice and question anyone who was lifted out. The intrepid Clare Hollingsworth, the Kate Adie of the day, penetrated into the Wadi

Taym to join the 1st East Anglian Battalion and camped out there, obviously charmed by their commanding officer, Jack Dye. The Press on the whole gave us a very full and fair coverage, though there was an element of frustration which occasionally showed through. As events turned out they could all have been lifted to the top of the Jebel Huriyah when we captured it. This would have been a big story, but by then a much bigger one had stolen the headlines – the death of Nehru – and they had all gone off to India.

A good many politicians followed Duncan Sandys to the Radfan. Chief among them was the shadow Defence Secretary, Denis Healey. We enjoyed his visit and took him everywhere we could; he was very interested and agreeable and took copious notes. I found later in the Ministry of Defence, when he was no longer a shadow, that he was usually agreeable to those of his own age or younger. His tendency to bully was reserved for officers weighed down by four or five stars.

During this pause the Radfanis, inactive elsewhere, turned their attention to Thumeir itself. About 25 men attacked – unusually – at night the piquets scattered about on small hills round the camp, and the brigade headquarters was treated to a firework display only half a mile away. On the afternoon before this I had been talking to a chirpy little lance-corporal of the Royal Scots perched in command of his section amongst the rocks on one of those hills. The main attack hit his position and a sharp close-quarter battle ensued. The defence was vigorous and spirited; so much so that the Radfanis fled and the lance-corporal was awarded a Military Medal for his leadership.

After one more unsuccessful attempt at night the rebels gave up the formal attack and sent individual snipers to creep about in the rocky plain around the headquarters. They had no success, for they were very bad shots, but meanwhile a story, probably apocryphal, went the rounds that, some years before, Arab tribesmen had crept within range of some latrines and had shot an officer using them. Our latrine builders had not concerned themselves with any nonsense about modesty and canvas screens; they had dug some holes, put a wooden rail across and regarded their task completed. In order to prevent the headquarters from witnessing its members performing their morning duty in full view, the various latrines were located in depressions in the ground. These depressions were surrounded by thorn bushes and rocks, and whilst engaged on one's business it was hard to blot from the imagination the thought of a Radfani, rifle at the ready, creeping through the cover behind. There was thus no hanging about; the whole operation was conducted very briskly. However, the rumour did have one excellent result; the Press no longer stayed the night.

The shortest route to the Jebel Huriyah was down the Wadi Misra, itself a rebel base which we had intended anyway to clear one day. The wadi is fertile, contains several villages, and is comparatively wide, though narrow enough to make picquetting of the high ground on either side essential before advancing up the middle. The operation would be quite different from the Wadi Dhubsan raid, much more deliberate, a step by step advance, building a route for artillery and vehicles and making sure that, before each stage was launched, adequate supplies were on the ground to support it. Monty himself, before one of his set-piece attacks, could not have surpassed the care and thoroughness with which this advance was planned.

We could only build a route for six miles. At this point the valley split into two much narrower wadis, each dominated by jagged peaks, of which the key was the heights of Shaab Sarah. Once through these peaks there lay, four miles ahead and up a comparatively gentle slope, the Jebel Huriyah itself, dominating the whole Radfan and, like the Wadi Dhubsan, a feature on which no European foot had ever trod. Again local opinion held that we should encounter fierce opposition.

We thus had to advance along the Wadi Misra until the wheeled vehicles could go no further and establish an administrative base for the final assault. We then had to capture the Shaab Sarah and make for the summit of the Jebel Huriyah.

The chief role in the attack was to go to the 1st East Anglians, in whose commanding officer, Jack Dye, I had great confidence. I also wanted the FRA to play a leading role and to be seen to have done so – 2 FRA were to advance parallel to the East Anglians, picquetting the north side of the Wadi Misra. Armoured cars were to push down the middle. The advance started on 31st May, and since the Belvedere helicopters were not to return till 7th June, we could not take on the peaks until then. Meanwhile we were given three Wessex helicopters, one of which crashed on a hillside.

Jack Dye's battalion faced some formidable climbs. For one of them he had to scour the ranks for expert rock climbers to make up a special team. They advanced slowly but surely. The villages had been evacuated and opposition was light, though a landrover was blown up on a mine. When they reached the end of the wadi, 2 FRA took over the picquetting on both sides while the East Anglians got ready for the Jebel Huriyah. It thus fell to 2 FRA to capture the dominating peak of Shaab Sarah which lay immediately ahead. The climbs they faced were so testing that I do not believe a British battalion could have done the job.

The FRA clambered up with great dash, but when they approached the summit they met a large force of enemy which ferociously attacked them. There followed the final, and decisive, battle. For once the Radfanis made the error of foresaking their sangars and advancing into the open. The FRA pinned them down and the RAF Hunters, for once able to see their target precisely, were highly effective. After a day's hard pounding the Radfanis had had enough and disappeared. Though we did not know it at the time, that was the end of the Radfan operation.

Two nights later the flags of the East Anglians and the FRA were flying on the summit of the Jebel Huriyah, with the lights of Aden visible 50 miles away. As I alighted on the Jebel at dawn to join the two commanding officers, the whole Radfan massif seemed to lie at our feet, glowering, jagged, grey-brown, unfriendly, but no longer menacing. It was a moment to savour. All three Services had worked together to achieve it, but the main credit must go to Jack Dye, a resolute and intelligent soldier.

The Radfanis offered no further resistance and a few months later formally agreed to cease their harassment of the Dhala road. By then I was on Salisbury Plain commanding the 3rd Infantry Division and able to look back with comparative detachment on an extraordinary six weeks. I had had the good fortune to have been served by a first-class and tireless young staff, and to have worked with outstanding soldiers of every rank. Throughout the operation my superiors had allowed me to make and to carry out my own plans; I received from them nothing but unstinted help and support, never interference. It was a truly independent brigade operation, perhaps the last that the British Army has fought.

Our success had rested on the shoulders – and the strong legs – of the British and Arab infantry soldier. Without his guts and his ability to fight through those hostile crags, cliffs and wadis, in that skin-flaying heat, to meet the enemy on his own ground, all the expensive aircraft, artillery, armoured cars, technical equipment and impedimenta might just as well have stayed in Aden. These all played their part in helping him forward; he could not have done without them but he alone could finish the job.

Reading through this account some may feel that to use our vast firepower – the Hunters with their rockets, the artillery, the armoured cars, the mortars, the machine guns and some six battalions – against a few hundred poorly armed tribesmen was a bad case of overkill. But I am certain that to try and pursue these tough fighting men into the heart of their own cruel, harsh domain, and to force them to abandon their rebellion would have taken not months but years – if it could have been done at all – without the fullest use of the firepower and mobility with which modern technology had provided us.

No sympathy need be wasted on the Radfanis. We would not have invaded their country and brought them to heel if they had not consistently murdered and cruelly pillaged innocent travellers along the Dhala road. The maintenance of law and order in the Protectorate was in the end the responsibility of the British government, and to stand by and allow the region to lapse into anarchy, as it was rapidly doing, was a course which our government rightly refused to follow. And, once British forces were brought in, it was their duty to end the rebellion in the shortest possible time and with minimum cost in lives. This we tried our best to do.

* * * *

The 3rd Infantry Division was the British Army's strategic reserve, with its headquarters in Bulford on Salisbury Plain. One of its brigades was based on the Tidworth/Bulford area, another at Colchester and a third at Plymouth. We worked closely with the 38 Group RAF at Odiham, and were organised and equipped to put a joint Army/RAF headquarters in the field if required. No one conversant with the way the world was moving could seriously have supposed that such a heaquarters would in fact be required in the foreseeable future, but we had to assume to the contrary.

I had however a personal reason for apprehension when the Prime Minister of Southern Rhodesia, Ian Smith, suddenly proclaimed UDI. Whilst in Northern Ireland I had been invited to Southern Rhodesia for some six weeks to run a course on show-jumping for Rhodesian riders, and I spent a happy and instructive time there based first on Chris and Jane Coldrey and then with Liz Warren-Codrington. I found that Mr Iain Macleod, the Commonwealth Relations Minister in London, was deeply distrusted there – I am unable to judge whether this was fair or not – and much of the evening chat centred round his determination to bring about a multi-racial society in the Rhodesian Federation. The friends with whom I discussed this were on the whole sensible and reasonable, devoting much thought to a genuine effort to comprehend how their life could be adapted to a multi-racial one. Nice, worried people.

The general in command of the Federation Army, Bob Long, whom I knew, discovered my presence and was kindness itself. When my riding instruction ended, I became a soldier again. He insisted on putting a light aircraft at my disposal, and with an escorting staff officer I was flown in it round the Federation, to Northern Rhodesia, where I went down a copper mine, and to Nyasaland. I talked about and discussed quite sensitive military and political subjects with senior and responsible people, black and white, all in a spirit of trust and mutual confidence.

Now UDI had cut the Gordian knot. There was outrage in British political circles, and wild talk of military intervention by the British strategic reserve. A glance at the atlas showed that the talk was indeed wild; the logistic and overflying problems brought up by a British invasion of Southern Rhodesia killed the idea stone dead. In the end we compromised by sending a battalion to sit, unproductively, on the Northern Rhodesia side of the Kariba Dam. Meanwhile I was greatly relieved that I was not going to become a latter-day Brigadier-General Hubert Gough presiding over a modern version of the Curragh Mutiny, for under no circumstances would I have consented to command such an expedition.

Such fantasies apart, the real task of the 3rd Division was to furnish and then run a military supermarket. Scattered round the world, in the Middle East, Africa, the Far East and Central America were British Army garrisons and commands facing situations which constantly changed. If they wanted reinforcements at short notice they asked the 3rd Division to produce them. 'A REME workshops, perhaps?' they would enquire. 'Certainly,' we would reply. 'We have just what you need, a nice, neat, efficient workshops at Colchester, with a charming commanding officer; it will be with you very shortly.'

Since any part of the division, including every brigade headquarters, was likely to find itself suddenly and unexpectedly transported to the ends of the earth, the atmosphere was inevitably somewhat unsettled. We were busy preparing for the unexpected, all the while conscious that when a call came, those who answered it would almost certainly not find themselves working with the 3rd Division colleagues with whom they were training.

The commander-in-chief, Southern Command, to whom I reported, was General Sir Ken Darling, once the scourge of EOKA in Cyprus. And a splendid commander he was – loyal, tough, cheerful and energetic. He had the same ability to inspire trust and confidence as had Perry Harding – at a far lower level – in the 23rd Hussar days. I would often have to visit him to discuss problems; an hour later I would emerge with solutions agreed and all doubts discarded on the floor of his study in Bulford Manor, where we usually met.

He conceived the idea that the 16th Parachute Brigade at Aldershot should be added to my command and, since he was an ex-commander of the brigade himself, he had no difficulty in bringing this about despite their traditional independence. But I was not a qualified parachutist, and was entitled to no airborne wings on my shoulder. I could not with an easy mind give orders to the 'maroon machine' unless this was put right.

A recruit, officer or man, for the Airborne Forces had in those days to endure a fortnight in their 'P' Company at Aldershot. 'P' Company had a reputation. The first week was passed in the gym, where sadistic members of the Army Physical Training Corps (APTC) set out to ensure that by Saturday evening the recruit had been exposed as unfit, weak-willed and a hopeless prospect for the Airborne – in fact to break him. If by that time they had not succeeded in their aim, the survivors were taken to the Brecon Beacons and there marched up hill and down dale with heavy packs on their backs for a week. Anyone still on his feet was then allowed to start parachuting. This was the reputation; the reality was not as bad as that – not quite.

Sergeant-Instructor Terry Macaree of the APTC was slim, dark and hard; courteous, intelligent but not one to mess about. He had newly arrived in a gym in nearby Larkhill, and to my joy I discovered that he was fresh from being one of the 'P' Company 'torturers'. I invited him to prepare me.

I was joined in this enterprise by a willing volunteer in my driver, Corporal Norman Craven. He had accompanied me from my regiment when I finished command and had been with me ever since. He had been smuggled into the rear of Frankie Festing's aircraft as we journeyed abroad; he had fished the Colebrooke river with a good deal more success than his master; he had accompanied me to the top of the Jebel Huriyah. Altogether he, with his wife Lillian and their two boys, shared our lives for 11 years.

He was a living condemnation of the British educational system. Emerging from a mine in the South Wales valleys and volunteering for the army, he had as a recruit been assessed by the army education authorities to be of such limited academic attainment that he was only fit to be a hewer of wood and a drawer of water – a general duty man. In fact he was as bright as the proverbial button but his brain had never been jerked into use. When it was, he could master anything that interested him and in particular he developed a flair for things mechanical. He was also tough, fit and full of enterprise; he left me eventually as a sergeant to run a successful garage in Gloucester, where he still is.

Together we were worked on by Terry Macaree. He started, I recall, by making us run to and fro across the gym, one press-up on one side, two on the other, then three, four and so on up to 20. By then we had done quite a lot of press-ups. This was just the start. We visited him every day and he put us through the 'P' Company routine as if we were already there. After three weeks Terry was prepared to agree that we could take our chance at the real thing.

First, though, I had to clear this plan with my superior officer. Ken was far from enthusiastic – not at all the sort of thing generals should do; anyway at 48 I was too old. But he understood how I felt and finally, with the greatest reluctance, he agreed – with the proviso that if I completed the course and qualified, I would do no further parachute jumps without first obtaining his permission.

Norman Craven and I duly reported to 'P' Company at Aldershot, where the instructors viewed me with a certain apprehension. I made them promise that they would treat me exactly like any other recruit, and that if I failed to make it, I was failed. They agreed, and they kept their promise. They were all, despite their hardness, wise and experienced men who knew when they had pushed an individual up to his limit. If that limit was too low to be acceptable, that man was out, then and there. They would say, off duty, that fitness was not the main requirement and that their job was to assess whether each of their charges had the guts and character to become an airborne soldier. I could see what they meant, but with respect to them this was not entirely accurate – a young bombardier from the airborne gunners on our course was so superbly fit that he never seemed to come under any strain at all. In racing jargon, he was cantering.

The week was tough and exhausting, but Terry Macaree had prepared us so well that at least nothing that they hurled at us came as a surprise. The Brecon Beacon week was for me far worse. Tramping day after day across the wet Welsh mountains, settling down for the night in the open, soaking wet, and then having to prepare one's own food, was probably child's play to the hardened infantry soldier, but certainly not for a pampered general. For the evening meal Norman Craven came to the rescue. I found that heating my food by means of a curious little pellet which you had to light, under a ground-sheet in the pouring rain, was not a skill easily mastered, but, tired as he was, he managed for both of us. I have seldom been more relieved when the week ended, but end it did with my feet still under me and carrying me forward – just. I flew back in my helicopter from Wales, again a general and no longer an exhausted recruit, in the knowledge that somehow I had struggled through. I also knew that I was never, repeat never, going to do anything like that again.

I had to delay my parachuting because the demands of the job I was supposed to be doing, commanding my division, had mounted up during my fortnight's absence. Norman Craven, however, continued and arranged that, should he qualify, he would combine his duties as my driver with joining the Armoured Corps Parachute Squadron, then located in Tidworth. One morning, therefore, I was dazzled by a figure straight out of glorious technicolour, regimental green trousers topped by a splendid new red beret, both outshone by the beaming grin of triumph on his face.

The parachute week was a push-over compared with 'P' Company. I had anyway done some jumps four years earlier at Sandhurst. But I was in a hurry to complete the prescribed eight jumps for plenty of work awaited me at Bulford. Annoyingly, the weather refused to cooperate, and the wind too often exceeded the safety limit of 20 mph. Drop after drop was aborted and by the Thursday I was well behind schedule. That day however was calm and I looked forward to putting two jumps behind me, one in the morning and one in the afternoon. I was based at the RAF Station at Abingdon for the week, and on that morning Ken Darling's office rang requiring me to attend a meeting with him that afternoon. I protested vigorously that I would have to miss my afternoon jump – must he really see me that afternoon? – all very tiresome and so on. He was adamant; I must cancel my jump and that was that.

Not in the best of moods I settled myself for the morning jump into the Hastings aircraft with the rest of my course, all young airborne recruits, some of whom had been through 'P' company with me and whom I now knew quite well. The three instructors in the aircraft had become friends; the RAF parachute men were outstanding, cheerful, kind and confidence-giving. Before our first jump, out of a balloon, as we had formed up to leave the hut to march across to the grey, sinister shape looming before us, our RAF instructor had made us sing, and whistle, the song from *The King and I*:

> When I'm shivering in my shoes
> I hold my head erect
> And whistle a happy tune
> And no-one then will know I'm afraid'

We had arrived at the balloon feeling much better.

Now, as I settled into the aircraft with a parachute on my back, I looked around at the familiar faces, young, eager faces outwardly cheerful, but unable to conceal a certain tautness round the mouth. I clearly remember thinking that it was about time that the RAF were given a rather more modern transport aircraft than the Hastings – the rod on the floor by my feet which controlled the tailplane looked distinctly worn. But the Hastings carried us safely over the dropping zone at Weston-on-the-Green and down I floated, able to look round at the Bicester hunting country over which I had galloped so long ago. I landed well, but the young man next to me, rather large of figure, had fallen heavily and twisted his ankle. He cursed as he realised that he would be unable to jump that afternoon, and I commented ruefully that that made two of us.

I drove back crossly to Bulford Manor where Ken was holding his meeting, which passed off uneventfully. As I walked out of his front door, there was a commotion. A car drove hastily up and disgorged an officer from my headquarters, rather white in the face. 'Thank God,' he said when he saw me. I was mildly surprised by this greeting, but then he burst out, 'A message from Abingdon, an aircraft has crashed.' With a feeling of dread I questioned him further. The Hastings from which I should have jumped that afternoon was lying in smoking pieces in an Oxfordshire field. No survivors. Abingdon had rung to check whether or not I had been in it.

Distraught, I drove at once to Abingdon. I arrived just as the pathetic corpses were being carried into the gym as a temporary mortuary. There was nothing I could do except say how deeply sorry I was. I learnt that one of the rods connected with the tailplane – perhaps the very one I had noticed that morning – had broken; the aircraft had reared uncontrollably skywards, stalled and plunged straight down. No-one had had a chance. All were dead; crew, those fine instructors, the whole course of would-be airborne soldiers. All save myself and the large young man who had twisted his ankle.

The mass funeral in the Aldershot Chapel was heart-rending – the rows and rows of coffins, the dignity of the parents in their grief, the serried mourners of shocked airborne soldiers. Accustomed as I was to war and to deaths in action, this was something different. Splendid young men were lying in their coffins, lives full of promise now ended, all because the aircraft to which we had entrusted them was too old and unsafe for the job.

I earned my airborne parachute wings and was from then on able to look the paras I commanded in the face. But I had been deeply shocked by this tragedy and there were no rejoicings, just gratitude. Life commanding the strategic reserve was busy, and I got on with the job.

Not long afterwards, we had arranged a large joint exercise with 38 Group RAF in the desert round El Adem in Libya. 'Duke' Mavor, the Air Vice Marshal commanding the Group, was to operate the joint headquarters and be in charge of the 'home' force, while I directed the exercise as a freelance. On the last day a parachute drop was planned behind the 'enemy' lines. Why, I asked myself, should not the exercise director jump with them; an admirable way of observing both sides of the mock battle. But first I was contracted to seek permission to parachute from my commander-in-chief.

I walked straight into it. Ken Darling was furious. 'Nonsense,' he stormed. 'Out of the question, Absolutely not. You're larkin', that's what you're doing, larkin'. When I commanded the brigade I never allowed it. And what's more,' said he, warming to his work, 'I was talking to Jim Cassels, the CGS, yesterday and he said you're to stop all this nonsense. He will want you for a job in London soon and if you go and fall on your head – which is the only part of you of any value to the Army now – you'll be useless to him. Larkin' – that's all it is.' So, with this blast of commonsense, my parachuting ended.

A few months later the call to London was confirmed. Apart from a short and happy spell in Yorkshire, I was to be a fixture in Whitehall for my remaining ten years in the army. High level military politics descended round me in a thick cloud, barely penetrated by glimpses of the world outside.

CHAPTER TEN

Ten years hard (1966–76)

During a busy morning taking over from Mike Carver in the office of the Director of Staff Duties, he pointed to a copy of *The Times* lying folded up on a table. 'Oh yes,' he said in passing, 'they do give you a copy of *The Times* but I never seem to have a moment to read it.' This boded ill. And correctly so. The title 'Staff Duties' could be made to embrace almost any activity in the Army Department, and I soon discovered that it very nearly did. The responsibility for 'organisation' alone could cover subjects ranging from the size of the army and its various components to the number of cooks on each unit's establishment. All these had financial implications, great or small, which had to be assessed and agreed. Whenever the Director of Military Operations wished to make a deployment, my department had to decide which units had to go and issue the necessary orders.

If there was a doubt which department was responsible for a certain decision, it was invariably solved by placing it under the wing of Staff Duties. Thus I found myself having to make some odd decisions. For example, whether a general's request for a helicopter to carry out a visit should be granted or whether he should be told to flog there in his car. As can be imagined this could cause umbrage. It was certainly not the only decision with this potential or worse.

By the middle 1960s, Denis Healey, as Secretary of State for Defence, had wrought many changes, but perhaps the most far-reaching by that time had been the drastic contraction of the Territorial Army into the much smaller Territorial Army and Volunteer Reserve. This dismemberment – for it was no less – had caused a considerable uproar amongst the territorials, who country-wide contained many prominent and establishment figures, aristocratic and military, headed by the Duke of Norfolk.

The detailed organisation of this much smaller reserve army, the decision on which regiments the cuts should fall, and the subsequent recasting of the survivors, were Staff Duties' responsibilities. Mike Carver, with his superior officer, Shan Hackett, had together fought their way through this prickly jungle, at the end of which some of the victims, retaining their sense of humour and fastening on the all too appropriate combination of the two names, had presented the pair with a suitably designed Hackett-Carver tie.

I had luckily arrived too late for this encounter, but there was no shortage of problems lying in wait during the three years ahead of me, the most serious being caused by the near-panic in government circles resulting from the Wilson devaluation crisis of 1967. After some of the more frantic expedients had been discarded, a rapid acceleration of the East of Suez withdrawal was decided upon, coupled with economies in the Defence vote which required a further reduction in the Army's strength. In all this I was the 'hatchet man', but not a particularly passive one. If the many proposals from above seemed to me to need opposing or modifying, I had no hesitation in saying so.

The Ministers with whom we worked played an important part in our lives. As a very general opinion – and there were several individuals to whom this did not apply – of the three governments under which I worked – the first Harold Wilson, Edward Heath and the Wilson/Callaghan – I found Labour Ministers easier to work with than Conservatives. They usually had the sense to realise that they had much to learn; they did their homework and concentrated on the essentials. Conservatives were fussier over detail and had all too often done their National Service in a 'smart' regiment; the military experience thus acquired had given them opinions on how the army worked, or should work, which they often considered to be more relevant than the views of serving generals. One or two made it clear that they had no very high opinion of the views of generals anyway, believing them ignorant of the real world and therefore tending to patronise. This criticism in no way applied to the Conservative Defence Secretary, Lord Carrington, who was invariably a pleasure to work with, but the Minister I most liked and respected was Denis Healey's Minister of State in the first Wilson government, Gerry Reynolds. Long since forgotten he died in office of cancer – a most admirable man, straight, decisive, intelligent and agreeable – a great loss.

The East of Suez withdrawal provided ammunition for the government to reduce the size of the Services, and Denis Healey would regularly come up with proposals for cuts which made our hair stand on end. I feel sure that often he was merely trying it on, and that this was his way of forcing us to justify by hard arguments the limits below which we did not feel it safe to go. Hard arguments did not in his view include heart-rending cries about the sanctity of the regiment and the regimental spirit and traditions, but they did include calculations about the number of army units which would be needed to accommodate the various world scenarios which he would devise.

Each commitment – NATO, Hong Kong and so on – would have to be evaluated in terms of army units and a reserve left over for the unexpected. This was more complicated than it sounds because the nature of the 'unexpected', its duration, how many troops it might need, where the replacements for these troops would in due course come from, thus how big the reserve would have to be, all gave rise to long arguments and to calculations which I soon got the feeling that only I and a very few others actually understood. All these discussions and calculations were of course based on assumptions about unknown events in the future and could only be guesswork.

We would invariably come up with force levels which were much bigger than Mr Healey considered necessary. 'The scenario against which you justify this force level is politically out of the question,' was a frequent retort. I recall however that the final allocation for Northern Ireland was three battalions; presumably more were politically out of the question. Three years later the number of battalions in Ulster was 17.

All too often the results of these calculations were due to be considered in Cabinet at very short notice, and the work tempo would reach Gerald Templer levels. My right-hand man was Lieutenant-Colonel Frank Kitson. He was a man of action whom military drama followed like a shadow wherever he went. Years earlier he had blacked his face and gone off into the bush after the Mau-Mau. Immediately after he left me to command his battalion in Cyprus the Greeks singled it out for a large-scale attack; later he arrived in Northern Ireland to command my old brigade just in time to bear the brunt of the explosive early months of the troubles there.

Although he was always complaining that he was not a Whitehall warrior, he was in fact an extremely good one. He lived in Hampshire and by the time he was trudging up several flights of stairs on arrival at the Ministry – he scorned a lift – he had already exercised his horse. He took all the changes of plan over force levels in his stride, mastered the calculations with little difficulty and remained totally unflappable, however frantic the time-scale.

If, at the right age, his army career had coincided with a major war, he was the sort of personality who could well have become a household name as a commander. As it was , he became something of a military maverick in his later years as a senior general and was sidelined, writing a book about the army which would have been better if he had had recent experience in Whitehall before he wrote it. It was, in my view, an error on the part of the army that this original thinker and tough operator was not more usefully employed.

I always enjoy an entirely typical comment of his which he made while commandant of the Camberley Staff College. He was receiving bitter complaints that there were not enough tennis courts and that it was difficult to book one; more should be provided. 'Oh,' he said. 'How odd. When I am exercising my horse at six o'clock in the morning they are always completely empty.' No more were built.

The Director of Staff Duties needed to master the details of deployment and force levels, organisation and reorganisation, costings, manpower, the effects of changes in equipment, and the general contraction of the army. He was thus in a powerful position when it came to an argument. The senior generals to whom I worked were able and helpful but, although discussions and disagreements took up many tedious hours, it was my ammunition supply which usually carried the day. The most difficult confrontations were the inter-Service ones, because I was dealing with equally well-informed officers of my own rank with their own force levels and budgets to protect, and with – of course in the nicest possible way – designs on a rather larger slice of the cake than mine.

These time-consuming discussions were eased when the Minister decided to short-circuit the usual channels and set up his own inter-Service team of able, youngish officers to mediate and report direct to him. This so-called Programme Evaluation Group (PEG) was regarded with deep suspicion by the Chiefs of Staff – Healey's spies was the kindest expression used about them – but as far as I was concerned they were a help. The ablest of its three officers was the airman, Air Commodore Neil Cameron, who soon became a friend and to whom I talked freely. I knew quite well that all I said went straight back to the Minister, missing out my superiors, but I was prepared to risk that and no harm resulted.

PEG however continued to be most unpopular with the Chiefs of Staff, very largely because they knew that Denis Healey was on close and familiar terms with these comparatively junior figures, and what, they wondered, were they saying to the Minister after the third whisky and soda?

Whatever was said or not said, the suspicion tainted Neil. As soon as Healey had moved on, the Air Marshals pounced, and consigned this able and personable officer to outer darkness. His career seemed finished until several years later an enlightened Chief of the Air Staff, Andrew Humphrey, extracted him from limbo, promoted him, and when he himself moved on to the supreme appointment of Chief of Defence Staff, ensured that Neil, Cinderella-like, became head of the RAF. Shortly afterwards and while still in office Andrew Humphrey died, and Neil took his place, later becoming Lord Cameron but also dying much too young. Sadly therefore, having achieved the military pinnacle against all the odds, he was given little time to enjoy it.

The late 1960s were, I imagine, comparable with the 'Options for Change' crisis in the early 1990s as a harassing period for the army. Abroad, though Hong Kong remained, the challenge, excitement and – sometimes – glamour of the postings east of Suez were no longer to be part of our lives. High officers were facing the prospect of leaving their palatial Singapore residences where their every wish, and that of their wives, had been anticipated by their indefatigable Chinese staff. British troops were considering how best to hand over their responsibilities to the local forces, hoping that the unhappy exodus from Aden would not be repeated on their patch. In the Persian Gulf sheiks were realising, somewhat incredulously, that shortly they would be on their own.

At home, regiments and corps were facing cuts, reductions, and amalgamations which were highly unwelcome, and which I had the unhappy duty of processing. Many resisted, some successfully – 'Save the Argylls' may be recalled – but only a few will remember the failed attempt to amalgamate the two Household Cavalry regiments. This was frustrated through a formidable onslaught on the CGS by the two Gold Sticks of the day, Admiral of the Fleet the Earl Mountbatten of Burma and Field Marshal Sir Gerald Templer – an interview which I attended to provide cannon fodder for the two great men. Other honorary colonels with less fire power were angry, some tiresome, most were just sad. A good many passed through my office, and I did my best to explain and sympathise. The DSD or his equivalent is never popular. To be considered fair and thorough is the best he can hope for.

Somewhere in the modern Ministry of Defence there must be an officer, differently entitled, but performing the same sad duties that fell to me in the 1960s. He has my sympathy. Indeed his task is probably more difficult than mine was, for the modern reductions and changes in army organisation are probably more savage. At least the situation that faced us in the 1960s was the result of very thorough and all-embracing Defence Reviews conducted by Denis Healey. As I know all too well, every commitment, every force level, every major equipment change in all three Services had been worked out, compared with alternatives, and argued out in great detail over a long period. As far as the Army was concerned the changes, severe and resented as they were, could at least be justified by facts and figures. However much the name of Denis Healey was execrated, the army took its bitter medicine knowing in its heart of hearts that facts had to be faced. It does not appear that 'Options for Change' in the early 1990s is enjoying the same acceptance.

Nevertheless the process was not as smooth as I have made it sound. Just as the regular and territorial forces were settling down to the changes of the early and middle 1960s, the financial troubles with which the Wilson government found itself beset brought further changes. Even after that the eagle eye of the new Chancellor, Roy Jenkins, continued to rove over the Defence vote. No doubt the army outside Whitehall felt as did Tony Farrar-Hockley, by then commanding the parachute brigade, when in an attempt 'To lighten the many difficult times of your day' he sent me a quotation from Petronius Arbiter 210 BC:

> We trained hard – but it seemed that every time we were beginning to form up into teams, we would be reorganised. I was to learn later in life that we tend to meet any new situation by reorganising, and a wonderful method it can be for creating the illusion of progress while producing confusion, inefficiency and demoralisation. Plus ça change ...

In 1969, to my great relief and joy, I was sent to York as the lieutenant-general in charge of Northern Command. York was a social and sporting paradise. We lived in the magnificent Claxton Hall with a domestic staff – believe it or not – of twelve. The surrounding landowners, headed by Charles Halifax, were immensely kind to us, and we were guests at, or took part in, every social, cultural or sporting event within reasonable reach. My command stretched from the Border down to Northampton, from the North Sea in the east to Cheshire in the west, where began the Western Command. Almost the whole command consisted of territorials; there were hardly any regular units.

The work-load was minimal. All I had to do was to travel round this large area with reasonable frequency and visit those for whom I was responsible. I was always made welcome but I cannot believe I achieved much more for them than their major-general district commander who had often just visited them. A great many chiefs were presiding over not many Indians. It was perhaps helpful to the army's cause that a 'Sir' – as I now was – should appear occasionally in mayor's parlours throughout the north of England. The mayors of such cities as Halifax and Bradford, usually strong Labour supporters, had often fought gallantly in the war and were sympathetic to the army – fine and friendly men whom it was a pleasure to meet.

But the days when a senior general could be provided with such an immensely comfortable and enjoyable appointment with little work to do were, sadly – and rightly – over. I had believed this to be so in my previous job and the reality was conclusive. At a time when regiments were being amalgamated, the army drastically reduced, thousands of soldiers made redundant for lack of money for defence, the commanders in-chief of the home commands had become an unaffordable luxury. Relaxing in Claxton Hall, I took comfort from the knowledge that I could expect another two years of enjoyable peace before the axe fell.

No such luck. Less than a year after our arrival I opened a letter at breakfast which told me that I was to return immediately to Whitehall as Vice Chief of the General Staff. The officers of Northern Command gave us a wonderful send-off at a large dinner in York. The house staff, sad and disorientated after such a short and, I believe, happy stay, made us a presentation and we were gone. We had been allotted a pleasant house in Kensington Gate, and to help us run it there came with us Sergeant Terry Geary, who had joined us at Tidworth and was to remain, loyally and cheerfully, with us until my service ended. Another member of the team was my faithful and splendid driver, Sergeant Charlie Humphries, who later rose to much greater heights by becoming driver to the Prince of Wales.

It is often said that in Whitehall personalities change but the problems remain the same. During my brief stay in York, however, one new problem had broken surface, Northern Ireland. I took over as Vice Chief in the winter of 1969, a few months after the initial disturbances in Londonderry and at a time when the British Army's honeymoon with the Catholics was ending, a time of street rioting and petrol bombs, a time when the IRA, after a slow start, had seen their opportunity and begun to make their influence felt. It was a time when the British government and people were starting to realise that the 'Irish question' was seriously alive again, but not many had the prescience to imagine how grim, how tragic, and how prolonged this emergency was to be.

The biggest personality change in Whitehall had ushered in Conservatives instead of Labour, Heath instead of Wilson, Carrington instead of Healey. The Chief of the General Staff was General Sir Geoffrey (George) Baker and he was to hand over to Mike Carver in the spring of 1970. He had borne the brunt of the effects on the army of the Healey cuts, and his quiet and sympathetic personality had contributed greatly to the settling-down process over which he was presiding. He felt it his duty before he left office personally to visit every army garrison world-wide as his 'nunc dimittis'. So committed had he become to this mission that nothing, not even a major crisis in Northern Ireland, was going to deter him. For the first few months of 1970, therefore, he was seldom in London, and I found myself heading the Army Department's end of the fast-deteriorating scene in Ulster.

In those early days there was no Northern Ireland Office in Belfast, and no Northern Ireland Minister; the situation was the responsibility of the Home

Office, headed by Reggie Maudling. The Home Office was not the ideal department to mastermind a fast-moving politico-military crisis, and its Minister, though doubtless very able, sometimes did not seem to have his heart in this aspect of his responsibilities. Indeed, I remember at the end of a meeting in the Defence Secretary's office Peter Carrington saying with a twinkle, 'Of course, Northern Ireland is not exactly Reggie's scene.'

Ian Freeland, an old friend from the Camberley bungalows, was the general in command in the early months of 1970, and we talked often on the telephone. As the situation worsened he would regularly ask for reinforcements to be sent across post-haste. On one Saturday morning I was at home preparing myself for a day's hunting in Leicestershire – for it was no good sitting with my head in my hands and brooding – when the telephone rang and there was Ian saying that there was a crisis; he must be sent two more battalions at once. Having cross-questioned him and satisfied myself I rang Lord Carrington, discussed it with him and got his agreement. My next call was to the Director of Military Operations, Ronnie Coaker, who lived in Leicestershire and was also readying himself for his day's hunting. Having given him his instructions I rang off. When later we met at the meet of the Cottesmore he was able to assure me that all had been set in motion; there was nothing more that either of us could do except to try and enjoy our day with hounds.

On another Saturday's hunting in the February of that year – a cold, bleak day – a car follower who had been listening to the radio stopped me and gave me the news that a British soldier had been shot dead on the streets of Londonderry, the first to die at the hands of the IRA in this emergency. Looking back over more than twenty years, across the gulf which has since swallowed thousands of lives to the point when such news hardly earns a comment, I still remember the cold chill of horror which struck me – here, unbelievably, here in Great Britain, in one of our streets in our own country, a British soldier had been killed in action.

This was the period when every night seemed to bring a fresh crisis. As I was dressing in our London house the telephone would ring and the Ministry duty officer would tell me that at nine am the Defence Secretary wished to be briefed by me on the events of the previous night. A dash to the office, a quick discussion about what had actually happened and what should be done about it, and there I was walking down the corridor thumbing through my briefs and talking them through with my Northern Ireland staff officer.

Peter Carrington's large office was furnished with enormous leather-covered armchairs and a vast sofa. When you sat in one of them a dilemma presented itself. Either you lolled back in an almost horizontal position, which seemed disrespectful, or you sat on the edge looking ill at ease. Usually I lolled. We would go through the night's events and decide what should be done. The Minister would often ring the Home Office to coordinate action. Under his veil of relaxed imperturbability there lurked a very sharp brain. He had the tiresome knack of asking the one question that you hoped he would not ask, but the lead he gave was always positive, urbane and reassuring.

Whatever our tribulations in Whitehall, the problems facing the commanders and troops on the ground soon put ours in perspective. While the casualties from actual gunfire or explosives were few and far between, the danger – an unpredictable danger – came from mass disorder in the streets. The Royal Ulster Constabulary had long since been overwhelmed by the size of the crowds, and the soldiers, as yet inadequately equipped with riot gear and protective clothing, were all that stood between a break-down of law and order in several parts of the Province. It was quite possible to envisage a build-up of events in which the numbers of battalions in Ulster would physically be unable to cope.

Later, as the casualties mounted, the situation began to take on the shape of an anti-terrorist operation, with crowd disorder gradually diminishing. At the time of which I am writing, the physical casualties were mercifully low, but the strain on commanders and troops was severe and ever-present as they waited for the incident, often small in itself, which could spark off a mass riot.

I visited Northern Ireland several times, and once or twice, as the acting head of the British Army, found myself in Stormont facing their Ministers. Mercifully, Ian Paisley was at the time no more than a turbulent priest, but the demands were always the same, for more troops and tougher measures. It does not seem, twenty years later, that much has changed. In fact, at the time, more troops, even if we had judged they were necessary, could hardly have been accommodated.

So many battalions and dismounted gunner regiments had been crammed into the troubled parts of Belfast that most were living in acute discomfort. Unheated and delapidated warehouses and sheds were all the accommodation that could be found for them in early 1970; manpower was stretched, hours of duty long and tense, rest periods all too short. Rough barricades of corrugated iron were being thrown up between the opposing factions. At the headquarters of battalions cheerful faces would greet me in decidedly cheerless surroundings; rain or sleet, blankets and boards achieving a rough cover and black-out, sentries, mud, watchfulness, furtive glances from faces at nearby windows, and above all the dreariness, the grey-brown dreariness of those streets. On a wall was scrawled the slogan 'No Pope Here'. Under it a humorist, probably one of our soldiers, had aptly written 'Lucky Old Pope'.

Ian Freeland was due to be replaced by a freshly-promoted lieutenant-general, Vernon Erskine-Crum of the Scots Guards. He met me in London to be briefed and we lunched together. I had never before met him, and found him impressive and charming. About a week after he arrived in his headquarters in Lisburn he rang me with a problem. On the following morning two IRA men were due to be buried in Belfast and it was expected that the IRA would make a point of firing a volley over the graves. Vernon had been told by the Northern Ireland Prime Minister, Chichester-Clark, that if they did so he was to arrest the firers. Vernon had pointed out that the resulting mass uproar would require at least two more battalions than he had on the ground. The Prime Minister was adamant. What, asked the new GOC, was he to do? It did occur to me that his voice sounded rather fainter than usual but thought no more of this at the time.

I then had to initiate the absurdly cumbersome ritual of walking down the passage to seek an audience with the Defence Secretary, who miraculously was still in his office late on a Friday. He then picked up the telephone and asked the Home Secretary – even more miraculously still in his office – to remonstrate with Chichester-Clark. Finally the Home Secretary rang Stormont and forbade the operation. This round-about procedure, which was then the only way of dealing with such problems, was so highlighted by this incident that shortly afterwards the government set up the Northern Ireland department, with a powerful Minister – Willie Whitelaw was the first – who had an office in Belfast, commuted there from London and took all such decisions himself. This was a considerable relief.

Meanwhile a tragedy had occurred. The unusual faintness of Vernon's voice on the telephone was explained when shortly afterwards he collapsed and died of heart failure – a very sad loss not only to his family and friends but to our affairs as a whole, for he was a fine officer who could well have risen right to the top of the army. The major-general Director of the Royal Artillery, Harry Tuzo, thus suddenly had greatness thrust upon him and rose splendidly to the challenge; the Defence Secretary was heard to remark how impressive it was that the army, having lost one top-class general, should be able immediately to replace him with another.

It was very interesting to have the duty of attending Defence Committee meetings in Number Ten in George Baker's absence and watch Cabinet Ministers at work, but trying to combine all this with the Vice Chief's normal duties meant a long day. The post of Deputy CGS had just been abolished and to my responsibility for operations and intelligence world-wide was now added my old department of Staff Duties and that for Operational Requirements, which planned the weapons of the future. It was a relief therefore when Mike Carver arrived as Chief, because he, immediately and entirely correctly, personally took charge of the Northern Ireland emergency and I could then do what I was supposed to do.

The situation in Ulster continued however to dominate our life in Whitehall.

I was still concerned, albeit now as the number two, with the explosive events which were about to unroll before us – internment and its violent aftermath, Bloody Sunday, Operation Motorman which disposed of the 'no go' areas, and always the continuing need to develop new equipment and suitable anti-riot and anti-terrorist weapons.

My fellow Vice Chiefs, Terry Lewin for the Royal Navy, 'Splinters' Smallwood for the RAF and I also had the duty of keeping our eye on the government's approach to the financing of the Services, and it is depressing to see now, in the early 1990s – before the 'Options For Change' reorganisation has had time to take effect – how little has been done, then and since, to grapple with a problem which even in the early 1970s was becoming all too evident.

The words 'Defence Review' were associated with Denis Healey and that has been quite enough to make succeeding Conservative governments avoid them like the plague. The Wilson/Callaghan government of the late 1970s also avoided using the words because they knew that the Conservatives would say that Labour always cut our defences. Thus, for 20 years, no radical and effective examination was ever undertaken to assess commitments and force levels against the money likely to be available for defence.

The original defence reviews of the 1960s saved money by abandoning commitments east of Suez, but although the Services each became smaller it could be said with reasonable truth, despite our deplorable economic performance, that our armed forces still gave us the right to regard ourselves as a great power. This remained the policy of succeeding goverments, but the necessary funds to support this policy were not forthcoming. Year by year, as the available funds fell short, there was a deterioration in the effectiveness of our defences.

No government ever nerved itself to ask, 'Can we now afford to continue with equal weight being given to an army, navy and air force, and an independent nuclear deterrent, and at the same time retain our present commitments? And pay more for defence per head of population than any of our Allies except the United States.' Or if they ever did ask themselves that question none has ever faced up to the political trauma – admittedly a very considerable trauma – of acting upon the answer. It would of course meant doing something perfectly horrible to at least one of the component parts of our defences, and to the, in my opinion, top-heavy and over-manned organisation which commanded, managed, and trained our Services.

As I well know, the Vice Chiefs of Staff in the 1970s were complaining bitterly about the line of least resistance that was invariably adopted – the so-called 'salami tactics' – with each Service every year slicing away another tranche of its effectiveness through lack of money. The results of 20 years of salami tactics became evident when it was discovered that to put one effective division into the Gulf operation in 1990 the two other divisions of the British Army of the Rhine, and most of the troops at home, had virtually to be grounded because their manpower, equipment, spare parts, ammunition, and supplies had to be removed from them in order that one division should be made fit to fight.

The victories in the Falklands and in the Gulf – luckily requiring no more than the strength of one division – were the best possible advertisement for the qualities and skill of the British servicemen. Our positive response and the success of both operations greatly enhanced our world reputation and strengthened our diplomatic hand. But the British taxpayer, if he thought about such matters at all, might have wondered why he had been led to believe that he was helping to pay for three armoured divisions in BAOR, all allegedly capable of fighting a full-scale war against the Soviets, when in fact he was getting nothing of the kind.

Now, of course, that the full horrors of the ill-thought-out 'Options for Change' are becoming apparent, the 1970s and 1980s are looked back on as a kind of defence golden age. In fact our defence posture then was largely a 'con', and we were lucky to get away with it.

Looking back, my time as VCGS was the least rewarding of the appointments which I held in Whitehall. The very nature of the job meant that I was not the man in charge, as I had been in Staff Duties and was to be again as Adjutant-General. I am not complaining, the job had to be done by someone, but to spend hours planning for contingencies that everyone devoutly hoped would never occur, though it does, I believe fascinate some officers, held little charm for me. The technicalities of the weapons of the future were usually beyond me, but my practical experience enabled me to contribute, I believe, and many years later, watching on television the operations in the Falklands I was able to see the fruits of some of our work. And of course there was the practical reality of Ulster with which to grapple, but on the whole I was glad when my three years were up and I went on to a much more congenial post.

Operational planning, with which I now ceased to be concerned, does not deal with soldiers as individuals. It deploys and organises battalions, brigades and so on impersonally; it deals with groups of soldiers, numbers of soldiers. As Adjutant-General I became responsible for individual people; for the practical, down to earth problems that interested my particular cast of mind. As the army's personnel officer I was in charge of conditions of service, pay, training, discipline, health, and for all the various corps which contributed.

However interesting his tasks may be to the Adjutant-General, nothing could be more boring than to have to read about them. I shall be brief. I was immediately involved in battles about Service pay. For several successive years governments, conscious of inflationary trends and the worsening economic situation, had laid down 'pay norms' for annual rises. These had been ignored by industry, which had consistently awarded itself pay increases considerably in excess of the 'norm', but had been rigidly applied to the Services and the Civil Service. Their pay scales had thus fallen considerably, indeed absurdly, behind the average outside. The forthcoming, and badly needed, rise due in April 1974 was being bedevilled during the previous winter by the oil crisis and the miners' strike; again a totally inadequate 'pay norm' rise was part of the package proposed by the embattled Heath goverment during that awful winter.

The good humour of the British soldier, particularly the married soldier, came under strain. I well remember during a visit to a sergeants mess, as usual welcoming and friendly, that I called for silence in order to bring them up to date with the latest news on their pay. In a moment their genial faces had become contorted into those of incensed and outraged shop stewards; the atmosphere quite changed. As I found in later years in appointments outside the army, money, sad to say, seems to have that effect on people.

In Whitehall I soon became as bad as they were. No trade unionist can have fought for his members more fiercely, or – it has to be said – more selfishly and ruthlessly than I did. Ever since I feel that I know why union leaders sometimes behave as they do. Frantic efforts were being made by the government, at the height of the miners' strike and the 'three day week', to find ways out of the impasse. The phrase 'unsocial hours' was coined. If you could prove that your members worked unsocial hours they were entitled to a pay rise above the norm. I maintained that if anyone worked unsocial hours the army did, only to see a minute from the then Employment Secretary, Willie Whitelaw – of all people, fresh from Northern Ireland – saying that the Services did not qualify!

Feelings ran very high; it was a bad two months. I did not feel that the central staffs in the Defence Ministry, who were supposed to fight our corner, were being nearly tough enough, and fell out with the four-star officer who had the job of coordinating the Services' efforts. I felt acutely my responsibility to the army for seeing that it was properly paid, and was all too aware that I was not delivering the goods. Just as I was beginning to feel that I must resign and make my views public in the process, the Prime Minister called and lost his fatal election. Mr Wilson instantly gave everyone, including the Services, all that they were asking for, thus having, I understand, a disastrous effect on inflation, but causing much satisfaction amongst the beneficiaries. Indeed, I may be wrong, but I do not believe that the Services have ever seriously fallen behind since that day.

The second Wilson government, if its choice of Ministers was any guide, took much less interest in defence than the first. Although the Secretary of State, Roy Mason, compensated for his total lack of charm by a decisive competence which we admired, the Ministers under him varied from the deadly to the wildly eccentric. How one or two of them could have been considered to be of Ministerial timber defeated us entirely. I made a point of seeing as little of them as possible and dealt mainly with the senior civil servants.

The very senior of these, the Permanent Secretaries, were nearly always extremely clever and very helpful and pleasant. They were the type of high quality men who could, as many have shown after retirement, master any task which they were likely to be given – not always great battlers, no sticking out of chins and thumping of tables. Smooth intellectual argument and charm were their weapons. There were exceptions – Frank Cooper combined his intelligence with a combativeness that could be devastating – no Sir Humphrey he.

The younger Assistant Secretaries with whom I dealt were often on their way to becoming Permanent Secretaries themselves, and were usually a delight to work with. I did however see all too much of the second layer down, the Deputy Secretaries, many of whom had reached their ceiling, and into whose soul the iron had long since entered. In the nicest and most civilised way they were experts at telling you that not only would your idea not work, it had been thought of by someone else many years earlier and had proved a complete fiasco then. Anyway it would cost too much money and mean a lot of extra work. I enjoyed trying to defeat their wiles and sometimes succeeded; indeed on one occasion I was delighted to be told that a certain DUS would never forgive me for having proved him wrong. That particular contest had concerned the provision of British television for the families of our troops in Germany, a measure which he had condemned as totally unnecessary, far too expensive and indeed out of the question. Nevertheless the families got their television.

It was possible in the personnel world to achieve, just occasionally, a change for the better which has stood the test of time and is now accepted as normal, and I can look back on some of these. I stand firmly by the thought 'You can achieve almost anything in this world provided you don't mind who gets the credit'. If you know in your heart that if you had not been there a certain change would not have been made, that should be quite enough. I can look back on my time as Adjutant-General with a clear conscience and with enjoyment, but with no wish to parade any trophies which I may think I won.

But nearly ten consecutive years in reasonably testing posts in Whitehall is draining. Civil servants spend their lives in Whitehall and seem to survive, so what, it may be asked, am I complaining about? But they do not have to make policy decisions, argue about them and then sell them to the customers; they exercise great influence but the buck passes on to the politician, through, in the case of the Defence Ministry, the senior officers. The latter are responsible not only to Ministers but for, and to, their officers and men. Civil servants, able and intelligent as they are, provide the ammunition; they do not have to fire it off and take the come-backs. In any case, though it was my fate to become a Whitehall warrior, I was by no means a 'natural' for the role as some officers are. The sun shining through my office window would mock me as I sat at my desk knowing that its rays would have long faded before I could escape. My thoughts would all too often turn to the fun and fresh air that I was missing.

Again, though, it may well be asked, what am I complaining about? Thirty years earlier the idea that one day I should become a four star general, and, to use Olympic Games language about the army hierarchy, win the silver medal in my age-group, would have been unthinkable. So, my complaints are not meant seriously, for in truth good fortune had ridden with me every yard of the way.

As my time in Whitehall drew to its close, I was asked if I would like to be considered for one or two prestigious posts overseas. I had no hesitation in taking myself out of the running. I retained no desire whatever for further high level business, high level functions, or high level society. I had had more than enough of the great and the good and the self-important. I had a fairly good idea that congenial, though not lucrative, posts in racing and the equestrian fields would await me as a civilian, and above all I wanted at long last to live with my wife in our own home in the country and enjoy – certainly not, I hoped, the evening of our days, more like the late afternoon – without being enmeshed any longer in official life.

And so, with absolutely no regrets, but with a great sense of past enjoyment and gratitude for all the opportunities which I had been given, I said goodbye to the army after 40 years.

CHAPTER ELEVEN

'Oh no, Monkey, not like that'

When I was working in the Joint Planning Staff in Whitehall I had a crashing fall at Kempton Park. My doctor shook his head over the resulting state of my neck and warned me that I should give up steeplechasing. For a while I believed him and during this period of comparative inactivity I started to put brush to canvas.

We had spent a good deal of time in London wandering round picture galleries, and although some of the works we saw were marvels of composition, colour and technique there were others which, I felt, could possibly be emulated if I tried hard enough.

So I bought a small box of oil paints. I also bought some books of instruction but found them so detailed and complicated that I soon flung them aside and never opened them again. I put an orange on a plate and began to portray it. After a messy interlude a recognisable if unappetising likeness was produced. I was hooked.

Encouraged by my early efforts I took my work to the talented and helpful painter William T. Wood. He encouraged me to 'be myself' and I am sure that this is the best advice on painting that I ever received. I had neither the time nor the opportunity to join a class nor had I, then or since, the temperament or the slightest wish to do so. Mr Wood criticised my paintings, made suggestions and allowed me to watch him at work. To sit at the feet of an expert and learn has been my method ever since.

Soon after that we went to live in the village of Dedham, the home of Sir Alfred Munnings. I never dared show any of my paintings to the great man, but the walls of his house were plastered with wonderful works of his ranging from the gypsy pictures of his early days to the mannered, and to my mind less attractive, hunting and racing portraits of his later years. From all these I learned.

He was an extrovert of remarkable force of character, who by that period of his life was not much concerned about other peoples' opinion of him. I

Christmas card from Violet Munnings

remember attending a dinner party at which at the end of the meal he decided, unasked, to regale the company with his recitations, starting with John Masefield's *Reynard the Fox* and continuing endlessly with his own hunting poems. On and on and on he went, hours passed and his audience, unable to converse, became restive. A Buxton cousin of Zulu's complained audibly, 'Fella's a bounder, fella's a bounder' – but he was unstoppable.

Lady Munnings was equally unorthodox. When her beloved Peke died she had it stuffed and continued to take it about with her. She once settled down in a London bus with it on her lap. As she had doubtless hoped the conductor thought it was real and asked her to remove it, which she declined to do. It was not until his fury had become ungovernable and the police had arrived that she revealed the truth. By then the bus had been delayed for at least 20 minutes but that did not concern her in the least.

The years passed and I continued to paint, though was kept too busy by my duties to make much progress. I persevered, awaiting the day – which has now arrived – when I could give painting a higher priority. Meanwhile I remained hooked. Other amateurs talk of painting's therapeutic effect on them and how it calms their spirits. I find it exciting, but not particularly calming. I experience frustration when the colours, so carefully and thoughtfully mixed, assume the colour of mud. I feel apprehension halfway through a picture that my plans are not working, and fury when they obviously haven't. I feel disappointed when the bright colours, which I have assembled as a decisive reserve to be hurled into the battle and to convert defeat into victory, fail to do the trick.

And yet – and yet – even in those days a picture which pleased me occasionally materialised. As it does in racing, every time you set out your palette for a new venture, hope springs eternal. For better or worse, what results is your creation and yours alone. A turning point upwards came when I met Paul Maze, a painter of unbounded charm and talent, some years before I left the army. Our friendship continued until his death in 1979. He was a Frenchman become an Englishman, equally at home in both countries.

He was born and brought up in Le Havre. Paul's father was intensely interested in painting, and gave the boy a paintbox with which to work. Georges Maze had many painter friends and took his son to watch Pissarro paint. Later Paul set up his easel on the beach and asked permission to sit next to Dufy, who would help him. Braque, described by Paul as a rather sombre boy, was a playmate. As a very young man he worked with Vuillard, Derain, and Segonzac. Thus, in the late 1970s, it was possible to converse in lively style with a personal friend of impressionists who were painting their masterpieces almost a century earlier.

His love affair with the British Army and with England had started at the age of twenty-one when, on the outbreak of the First World War, he saw the horses of the Royal Scots Greys disembarking at Le Havre. At once he made up his mind to join them, and this gangly young Frenchman had no qualms about walking up to the commanding officer and asking if he could become their interpreter; somewhat surprisingly he got his way. He borrowed scraps of Greys uniform and attached himself to them without concerning himself with such tedious details as badges of rank or identification papers. In a way which he made his own throughout his life, his openness, gaiety and self-confidence soon ensured his acceptance into this most 'cavalry' of cavalry regiments. Having apparently no fear, he was soon as useful to them as an unofficial and French-speaking scout as an interpreter. He would unconcernedly swan here and there on his motor-cycle, and predictably he was soon in trouble.

In his book *A Frenchman in Khaki* Paul gives a vivid description of the retreat from Mons in 1914 – the terrified civilians, the exhausted but determined British regular soldiers, the confusion. Whilst out on his motor-cycle he narrowly escaped capture by the Germans, and then fell into the hands of the provost-marshal of the retreating British 2nd Infantry Division, who promptly arrested him as a spy.

Since Paul wore no recognisable uniform and had no identity papers, the provost-marshal seemed to have every justification, and when a German razor was found in Paul's haversack, a firing squad seemed certain. The Scottish soldier placed in charge of him commented realistically, 'Dinna worry, if ye're a spy ye'll be shot all recht; if ye're no, ye willna be.' Just as Paul was being led away for execution the sound of trotting horses was heard, and round the corner came a squadron of the Royal Scots Greys with Major Foster Swetenham, a friend, at its head. 'Paul,' the major shouted, 'what are you doing here?' – and all was well.

But clearly this unofficial masquerade could not be allowed to continue. He had to enlist in the French Army but immediately wangled his way back to the British – this time to the headquarters of the 2nd Cavalry Division, commanded by Hubert Gough. When the general was promoted from division to corps and then to command of the 5th Army, Paul went with him. Described as a liaison officer but using his skill as a draughtsman to draw sketches and panoramas, he did useful operational work and became a close friend of his master. Sir Hubert Gough remained his hero for life and Paul would vigorously defend his handling of the 5th Army in its débâcle during March 1918, for which the general was sacked. Hubert Gough, not only in Paul's eyes, was made the scapegoat when the fault lay with others – an enormously long and weak line with too few men, and it broke.

When I first met Paul and was privileged to become one of his countless friends, he obviously took a special liking to me. This was explained when he wrote to me about a year before he died, 'Your letter expressed so much of what I immediately felt on seeing you when you entered the house for the first time. You evoked at once what I felt about Gough when I reported to him in 1914 – at once I felt devoted.' The feeling was mutual and I spent many happy and enlightening hours watching him paint and discussing his pictures with him. Eventually I was greatly honoured by his offer actually to help me with my work. 'I will show you how to avoid the pot-holes,' he wrote. I was all too aware that the only other 'peintre de dimanche' – as he called the amateur – on whom this honour had been conferred was Winston Churchill, whom he had met in the Great War. They had become life-long friends linked by a love of painting.

In the 1920s and the 1930s Paul alternated between England and France, painting with Vuillard, Derain and Segonzac, and exhibiting in London, Paris and New York. He attracted friends like a light attracts moths. During his travels and work the statesmen, the aristocrats, the industrialists, the millionaires, the high-ranking Service officers he met had not only bought pictures from him but had fallen under his personal spell. He loved company and his house was usually full of guests; many were painters themselves.

Paul would recount how one day a group of painters gathered round Churchill who was working at his easel, when the statesman stood back, handed four of them each a brush and said, 'Come to my rescue. You, Paul, shall paint the trees, Segonzac the sky, Simon Levy the water and you, Marchand, the foreground. I shall supervise.' Which, lighting a cigar, he did, the whole group watched benevolently by Vuillard with his bushy white beard. The result, signed by all of them, at least had the value of novelty, but was not, I understand, a great work of art.

When I knew him 40 years later he lived beneath the Sussex Downs with his second wife, Jessie – a graceful, smiling presence dedicated to making Paul happy. Although his personality was powerful and his ways eccentric it was Jessie's unbreakable calmness of spirit which pervaded the elegant cottage in which they lived.

I would often stay in their detached annex crammed with Paul's paintings. After breakfast and before he had risen I would take my easel to a spot in the garden from which there was a view to paint. The South Downs gazed calmly down upon me.

Later on a presence would make itself felt behind me, a tall, angular figure, floppy hat, loose-fitting shirt, baggy trousers, beaky nose – the whole slightly resembling a stork. 'Oh no, Monkey, those trees, not like that – give the brush to me.' A few dabs on the palette, a vigorous flagellation of the canvas, and there, produced in a couple of seconds and with four or five brush strokes, were trees, living and moving. Sometimes he would seize the canvas from me and repaint parts of the picture himself, often ignoring the light and shade produced by me in the morning. His contribution, which might be added in the afternoon with all the shadows pointing in a different direction, did not always combine happily.

We would spend hours together in his studio looking through hundreds and hundreds of loose canvases and pastels, flowers, landscapes, seascapes, military parades, racing scenes. Many were the fruit of hours spent behind his easel at Goodwood races, Cowes regatta and the Horse Guards parade-ground. He held two exhibitions in London, organised by his great friend Michael Gow of the Scots Guards, consisting almost entirely of lively sketches, water colours, pastels and oil paintings portraying the Trooping the Colour and other parades.

Every one of these hundreds of paintings, in all their variety, was so evidently inspired by sheer enjoyment of the beauty of his subject – enthusiasm in every stroke. Many were of Jessie – Jessie in the garden, Jessie having a picnic, Jessie at her toilet in front of her looking glass, Jessie in the nude. He once showed me a pastel sketch of their sitting room which included a sofa with their King Charles spaniel recumbent upon it and remarked, 'See, dear little Neva lying there, see with what love I have sketched her.' His voice would soften as he used the word 'love', as he often did when describing his work – a boyhood memory of watching Pissarro at work, and of his father telling him to observe not only what the master was painting but also with how much love.

Out walking, although in his eighties, he would stride along looking up at the Sussex hills for inspiration. 'See, Monkey, how that little strip of trees creeps so gently down the side of the valley and how it looks so shyly up to the strong cliffs and rocks above it, how it moves with such rhythm – always you must have rhythm – and look at that lovely sky, see how it sings.'

His best work, it always seemed to me, was in pastels; their lightness and freshness suited so well the sponaneity of work inspired by his own sensual joy of living. His intellect, and his remarkable gift for friendship, expressed as effectively to the humble as to the grand, never flagged, but in the end his body refused to carry him any further along life's road. He died having cut a larger swathe of human happiness throughout his life than very few others can have done. I shall always be grateful for having been one who was captivated and inspired by the unique personality of Paul Maze. As Michael Gow concluded his eloquent tribute at Paul's memorial service, 'He died ninety-two years young.'

CHAPTER TWELVE

Grandstand jockey

When I retired from race-riding in 1954 I was elected to the National Hunt Committee. This committee governed steeplechasing and hurdling, and was the partner – very much the junior partner – of the Jockey Cub which ran flat-racing. In the mid-1960s the National Hunt Committee was absorbed by the Jockey Club and all racing came under its one authority.

I was elected in the hopes, presumably, that in due course I would have the time to assume some responsibility within the management. 'In due course' lasted some 26 years. Meanwhile I sat as a backbench member and attended meetings when I could.

The modern Jockey Club is criticised for being too aristocratic and autocratic, but compared with the 1950s version it is democracy personified. The National Hunt Committee had its share of the aristocracy – indeed some of the more senior and eminent Jockey Club members belonged to both committees – but consisted mainly of fox-hunting country gentlemen. Informality was never allowed to percolate through the portals of No 15 Cavendish Square where the meetings were held. If, greatly daring, you wished to contribute to the discussion you rose to your feet and started what you had to say with 'My Lord Chairman (he was usually a lord), my Lords and Gentlemen ...'

This formality was oppressive and there was not much discussion. The Stewards – the ruling body – told us what they proposed to do and we were expected to agree, which we submissively did. There were a few 'turns' to look forward to. Bill Anstruther-Gray, later Lord Kilmany, was for much of that period Deputy Speaker of the House of Commons, and would rise portentously to address us in his best parliamentary manner. 'If I may make so bold as to trespass on the valuable time of the committee? Whilst expressing the utmost respect for my Lord Chairman, who has of course unrivalled experience in the matters on which we are deliberating and who has put his proposal so clearly and persuasively before us, I venture to put forward perhaps a somewhat contrary – indeed I might say an opposing view – regarding the policy which the Stewards in their wisdom are seeing fit to pursue. Again with the utmost respect and without wishing to detain the committee, I cannot refrain from expressing my concern – indeed, I have to say, my strong concern – at the position in which the small owner will find himself...'

General Dick McCreery was another champion of the small man, and would rise to his feet not only to further the cause but to propose that more representative members, such as yeoman farmers with racing experience, should be elected to the committee. Alas, he and Bill, both usually going much further down the road to democracy than racing's rulers were then prepared to travel, were invariably losers and this could be sensed from the atmosphere the moment either of them rose.

The National Hunt Committee in the early 1960s did break fresh ground in electing as its Senior Steward Wing-Commander Peter Vaux. He was a Yorkshire landowner but not an aristocrat, and he had recently been a tough amateur steeplechase jockey, riding mainly for trainers in the north. Although his appointment raised some eyebrows he proved to be an effective and successful holder of the office, his main achievement being to cause the Grand National fences to be radically altered for the better. Instead of the upright cliffs which I and so many others had grown to know all too well, the fences were now sloped. Although no less stiff and no smaller, they became far more inviting to jump and caused many fewer falls. This change was more important than the recent alterations to Bechers Brook and other fences which have caused so much publicity.

These days of successful innovation were however in the future when Peter Vaux rather nervously took his place to open his first meeting as Senior Steward of the National Hunt Committee. I happened that day to be sitting just behind two eminent Jockey Club members who had decided to go 'slumming' in this altogether inferior gathering of which they had deigned to be part – Lord Rosebery and another elderly peer. As Peter rose, a youthful, slight and somewhat self-conscious figure behind the lectern, the elderly peer turned to his neighbour and asked abruptly, 'Who's this fella?' Lord Rosebery raised his eyes and doubtfully surveyed the new Senior Steward. After a puzzled pause he replied, 'I dunno, Peter Thrale's 'stopping' jockey, I believe.'

The years rolled by. National Committee members became Jockey Club members as the two organisations merged; Cavendish Square was abandoned for Portman Square; Weatherbys – the Jockey Club's civil servants – died and were replaced by other Weatherbys. I continued to sit in silent obscurity as a back-bench member – silent because my soldiering had made me too out of touch with the racing scene to have anything to say worth hearing. I occasionally found time to act as a local steward at Windsor races, but otherwise could make no contribution to justify my membership.

I retired in 1976 from the army and was at last available. Rather disappointingly four years passed without any sign of recognition from the Senior Stewards of the time. This delay meant that old age would have crept upon me before I could myself be considered for the post of Senior Steward. Racing was run by six Stewards – the senior, the deputy and four others variously responsible for Discipline, Race Planning, Finance and Licensing. An aspirant for the top post had to spend at least three successful years as one of the four junior Stewards before reaching a list of 'possibles' stretching some years ahead. Mystery surrounded the final selection for Senior Steward. Like the Conservative Party in years gone by, the new man 'evolved' after a series of clandestine discussions amongst the Jockey Club 'great and good'. By the time I could have been considered I was too old. As it was, my eventual appointment as deputy Senior Steward was the result of accelerated promotion.

The break came when I was asked to chair a committee designed to establish the riding fees paid by owners to jockeys on a fair basis. This task was right up my street and after my battles over the Services' pay presented no problem. From this I progressed to responsibility for racing's Security Service, into the world described by Dick Francis so much more entertainingly than it really is. My colleagues were mostly ex-policemen, the senior a lively character and lately a Special Branch officer from the Met, Bob Anderson. The many 'cause celèbres' in which he had been involved included the Great Train Robbery and he was a marvellous raconteur – sadly the laws of libel prevent me from quoting from his repertoire. I was struck by the different view of his fellow citizens taken by Bob and his police colleagues, and that shown by the ex-army officers who, as stewards secretaries, were responsible on racecourses for detecting irregularities during the meeting. The latter instinctively believed that all concerned with racing were on the whole decent chaps, and were reluctant to believe that jockeys would ever get up to anything worse than the odd bump or two in the course of a race. Bob and his colleagues held everyone employed in racing to be guilty until proved innocent and much more likely to be villains than not. Bob was writing his memoirs but his account of episodes well remembered in racing history were, I suspect, too much for the lawyers and, as far as I know, they never appeared.

I was also the non-technical authority in charge of the dope-testing laboratory at Newmarket, though the real authority under which it works is a committee of professors including technical experts concerned with the whole campaign against doping, not just within horseracing. On the whole – I can only speak for racing – it is effective. On the whole.

Our precautions against doping are as good as, and in most cases far better than, elsewhere in world racing. I do feel, though, that the British racing authorities are inclined to assume too readily that if a dope-test proves negative that horse has not been doped. There have been several examples in recent years of horses which ran inexplicably badly but were dope-tested negative and whose running has never been explained. If athletes and their trainers can keep ahead of detection – as they clearly do – so can those who make their living from racing. I hope that research into the unknown is given more attention and money than it used to be.

In 1980 I was asked to take over from Jakie Astor as one of the two Jockey Club members on the Horserace Betting Levy Board. This board was set up by parliament in the early 1960s and is a 'quango' – a quasi-government body with the duty of extracting and then distributing the money (known as the levy) which bookmakers are required by law to return to racing.

Besides paying their annual tax to the government – in 1992 some £500 million – the bookmakers have to hand over a small proportion of their annual turnover to racing. In 1991/1992 off-course bookmakers above a minimum turnover range paid 2.2 per cent of their betting turnover to the levy, which in that year contributed just over £40 million to racing.

The levy pays for the integrity services – the officials and the technology operating in their different capacities to keep racing straight, and the dope-testing laboratory at Newmarket. It loans money to racecourses so that they can modernise their stands and their facilities. It finances the veterinary research into ways of encouraging soundness in racehorses and in keeping racing and breeding disease-free. But over half of the levy is made over to prize money, contributing just under 50 per cent of the financial rewards available to the owners of racehorses.

Without this levy on the bookmakers, whose livelihood comes largely from horseracing, racing would have to finance itself through the entry and licensing fees paid by owners, through sponsors and through prize money contributions by racecourses from their profits. The sum which could realistically be raised by these means would either impoverish racing in this country and reduce it to third eleven status on the international scene, or vastly reduce the number of owners because the gap between costs and rewards would become a chasm only bridgeable by the seriously rich.

As it is, with the annual levy of some £40 million in 1992, owners will fork out some £200 million in expenses and receive back under £50 million in prize money. Only six per cent of horses will show a profit and a high proportion of owners, whose horses fail to win a race, will receive back virtually none of their costs. With training expenses (excluding entry fees and travel) running at £12,000 per horse per year, it is not surprising that owners are under strain. Some are giving up the game altogether, a few of the richer owners are moving their horses to France or the United States and most are unhappy. And the sport of racing, a national heritage giving pleasure and excitement to millions, cannot flourish, or even exist, without enough people with the will and the means to own racehorses.

Other racing countries, France for example, have no bookmakers. The money that is raised from betting on their Tote monopoly can only go in two directions, to the government in tax or back into racing. In this country, all but the tax and the betting levy go into the pockets of the bookmakers. Prize money in France is thus some two and a half times higher than it is in England, facilities for the racegoer far superior and the cost of a day's racing far lower. It will cost you £40 to watch the Cheltenham Gold Cup from the members enclosure, and £5 to watch a big steeplechase at Auteuil in far greater comfort.

The reason for this disparity – which is certainly not confined to France – is the existence of bookmakers and the inadequacy of the levy which they are required to produce in support of horseracing from which they earn the bulk of their living.

Why then don't we have a Tote monopoly here? Bookmaking, established in this country centuries ago, is now big business. It is hard to imagine a government, with all its other preoccupations, prepared to face up to the powerful bookmaking lobby and all the hassle that it would cause, in order to put a bill – and find parliamentary time for it – before the House of Commons outlawing bookmaking and putting thousands of their employees out of work. I fear that this idea, although attractive in theory, will remain a mirage.

It is of course unsatisfactory that the racing industry – for that is what it is now – should suffer from divided control. Indeed, until recently there were three bodies concerned in the management of racing, not two. The Horserace Advisory Council represented the participants and the workers – the racecourses, the owners, the trainers, the jockeys – and established itself as the third member of a triumvirate.

There seems to be a general impression that the Jockey Club, motivated by what are called its backwoodsmen, was only interested in clinging to its present powerful position governing racing. In fact, in the past 25 years it has taken at least one initative designed to do exactly the opposite – to broaden the base of racing's management. In 1967 Sir Henry Benson produced a report designed to suggest a way of simpifying this system. He recommended the setting up of one racing authority on which all concerned would be represented. The Jockey Club, far from clinging to power, was content, provided it was sufficiently strongly represented, for this body to assume control of racing. But the idea came to nothing. The government would not agree to hand over control of the levy – considered as semi-public funds – to an authority for which they were not responsible. Thus the smooth management of racing continues to depend on the warmth or coolness existing between the bodies concerned – which over the years has varied according to the personalities in charge.

The Levy Board consisted of a chairman and two members appointed by the Home Secretary, two Jockey Club members, the chairman of the Horserace Advisory Council, the chairman of the Tote and a bookmakers representative.

Every year there is a dispute between the bookmakers and the rest of racing about the size of the levy. Racing puts its case for so many millions, the bookmakers protest that the sum requested is altogether exorbitant, would bankrupt the small bookmaker, and anyway racing has greatly exaggerated the size of their annual turnover. If no compromise can be reached the Home Secretary has to adjudicate, with increasing and understandable reluctance for he is apt to feel that he has more important things to do.

Thus the relations between the bookmakers and the racing authorities remain in a cold war mode for most of the year; a somewhat suspicious calm punctuated by bouts of bickering and culminating in open hostilities during the period for settling the levy. The battlefield is the committee room of the Levy Board. The chairman is appointed by the Home Secretary, who selects a figure from public life sufficiently interested in racing to be content to head this quango. His duty, with the help of his board, is to extract and then distribute the sum raised by the levy. Before he takes the chair he will have been warned by his friends amongst the mighty that he must stand up to the autocratic Jockey Club and impose his own personality on racing. There is less advice given to him about standing up to the bookmakers, though that is really his main task.

My first chairman was Desmond Plummer, who had previously run the Greater London Council. He was tough and forceful. He certainly stamped his personality on racing, and I would judge that he was very successful, with the important exception that, like all chairmen so far, he failed to make any impact on effectively increasing the size of the levy. By the time I joined his board he was battle-scarred by his annual disputes with the bookmakers and was barely on speaking terms with them.

He was succeeded by Ian Trethowan, fresh from being Director-General of the BBC. Ian was a natural conciliator, possessed of a most agreeable and friendly manner, and was confident that his wiles, tact and personal charm would serve him as well with the betting industry as they had with the BBC and with his parliamentary contacts. He launched a peace initiative with the leading bookmakers. The first move was to have an evening get-together with them over drinks. He asked me to accompany him but otherwise went into the lions' den without the rest of his board.

It was an immensely enjoyable and entertaining party, the bookmakers seemed pleased with us, stories were told, jokes cracked, the drink flowed well into the night. In the end it all became rather like one of those regimental parties which had gone on a shade too long, arms round each others' shoulders, each assuring his neighbour of undying loyalty, friendship and respect. The atmosphere when we broke up should have ensured the start of eternal peace.

Sadly, it did nothing of the kind. The most that could be said of the party's results was that after it we spoke to each other with greater cordiality, but not one extra penny did it extract for the levy. Many individual bookmakers are agreeable and friendly, but as a body their motto should have been taken from the battle of Verdun 'Ils ne passeront pas'.

Ian did many excellent things for racing, everybody liked him, and his premature death before he finished his tenure is greatly mourned. But he never cracked the bookmakers and by his last year he was as disillusioned with them as had been Desmond Plummer.

Levy Board meetings were no more exciting than the myriad committee meetings which I have sat through during my life, but for me they were enlivened by the chairman of the Tote, Woodrow Wyatt. He had been a well-known maverick as a Labour politician and by then was embarking on an active and influential Indian summer, retaining a robustly independent spirit. He would wander into meetings rather late, pick up his papers and peer at them myopically, giving the impression, rightly or wrongly, that it was the first time he had looked at them. When during his perusal he found a passage that aroused his interest, he would disregard the discussion proceeding around him and would ask a question which had the effect of diverting business into an altogether unplanned stream. Inevitably, and deliberately, he would sooner or later provoke the bookmakers' representative into a furious retort. With the satisfied smile of an angler who had hooked his catch, Woodrow would play the infuriated bookmaker with humorous sarcasm, to my, at least, great enjoyment, until the chairman asserted his authority and diverted business back to the subject which we were supposed to be discussing.

Woodrow was later a staunch and effective mover in the campaign to bring about Sunday racing, and altogether did much for racing as a whole. My Jockey Club colleague when I joined the board was Piers Bengough. Years before he had succeeded me as Alec Kilpatrick's chief amateur jockey and we would conjecture about our late and now deceased trainer's pleasure in discovering that his two protegés were occupying together such a dizzy pinnacle in racing – pleasure which would have been well camouflaged under comments designed to deflate any swelling of heads. The contribution which Piers has made to racing is not always appreciated. He left the army early and has since worked untiringly, voluntarily and often much too hard at various demanding tasks, combining at this moment the chairmanship of the Disciplinary Committee with Her Majesty's Representative at Ascot – which means he holds the responsibility for all that goes on there. He was succeeded on the Levy Board by Chris Collins, a noted horseman and shrewd businessman who eventually was responsible for reviving the Grand National meeting at Aintree. It will be a sad day if racing could no longer call upon the voluntary services of able and dedicated men like these. Professionalism is not everything.

During my time on the Levy Board, in 1982, the operation known as 'saving the Grand National' took place. Mrs Mirabel Topham, the former gaiety girl and the owner until 1974, had played a 'will she sell, won't she sell?' game since her acquisition of the Aintree course in 1949. She was a self-willed and contrary lady, and she obviously enjoyed the suspense and uncertainty about the future of the great race caused by the brinkmanship in which she indulged every year. Eventually she got tired of the game and sold the course to a Mr Bill Davies. He had contracted to continue racing there but his heart was clearly not in it. Aintree was run on a shoestring and Ladbrokes, the bookmakers, took over the running of the meeting on his behalf.

In 1982 Mr Davies announced that he was going to sell the course, if necessary to a property developer, for £4 million. It was soon clear that no one was going to pay this sum to buy Aintree as a racecourse. The ball had thus been played firmly into the Jockey Club's court. Unless the required sum could be raised to buy the course in 1983 one of the outstanding events in the British sporting calendar would disappear.

After discussion with Mr Davies the asking price came down to £3.4 million. He would go no lower and this became the Jockey Club's target. I was able to inform the Stewards that the Levy Board would contribute a £1 million loan if the alternative was to lose the Grand National. In some haste the Jockey Club now had to mount a fund-raising campaign to acquire a sum of £2.4 million.

The two heroes of the ensuing campaign were its coordinator and moving spirit, Johnnie Henderson, banker, once ADC to Monty and father of Nicky, the trainer, and Sam Vestey, who master-minded the fundraising. Without the work and initiative of these two there would now be no Grand National. The appeal raised £2 million, of which the members of the Jockey Club personally contributed nearly a quarter. Considering that a good many members were only interested in flat-racing and did not contribute, this is a matter for pride. Jockeys gave up their riding fees and racing as a whole rallied to the cause with generosity. But time had run out, we were still short of £400,000, Mr Davies stood firm and the property developers were lying in wait.

Then, in the nick of time the drinks firm of Seagram stepped in and provided the balance. This gesture, made on the initiative of Ivan Straker, was generous and taken at short notice. Without it our efforts would have failed and so it is fair to say, as the Press have consistently done ever since, that Seagrams 'saved' the Grand National. No-one ever seems to remember the £2 million that the Jockey Club raised.

During my time with the Levy Board I was invited to the annual William Hill – the bookmakers – luncheon at the Savoy. I found myself seated next to a diminutive figure with an aggressive ginger beard turning white, horn-rimmed spectacles and a bow tie. As I knew well, this was the redoubtable Phil Bull, master of the Timeform organisation, possessed of a brilliant brain, Yorkshire forthrightness, and a deep contempt for the Jockey Club – a racing personality of the first order.

He did not know who I was, so picked up my name card and regarded it disapprovingly. An army general, and a Jockey Club member at that – too good a target to miss. He instantly asked for my views, as a general, on the nuclear deterrent. I soon became aware that his opinions on the subject were if anything to the left of those held by the Campaign For Nuclear Disarmament. I was also aware that he was keenly awaiting the moment when I should burst into flames of wrath, thus ensuring a lovely row. No row in fact ensued. I was much interested in his point of view, and he soon became interested in mine. We fell into a deep and absorbing conversation; the nuclear deterrent was soon abandoned as a subject and our neighbours never got a word out of us for the rest of the meal. Afterwards he wrote to me, I wrote back and there started, not just a friendship, but a close one. I would often stay at The Hollins, his Victorian mansion near Halifax, usually when he was alone there, and we would talk far into the night on all manner of subjects. Letters passed regularly between us until his death in 1989.

Phil's father had been a Yorkshire coalminer of a strong ecclesiastical turn of mind. His way of life changed on the day that he saw a poster in Doncaster asking, 'What shall we do to be saved?' Underneath someone had written,'Back Doricles for the St Leger.' He did so and the horse came home at 40 to one. From then on he developed a passion for racing and communicated it to his son.

Phil graduated in mathematics in Leeds University and went to London as a school-teacher, combining lectures on sociology with visits to the races. His formidable intellect, retentive memory and thoroughness soon brought him success as a gambler and he lost interest in teaching. His new career was largely based on his discovery that the timing of races and the resultant data could be interpreted by a mind as agile as his to spot winners. He was the first to think of this, and it proved to be the foundation, secured by his mathematical skills, on which his life as a gambler, a writer on the comparative merits of racehorses, a racehorse owner and far-seeing critic of racing's management, rested. His crowning achievement was the establishment of Timeform, the largest organisation in the world devoted to assessing and supplying information about racehorses, based on Halifax and employing a staff of 100.

By the time I knew him his reputation in the world of racing had earned him the title of the 'sage of Halifax'. He had predicted and pressed for nearly all the improvements which, usually much later, came to pass, and he had strong opinions on everything. The Jockey Club in his view was compounded of tradition, inertia and stupidity. As a member of the body concerned I would protest when he said this, but in truth he only half meant it. He liked some members personally and sometimes entertained them at The Hollins. He was wise enough never to cause an outright breach with the club itself. But inevitably late at night some remark would set him off and like an elderly actor reciting a well-known part he would launch into a diatribe against those lordly 'twits', a diatribe which, when I knew him well enough, I could usually stop by pulling his leg.

He had the kind of powerful mathematical intellect which was quite beyond my ken – he played chess with a computer and usually beat it. His interest in world and national events was lively, and he coined a phrase which became well known, that against matters of real importance racing was 'a great irrelevance'. Quite right of course, and directed against the obsession with racing which leads too many to have no other subjects for conversation. It did however sometimes occur to me that the comment might perhaps have come better from someone who had not made a fortune from the sport.

In his last years he handed over Timeform and sat back at The Hollins, his letters no longer fulminating with criticism and rather sad. His family life had not been happy and he was lonely, with nothing to look forward to. His father's ecclesiastical bent had certainly not been passed on to the son, for Phil was a firm and convinced atheist. 'When our life ends it's no different from a fly being swatted on the wall – nothing more.' And again, 'When I die I've given instructions that there is to be no nonsense about services; someone must just put me in a sack and chuck me into a hole in the ground.'

The last letter which I had from him ran to ten foolscap pages. It discussed my work for the Jockey Club, expressed his fury that inferior minds had not yet changed a rule of racing in the way he desired, went on to say that it didn't matter because racing was trivial anyway, and concluded with several pages on how his thinking had been influenced by Shaw and Bertrand Russell. I miss these effusions, a powerful brew of wisdom, prejudice and mental vigour.

When I became deputy Senior Steward, there were a number of issues which seemed to have been put in the 'too difficult' tray and left there. One by one I asked the Senior Steward, Rupert Manton, if I could take them out and he agreed. These issues included the pay of officials, judges, starters and so on, which was far too low and was in due course improved; whether we should examine the much criticised system of amateur local stewarding at race-meetings and should we copy other countries and introduce professional stewards?

Another unresolved issue was the interruption of racing by snow, frost or floods – a possible answer being all-weather tracks. And should we use the government's flirtation with legalising trading on Sunday as an opportunity to raise the thorny question of Sunday racing? Did we even want Sunday racing? No one knew.

In the mid 1980s the confusion caused by the existing laws on Sunday trading – a confusion which persists to this day – was encouraging Ministers to consider introducing a Sunday Trading Bill which would permit shops to open legally on Sunday. As far as sporting events were concerned it is illegal to charge for admittance on the Sabbath, but most sports were by that time turning a blind eye and still are. Although racing could have followed suit, there was no point in doing so because betting was strictly forbidden on Sunday by law. The existing laws were therefore discriminating against racing, both horse and greyhound, whilst other sports, not affected by betting, were getting away with it.

When the Sunday newspapers announced that a Sunday Trading Bill would in due course be put before the House, I returned to London on the Monday determined to raise the question of Sunday racing. Woodrow Wyatt had simultaneously come to the same conclusion. Very soon I was charged with examining the whole problem, with deciding whether we indeed wanted to race on Sundays, if so whether the public would be likely to come and if we all wanted to go ahead, how it was to be brought about. I was closely associated with Woodrow in all this, and with many other helpful and enthusiastic people.

We launched a national opinion poll and soon found that the public would indeed favour racing on the day of the week on which most people are free. The racing industry, as always conservative, took some persuading that their accustomed Sabbath rest should be violated and were apprehensive about the extra labour costs, but appreciated that the extra crowds and public interest that Sunday racing would bring would benefit their sport and their livelihood. The bookmakers were far from sure that there was much in it for them, but did not wish to spoil the party and at least paid lip service to our campaign.

Sunday racing takes place everywhere in the world except in the United Kingdom. Ireland had recently been converted and Sunday meetings there were already a success, with much larger crowds than on a weekday. On the Continent Sunday racing is a part of national life. French men and women, Germans, Italians, Belgians – all go to church on Sundays in much larger numbers than they do here, and after a good meal many of them proceed to the races. Nearly all the Continental prestige races take place on the Sabbath before much larger crowds than are seen here on weekdays – fun for the family and the money rolls in.

If our government was intending to legalise Sunday shopping, surely it must legalise Sunday betting? Was the betting shop to be the only one closed in the High Street on that day? But there was already considerable opposition in certain quarters to opening any shops on a Sunday, and the idea of actually in addition legalising betting as well brought the passions and the prejudices of a certain type of puritanical Englishman to fever pitch. The Churches, of all denominations, were adamantly opposed.

I asked representatives of the Churches to come and discuss their point of view with us. No very senior figures attended the meeting and those who did had been heavily briefed to give no ground. I asked them the question, 'Why is it that Frenchmen, Americans, Germans, Irishmen and citizens of every other country in the world are trusted by their churches to race and to bet on the Sabbath, and that the British are not so trusted?' Only negative mumbles could be heard in reply, of which 'It's different here' was the only one I caught. In desperation I asked the Roman Catholic representative, 'The countries that race on Sunday in Europe are nearly all Catholic – why can Catholics be permitted to bet on Sunday races there but not here?' Again, no coherent answer. I gave up.

Woodrow and I called at the offices of Keep Sunday Special and were received with courtesy but got no change. I used the Jockey Club's annual briefing in the House of Commons to the All-Party Racing Committee to put our case. This was the first that MPs had heard of the idea and most were unenthusiastic. 'Constituents won't wear betting on Sunday, you know.'

To start with, therefore, it was uphill work, but our campaign began to go well, generating a good deal of publicity in the Press and on TV, and even politically. Then the blow fell. The Sunday Trading Bill, overconfidently presented by the government and without sufficient lobbying of waverers, was thrown out by the House of Commons. No Sunday trading, no Sunday racing.

Or so it was thought. We decided not to give up and to pin our hopes on a possible Private Member's bill in the future. Woodrow Wyatt, with his parliamentary knowledge and influence, now did far more than I could to push the campaign forward. On his initiative we had several audiences with the Home Secretary, first Leon Brittan and then Douglas Hurd. Both were on our side and did all within their power to help us forward, but after the defeat of the Bill could not do so openly. Briefing of MPs and peers in the following two years brought about a considerable movement in our favour; their initial lack of enthusiasm had changed, in many cases, into warm support.

Otherwise I and my committee spent most of the three years over which the campaign ran in working out how Sunday racing could in practice be best introduced, and having helpful public and private discussions with those who earned their living from racing. There was a strong view that racing on the Sabbath would be much more presentable to the public if betting shops were closed and all betting, other than that by credit on the telephone, took place on the racecourse. This system works happily in Ireland. But the bookmakers were adamant; if betting shops were closed they would withdraw their support from the project. Since the government was insisting that racing spoke with one voice this was decisive, but I believe that one day this might be the way forward.

In the end both Private Members bills failed, as I believe such bills are apt to do. After the second failure we decided to put the whole enterprise into cold storage and wait for a better moment. I handed over to an enthusiastic and highly competent member of my committee, Nigel Clark, and I know that whenever there is a chance of moving forward he will seize it – indeed he is doing so.

Our Sunday initiative failed because the final decision lay with the House of Commons and not with the racing authorities. The issue of all-weather tracks was however within the power of the Jockey Club and the Levy Board to sanction, and now these tracks are an established feature of British racing.

In January 1984 there was a two-month freeze-up and all racing stopped. Jockeys were idle and not getting paid, trainers could not run their horses, owners were paying large monthly bills for horses restricted to chilly walks round a straw ring. Frustration reigned. Surely, I felt, the technology of the 1980s must be equal to devising a surface which would not freeze or become water-logged, and on which horses could race when the use of grass was not feasible.

A committee was assembled which I chaired, representing all those who earned their living from racing, and a very good committee it was. As in the case of Sunday racing I was fortunate to have available the Levy Board Chief Executive, Tristram Ricketts, an able and delightful man, to help keep me on the financial rails and in the realms of the practical, together with bookmakers, the Tote, trainers, jockeys, owners, racecourse managers and vets. Peter Walwyn, the trainer, was outstandingly forward-looking and practical and so later was Ian Balding. From the jockeys Joe Mercer brought his knowledge of racing on 'dirt' in America. Enthusiasts were rare in those early days. Never has the instinctive conservatism of the British racehorse trainer been more in evidence and, it often seemed, the younger and more promising the trainer the more reactionary he or she was. A leading lady trainer complained crossly to the Press that the whole idea was a waste of racing's money. I hope that somebody broke the news to her that one of the main objects of the idea was to bring more money into racing, which in the event it has done.

Their main objection was the belief that we would never find a surface on which they would be prepared to run their horses. Indeed the only artificial surface then being used was the 'dirt' on which American horses race. This is a mixture of loose sand and loam, and when it rains heavily the surface is liable to become liquid mud, which the horses' legs penetrate until they come suddenly into contact with the solid surface on which the 'dirt' rests. The mixture is notorious for causing unsoundness and would never be tolerated here. Preventing it from freezing requires machines to circle the track continuously throughout the previous night, at vast expense.

We sent expeditions to the United States and Japan and learnt a little but not much that we did not know already. Then, as usually happens when a potential market is sighted, two firms in this country came up with two different surfaces, one called Equitrack and the other Fibresand. After a good deal of trial and error both were found to meet our needs, and now one is well established at Lingfield and the other at Southwell, with another planned elsewhere. National Hunt races take place on both, and they enable flat racing to continue throughout the winter. Whilst in no way replacing grass, they have achieved their object, despite the early misgivings and apprehensions. I handed over to Andrew Parker-Bowles before the difficult task of actually bringing these meetings into being began, and he did most of the hard work.

The third and by far the most contentious change in which I took the lead was an examination of the system for stewarding at race meetings. At each of the approximately 1100 meetings that take place during the year four so-called local stewards are appointed. A chairman is selected and he is virtually for the day in charge of the conduct of that race meeting. The local stewards closely watch each race and, with the help of their professional stewards secretaries, are responsible for seeing that the rules of racing have been applied during each race and during the day's programme. The chairman of the panel is in charge of any enquiry into a breach of the rules, and after consultation with his colleagues metes out any punishment that may be called for. These enquiries can become difficult, with the livelihood of jockeys, of trainers and a good deal of prize money at stake. Local stewards can fine, suspend, disqualify horses or alter placings and, in the last resort, refer the whole case to the Disciplinary Committee in London. They, and in particular the chairman, have a great deal of power.

In nearly every other country these tasks are carried out by highly paid professionals with considerable racing experience who cruise from course to course. Here we rely on ladies and gentlemen usually located in the vicinity of the race meeting, assisted by professional stewards' secretaries whose advice they do not necessarily take. They are supposed to be knowledgeable racing people and they are not paid – not even for travel there and back.

At this time, in the early 1980s, these amateur stewards were under heavy attack from the racing professionals and from the racing Press. Too many enquiries had produced, in their view, the wrong result, too many misdemeanours were going unnoticed, and amateur incompetence was blamed. All the Jockey Club's fault, as usual. Why can't we have professional stewards in this country like everywhere else?

My investigation into all this lasted for a year. My hand-picked committee, which fortunately included Johnnie Macdonald Buchanan, an ex-Senior Steward and with more experience of local stewarding than, probably, anyone in the country, was a strong one – open-minded and knowledgable, the Jockey Club at its best. A seemingly endless procession of representatives from every conceivable part of racing, including the punters, appeared to give evidence.

We were quite prepared to recommend the adoption of professional stewards, even at an estimated cost to racing of nearly a million pounds, and expected that the weight of opinion would so convince us. Surprisingly it did nothing of the kind. The great majority, including jockeys and trainers with experience of racing overseas, firmly upheld the amateur system as being fairer and more even-handed than a professional one. Only very few indeed, not more than four or five out of a total of some 100 witnesses, favoured going professional.

The general view was that this country was unique, except possibly for Ireland, in having scattered throughout it quite sufficient experienced and respected racing men and women to produce a good amateur stewards team at every meeting. But the system required a drastic overhaul. The wrong people, often for social reasons, were being selected as stewards at racemeetings. Worse, the system of Buggins' Turn for the chairmanship of panels was leading to people trying to run an enquiry who were manifestly incapable, for lack of judgement, knowledge or personality, of doing so. In too many cases, it was alleged, the defendant, particularly if he happened to be a trainer of strong personality, was apt virtually to take over the running of proceedings from the hapless chairman.

I have greatly simplified what was in fact a long and detailed enquiry resulting in a voluminous report with many recommendations, but the rectification of the system of selection was the key proposal. This recommendation contained within it, as we were to discover, a time bomb.

The Jockey Club formally approved the report, decided that the selection of stewards should be put right and we were all congratulated on a fine bit of work. It then had to be implemented, and the ticking of the time bomb, unheard as yet by members, became all too audible to those of us who had the task of actually putting our recommendations into effect. Bill Dugdale, the chairman of the Disciplinary Committee, and I were handed the duty of raising to an acceptable standard every stewards panel of the 60 racecourses in the country. This meant that we had to decide which existing stewards would have to be told that their services would no longer be required. Even worse, a system for disqualifying existing or would-be chairmen of panels deemed to be inadequate would have to be devised. The ticking grew louder.

We embarked on what eventually became one of the most disagreeable and embarrassing tasks I have ever undertaken. Bill and I personally knew a good many of the local stewards, but the great majority were simply names to us. We could only ask senior local stewards in whom we had confidence to give us their views on the competence of the stewards, mostly personal friends, with whom they worked. To fill in gaps we had to ask the stewards secretaries for their opinions, and we had available the Disciplinary Committee's records of recent enquiries which had gone wrong.

We did our utmost to be fair, but we had to remember that half-measures would not suffice. The evidence to our committee had made it resoundingly clear that all was far from well at present. The livelihood of jockeys and trainers – indeed the good name of racing – depended on our success in bringing about this change. This unpleasant nettle had to be grasped for the good of racing. It stung.

When the names of those who had to be told that they were no longer to act as stewards were listed, the ticking became much louder, for some were personages of repute in industry or were local magnates. They were not at all pleased, and soon were loud in their protests. But when we looked at the names of those to be disqualified from acting as chairmen, and found that the list actually contained members of the Jockey Club, the ticking became deafening.

I felt extremely sorry for the local stewards who were to be stood down.

Nobody likes, particularly if they have reached a respected, even eminent, position in life, to be told that their services are no longer required in a post, however unimportant, for which they have volunteered and been selected. Although the position of local steward at a racemeeting is of no real consequence to the outside world, the holders regard it as a minor privilege and it carries within a limited circle a certain prestige. Resentment was inevitable.

The Senior Steward of the day, Ailwyn Fairhaven, did his duty without flinching, wrote to those rejected and broke the news. All hell broke loose.

The umbrage taken by the individuals concerned infected their many friends. Feeling within the Jockey Club became so intense that before the April meeting of the Club at Newmarket, officials in Portman Square were receiving telephone calls from elderly members saying that in all their long experience they had never known such resentment in the Club. When I attended the races before the meeting several senior members cut me dead. At the meeting that evening the bomb went off.

For some reason the attacks were all directed at me personally. I had been unfair and had not correctly assessed the merits of the gentlemen – there were no ladies – affected; if there had been consultation I had been advised by lowly stewards secretaries who had no right to judge their elders and betters; an utter disgrace and an insult to members; anyway there wasn't much wrong with the present system. The attack was launched by elderly, mostly aristocratic members. The younger ones sat on their hands, spellbound as the blue blood boiled around them. They knew perfectly well that what was proposed was necessary and right but certainly were not going to say so. Only Chris Collins bravely rose to his feet and defended me.

I now realised the truth of the comment that when an aristocrat really sets out to be rude, he is in a class of his own. An elderly peer rose to discharge ten minutes of concentrated vitriol, ending with the memorable words, 'Let's get rid of the army and go back to being a gentleman's club.' This of course gave the game away completely. I, and I believe most others in the room, regarded membership of the Jockey Club as an opportunity to serve racing, and not an extension of White's.

I rose and defended myself and in due course the storm subsided after one of the most unpleasant hours I have ever spent. But, despite the sound and fury, no attempt was made to change the decisions and they all went through unscathed. When the conclusions of my committee were released to the Press, there was immediately a howl of contempt that the Jockey Club had lost their nerve and failed to do what was obviously needed and introduce professional stewards. I sometimes felt like telling them that there would have been a lot less blood on the carpet if we had.

Five years later, the recommendations having been implemented, an official review of the then standard of local stewarding had no hesitation of saying that the situation had vastly improved and was now satisfactory. Some mistakes are inevitably still made, but far fewer. There has been little more talk about professional stewards.

Somehow, though, I doubt if we have heard the last of this. The amateur basis of the stewards' panels still shows through, particularly in the punishments meted out for excessive use of the whip. No-one is more adamant than I am that flogging a tired and beaten horse deserves severe punishment, and no-one, I am sure, appreciates more than I do the difficulty of where to draw the line. Only knowledgeable, experienced and self-confident stewards can assess this limit and there are not enough of them.

I entirely disagree with the so-called experts, usually elderly, who say that the use of the whip in a close finish makes no difference to the effort that the horse exerts. There are some particularly gallant and competitive animals to whom this may apply, but no-one can convince me that a few sharp and expert cracks of the whip – which is now shortened and less severe – at the right moment and in the right place do not encourage most horses to pull out a bit more. The jockey is employed to win the race and will be heavily criticised by his connections if he loses without in their view having done all in his power to win.

In their difficulty local stewards have been instructed to count the number of strokes of the whip and if a jockey uses it more than five times in a race they should take action against him, win or lose. I am well aware of, and sympathise with, the public's dislike of seeing horses hit, but so long as a jockey is allowed to carry a whip – and there is a reasonable argument that he shouldn't be – we should not lose sight of fairness and commonsense.

Every case is different and should be judged on its merits. They range from the highly skilful and humane use of the whip which leaves the horse unmarked and without which the horse would not have won, to a dreadful belabouring of a beaten animal – a wide spectrum of variations.

My point here is that to apply a 'rule of thumb' of so many strokes is simply masking the reality that a number of stewards are not knowledgeable and experienced enough to make an informed judgement of what is, I admit, a very tricky decision. The day may come when the amateur panels have to be strengthened by the inclusion of one professional steward – as indeed my committee suggested as an alternative to retaining a completely amateur team.

The Jockey Club, which has considerably widened its base in the past 15 years, has all the virtues of an experienced, conscientious and impartial amateur body. Several members work very hard in various capacities for no material reward. Its effectiveness compares well with the authorities governing other leading sports and much of the abuse levelled at it is unfair. British racing is admired for the discipline wielded within it, for its comparative straightness, for its variety, and for the traditional and unique atmosphere of its great occasions. All these attributes, reaching back over many years into the distant past, have been nurtured by successive generations of the sport's ruling body, the Jockey Club.

As I found, though, during my years in 42 Portman Square the innate conservatism of so traditional an assembly puts a brake on progress. Any suggestion for a significant departure from established policy is invariably and instinctively opposed, at least initially, by most members, though some are invariably forward-looking and receptive of new ideas.

The introduction of all-weather tracks, the concept of racing on Sunday, the idea of a review body above the Disciplinary Committee, the reorganisation of the system of local stewarding, the recruitment of a badly-needed chief executive – all these and others were a break from established custom and so to many members, not by any means all elderly, automatically unwelcome.

Apart from Sunday racing – which is not yet legally permitted with betting but which most members now support – all these innovations are in place. But, before they were, imposing personages rose to their feet in condemnation, uttering in measured and portentous terms dire warnings of fateful consequences in store should such changes come to pass. None of these dreadful forecasts have materialised.

Perhaps the most significant failure to look ahead and adjust established policy occurred in the early 1970s. The key constituency in racing of owners, racecourse management, trainers and jockeys has never been part of the elected Jockey Club, though many Club members own racehorses. This constituency, although in their different ways its members have an important financial stake in racing, was at the time neither coordinated nor organised. It was, however, becoming restive about its lack of influence in the running of racing.

Unhappily a way was never devised of associating it more closely with the Jockey Club and bringing it into the Club's organisation as an integral part of racing's management. Perhaps an extra steward should have been appointed with the sole responsibility of looking after it and championing its cause. This is not hindsight for I very nearly proposed myself, as the ex-Army personnel officer, for the job. But I decided not to, largely because I knew that the Jockey Club chiefs of the day would have regarded such a suggestion as unwelcome, unnecessary, and indeed, for an unknown backbencher, impertinent. Perhaps I should have been bolder. The idea might not have worked, but I am sure that it would have been worth a try.

As it was, unwooed at a time before it was effectively organised and when their hearts might have been won, predictably this large and crucial constituency went its own way, became officially organised as the Horserace Advisory Council with a seat on the Levy Board and grew mightily in influence.

So powerful did it become that in the new British Horseracing Board, designed to take over the running of racing from the Jockey Club, its representatives will outnumber those from the Jockey Club and be in a position to take control. When, and if, the government passes the legislation necessary to enable the Levy Board to join the British Horseracing Board, there will at last be a body in charge of British racing which will be in a better position, with parliamentary help, to extract enough money from the bookmakers to usher in a new dawn.

Racing, which is called a sport but is in large part a commercial enterprise, must of course be run for the most part by representatives of those who as owners provide the racehorses or of those who earn their living from the Turf. I hope, though, that there will still be a place in the new hierarchy for the enlightened, experienced and hardworking amateur. If so, the Jockey Club could still be the breeding ground for such talent and leadership, and could continue to exercise a decisive influence on policy despite being numerically in a minority. It all depends on how well its future leaders play their cards.

Otherwise ... I suppose it could always 'go back to being a gentleman's club'!

CHAPTER THIRTEEN

'Why don't they smile?'

That perceptive sports writer for *The Times*, Simon Barnes, asked after the 1990 football World Cup, 'Why did the world switch on, millions upon millions of them? Because we like sport, because we like football, because sport is interesting, because sport is entertaining, because sport is *fun.*' And later, 'The mood of the World Cup was of grim purposefulness. And when sport is merely purposeful, it serves no purpose. We turn to sport for joy. If a sporting event cannot bring joy to the world, the world will simply seek its joys elsewhere.'

I shall be writing about show-jumping, not football, but the words have some relevance. It would be unfair to say that there is no joy in show-jumping – a win, particularly a team win in a big competition – brings joy to many. But it has become a profession rather than a sport, and it shows. Too many of its former aficionados have sought their joys elsewhere.

It is not surprising that the riders, especially the international riders, are less relaxed than their amateur forebears, for the financial pressures under which they earn their daily bread are immense. The cost of keeping, and touring with, a string of show-jumpers round the leading shows has proved impossible to meet without large private means or a wealthy sponsor. To acquire a sponsor, whether corporate or private, the rider has to become well known through winning important prizes on which 30 or 40 highly skilled opponents also have designs. Once a sponsor has been acquired he wants his publicity; the rider must go on winning or he loses his sponsor and sinks back into obscurity. The rider will not satisfy his sponsor if he fails to be selected to jump at the televised shows or for international teams to perform abroad. He worries about this.

If he does not own the horse which he rides there is always the risk that the owner will be tempted to sell it to a foreigner at a large profit. If it is the rider's best horse – which it usually will be – he has to start looking for a replacement. Unless he is lucky a novice horse with international promise will cost him or his owner upwards of £50,000. Top international show-jumpers have fetched as much as a million dollars. No doubt one will soon fetch a million pounds. To keep this in perspective the jumper Milton had already won by mid-1992 nearly a million pounds, far more prize money than Desert Orchid ever did. Those who watch jumping competitions on the television or at horse shows have been known to complain, 'But they all look so serious. Why don't they smile?' With what is at stake, would you? In any case they seem to regard it as unprofessional to show emotion – triumph and disaster are treated just the same. But this is not enlivening for the spectators.

Riding at speed over enormous fences may be a thrilling way of earning a living, but the 'clonk' of a fallen pole behind you can suddenly make that living less secure. There are one or two, like the Whitaker brothers, who have arrived at such a peak of eminence that their financial, if not their competitive, pressures are for the time being of no great concern. Below them hundreds struggle to reach the same happy position. At the bottom end of the sport the local riders compete in local shows with less pressure, but apparently with little more contentment, for they feel strongly that too much of the available money is lavished on the spoilt internationals. They count the Volvos and the BMWs – the prizes which the top riders drive victoriously round the arena after a big win – and grind their teeth in envy. So they don't smile much either.

Terence Rattigan used to say that when writing a play he aimed his work at Aunt Edna sitting in the matinée stalls. If Aunt Edna was pleased, so would everyone else be, by and large. Whether by design or by luck, the 25 years during which Mike Ansell presided over showjumping and popularised it through television had attracted thousands of Aunt Ednas to the sport. Show-jumping from the White City or Wembley would be available to them after the nine o'clock evening news, and from Hickstead in the afternoon.

Viewers began to identify themselves with Pat Smythe and Prince Hal, Wilf White and Nizefella, David Broome and Mister Softee, Peter Robeson on Craven A and Firecrest, Harvey Smith on O'Malley, Ann Moore on Psalm, Marion Coakes on Stroller, Dawn Palethorpe on Earlsrath Rambler. They lived through their triumphs and disasters, groaned when their favourite hit a pole, rose in joy from their chairs at a vital clear round, and soaked up the inside information about the leading horses which Dorian Williams purveyed so stylishly and so comfortably.

The personalities of the riders made an impact on viewers. Enthusiasts young and old joined Aunt Edna round the set and show-jumping became a television highlight. Viewers voted David Broome to be the BBC's Sportsman of the Year.

Bob Dean, Mike Ansell's man of commerce, soon realised that this excellent publicity could be converted into sponsorship, and industrial firms were not slow to respond. By the time I had, like Rip Van Winkel, emerged after 20 years show-jumping slumber – as president of the British Show-Jumping association in 1976 – sponsors had begun to change the world of which I had once been part. It cannot be said that they had changed it for the worse, for they had injected all that lovely money, but the downside was becoming all too evident. Mike Ansell had by this time gone back to Devonshire, but Bob Dean, although himself semi-retired, was beginning to utter warnings.

By the middle and late 1970s the corporate sponsors were becoming so determined to extract every inch of publicity that some firms were insisting that as well as the horse bearing its sponsor's prefix before its name, the actual name of the horse should be associated with the goods purveyed by their firm. Thus you could have a pulsating jump-off on the television between Jones Electronics Limited's Fuse Wire and Smith's Engineering's Gearbox. Then Jones Electronics would get fed up with sponsoring and the same horse would appear as, perhaps, Chemical Products' Stayfresh. Aunt Edna no longer knew which horse was which. They changed their names too often, not always very attractively.

She became disenchanted and transferred her affections to the three day eventers, some of them attractive young ladies liable to embrace their horses ecstatically after a competition, unlike the show-jumpers. Plenty of joy there. But there were too few three day events in the year, so she searched the channels for alternatives. Possibly she took up with snooker – all those well-dressed young men with nice manners – and a sport which, even if she did not play herself, her brothers and nephews did and she could discuss the matches with them.

Bob Dean eventually convinced the show-jumping authorities how disastrous for the sport's image it was that horses should be called Fuse Wire one minute and Stayfresh the next, and the rules were changed. Now if a rider has a mare called Meg, Meg she will remain, though she may progress from Jones Electronics' Meg to Smith's Engineering's Meg and then to Chemical Products' Meg – 'and don't forget to mention Chemical Products'. But by then it was too late, Aunt Edna had gone.

There are, of course, other reasons for show-jumping's fall in the TV viewing ratings and in public interest to the point now reached at which you have to wait up till midnight to see any evening events on the screen. Rumours, not entirely unfounded, that riders have been known to ill-treat their horses in order to make them jump more cleanly have not helped. And fashions change. All horse sports are less popular than they were and those which the viewer actually plays, such as golf, snooker and darts, now prosper on the box. All that can be done is to chase the publicity, and try to win an Olympic gold medal in front of the watching world.

The BSJA's president was almost entirely an honorary post, but I was also asked to chair the selectors of the international teams and to direct the international team effort. This I did for 14 years, and since we are amongst the three or four best show-jumping nations, medals of all three hues – though never an Olympic gold – regularly came our way.

Watching show-jumping can range from the excruciatingly boring to the intensely exciting. For me the biggest thrill came in the team event, the so-called Nations Cup. Four riders from each competing country aim to finish, after two rounds, on the lowest score. Each rider's round is crucial from the very first fence – unlike a race the suspense is continuous from start to finish – and as one of our home riders crossed the start line for what might be a decisive round, my watching body seemed physically to elevate out of my seat in sympathy and anxiety as he jumped each fence. Sometimes the championship will depend on whether one fence – quivering on its rest after it has been struck by a hoof – stays in place or falls. For those, like myself, who identify with the British team these competitions can be agonising.

No rider who has not the nerve for the big occasion competes with success in these Nations Cups. As tennis players find in the Davis Cup, competing for a team can be far more demanding than an individual competition. Some who excel when their efforts only affect themselves can be overwhelmed by the tension of a team event. Others thrive on it, and some very rare competitors actually revel in being the anchor man, the last of the four to jump. David Broome reserves his best efforts for desperate situations when only a clear round over an enormous course can win the gold medal, or when one fence down can mean team oblivion. John Whitaker only seems to wake up when he is confronted with the near-impossible. Such temperaments belong to the real champions.

Although 20 years had passed since I had competed internationally myself, there were still a few of my old team mates jumping at the top level, if ruddier of face and broader of beam. Harvey Smith, of course, was one but now a very different Harvey from the gauche young fellow lumbering round on Farmer's Boy. He had learnt to win competitions against the clock by cutting corners in a combination of muscular power and judgement which, at his peak, no-one could match. He now owned a string of horses, many from as humble an origin as Farmer's Boy, but Harvey had converted them into winners worldwide. Throughout the 1960s and the 1970s the names of Harvey Smith and David Broome were synonymous with show-jumping.

Much more, Harvey had become a 'personality'. His strong character contained more than a touch of Yorkshire bloody-mindedness, and his successes were accompanied by attitudes towards authority which increasingly hit the headlines. It is said that there is no such thing as bad publicity and Harvey went some way to confirming this, for he became an *enfant terrible* and the crowds loved it. Indeed, when he made his two-finger gesture at Douglas Bunn on the television after a round at Hickstead, his name became immortal. To do a 'Harvey Smith' at someone is now part of Britain's vocabulary.

He became a favourite of the media, and the results did not always endear him to those in authority in his chosen sport. Despite being the best-known character in show-jumping by far, I doubt if Aunt Edna really approved of him, although her nephews and nieces undoubtedly did. Harvey has an abrasive and overbearing side to his character, but I know that if I had to find a companion to accompany me into a dangerous jungle, I would pick Harvey Smith every time.

He had a few more years as a team member when I returned to the scene but his best days were over. Derek Ricketts, Malcolm Pyrah, Caroline Bradley and others were beginning to join the ever-green David Broome. Commanding this disparate and often temperamental expeditionary force was a man without whom our international show-jumping would barely exist as a coherent effort, Ronnie Massarella. He is a Yorkshireman of Italian origin, from the ice-cream family by then well-known in the equestrian world. Effervescent, enthusiastic, knowledgeable and impeccably mannered, Ronnie is also an outstanding leader. When a team in a Nations Cup has underperformed and is despondently awaiting the closing stages of the competition, tails down, Ronnie has the ability – unrivalled anywhere else in the international equestrian world – of cajoling, scolding, charming and encouraging them to snatch victory against all the odds.

He is still, after a quarter of a century, the team manager – unpaid, immensely experienced, a friend to all his charges and irreplaceable. I had the happiest of partnerships with him for 14 years. Now it is over I miss those telephone calls, those endless, bubbling telephone calls – sometimes despairing about riders or owners who would persist in putting their own interests before those of the national team – sometimes from Rome, New York or Madrid exultantly announcing a victory – sometimes conspiring with me how best to achieve an aim which the show-jumping authorities, not all as enthusiastic about the national team as we would wish, were endeavouring to frustrate.

For as president I had no power, and exerted such influence as I possessed from my international team base. Mike Ansell had for years been the sport's dictator. He had decided everything, his word was law and his powerful personality demolished all opposition. Now he had departed, and just as nations ruled by dictators swing, once the great man has gone, to ultra-democracy, show-jumping was now entangled in a spider's web of committees. Nothing could be decided unless several committees had considered and agreed it. These committees were large, and some of the more argumentative and talkative members belonged to several. Over these bodies had been set an executive committee under the sport's elected chairman of more than twenty strong. Meetings of this committee would go on all day, everyone talked at once, and very little got decided. As president I suggested that this governing body should be reduced to six or seven members, as in racing. Everyone nodded their heads and said how right I was. Needless to say, nothing was done.

When I took over as chairman of the selectors the Olympic Games in Moscow were only three years away. Alone in world equestrian circles British show-jumping had by this time placed round its neck a heavy millstone as far as the Olympics were concerned. The British Show-Jumping Association had some years earlier decided that all those riders who earned their living from the sport should turn professional. The amateur/professional distinction was indeed extremely blurred at the time and theoretically this idea had much to be said for it. In practical terms, it was a nonsense.

All riders unable to prove that their livelihood did not depend on show-jumping were forced to turn professional. No-one got the benefit of the doubt. Almost all our leading riders were at a stroke rendered ineligible for the Olympic Games. A quicker way of committing Olympic suicide could not have been devised. The policy was based on the highly unrealistic assumption that every other equestrian federation would conscientiously follow our lead and force their leading riders, some of whom were blatantly earning their living from their sport, to turn professional. Predictably, none did. The British authorities were thus left in the position of the platoon commander who rises to his feet and advances upon the enemy, only to look back and discover that his troops have remained firmly in their slit trenches.

This move had no practical effect for better or worse in a normal year, but in the Olympic year made the selectors' life more than difficult. In 1978 we had won the World Team Championship but in the Moscow Olympics we would have to take on the same or better foreign opposition without any of the four riders who had won it for us. All were ineligible. Indeed we were only able to field a third or fourth eleven against the Test sides of other countries.

Raising a team for Moscow thus caused problems and Ronnie's telephone calls grew more frequent and ever longer. Then in 1979 the Russians invaded Afghanistan and President Jimmy Carter called for a boycott of the Moscow Olympics. Mrs Thatcher flung her weight behind him, and there followed a confused and unhappy period, in which opinion within every sport was divided. A good many sportsmen and women were not prepared to kow-tow automatically to Mrs Thatcher who, they felt, knew very little about sport and who was mainly interested in keeping in with the Americans. They had been training hard and to them the Olympics was the pinnacle to reach which they had sweated and poured out money they could ill afford for years. Some were all too aware that this would be their last chance to compete at the Games.

The British Olympic Association rebelled and its campaign was led most effectively – and to me surprisingly – by its chairman, Denis Follows. I had formerly known him when I was a vice-chairman of the Football Association, of which he had been secretary. A delightful, mild and helpful man of modest presence, I had quite failed to appreciate that he had within him the steel to take on the whole British political establishment and force at least a partial win. He showed himself to be a real hero.

The decision whether to oppose the government's wishes and send teams to Moscow in support of Denis Follows had to be taken by the various sporting authorities individually. Responsible internationally and to our government for all horse sports in this country is the British Equestrian Federation. Although he was shortly to hand over the leadership of this body to me, Harry Llewellyn was still at the time the man in charge.

He was, I believe, in favour of joining the rebellion but surprisingly the equestrian sports took quite a different line from the majority of the national sporting associations. The ladies and gentlemen of the three day event, owners and riders alike, staunchly and patriotically supported Mrs Thatcher and would not hear of rebelling. The dressage competitors felt likewise. So did the show-jumping owners but the riders were divided. Harvey Smith, predictably, was all for defying the government and going to Moscow, but was heavily outnumbered.

Again surprisingly, all the leading foreign equestrian federations fell into line with Jimmy Carter. Though some western European countries sent teams for athletics and other sports, none sent any horses. In the event the riding medals were competed for only by the Russians and some eastern European countries, all very weak in equestrian terms. The winning of such devalued medals would not have been worth the expense and effort of sending our horses all the way to Moscow.

Looking back, the boycott seems to have been an impulsive reaction stemming from the misapprehension that governments had the power, if they so ordered, to stop their nationals from competing in the Olympic Games. In fact the sportsmen of most countries were perfectly within their rights to ignore their governments, many duly did so, and went regardless. The boycott thus resulted in the worst of all worlds. It was largely ineffective, spoilt the Moscow Olympics, had no discernible political effect on the Russians, made the West look rather silly, and was, in hindsight, an error.

To be the supremo of British equestrian sports, the President of the BEF which I became in 1980, sounds more important than it is. Foreign teams speak with awe of their federations; British riders have hardly heard of ours. They acknowledge the authority of the British Show-Jumping Association, or if they are three day eventers, dressage riders or drivers the British Horse Society, but barely register when their federation is mentioned. British equestrian sports operate with typical British independence. Their associations are steeped in tradition and many worthy men and women work hard and voluntarily in the interests of their particular sport without paying much regard to the others.

The BEF was grafted on to this time-honoured structure when it became necessary to have one body to speak to the Federation Equestre Internationale (FEI) or to the government. But it has always been regarded by the existing organisations and by the riders as something imposed on a perfectly satisfactory arrangement by interfering foreigners, and they only rarely wake up to its existence.

The BEF's small staff was headed at that time by an old friend of ours from the Camberley bungalows, Major-General Jack Reynolds, a most able and pleasant man who had, as perhaps one of the best staff officers of his rank in the army, shrewdly been recruited by Mike Ansell. He was a much bigger catch than the horse world ever appreciated; it was lucky to get him. During the recruiting interview Mike persuasively laid out all his wares and had ended by playing his final card, 'And, Jack, don't forget you'll meet such *nice people*.' Mike always did tend to let his enthusiasm run away with him.

As the channel between our hyper-active international effort and the FEI, the BEF staff was kept busy, particularly as the Olympic Games and the World and European Championships approached. I soon found that the president operated through persuasion and lobbying, not by power. The executive committees of the sports over which I presided were always terrified that I would try to take them over. Logically, if I had tried and succeeded it might have made for a more economical arrangement but, as I had found in the Ministry of Defence, the logical solution is often far from being the most sensible or practical. We jogged along perfectly happily as we were and quite efficiently enough. I knew very little about the three day event, the dressage and the driving, but enjoyed attending their championships and meeting their competitors. Nice people.

I went on selecting the British show-jumping teams. As the 1984 Olympics in Los Angeles came into view we were still handicapped by the self-imposed ban on our top riders, but Ronnie and I had managed to prevent the two young Whitakers from turning professional. Michael had only just emerged from the junior ranks, but John had several big wins to his credit, mainly on Ryan's Son. This was the only experienced horse which we had available for the Olympics, but he was 15 and feeling his age, with a good many miles on his clock. Michael had the mare Amanda, potentially brilliant but with an ingrained dislike of a water obstacle.

These two formed the backbone of the team. Tim Grubb, still British though based in the United States, had a fair horse called Linky. For the two remaining places we had to look well down the ranking list – Harvey Smith's younger son, Steven, had only ridden in one Nations Cup in his life. Nobody gave us any chance at all against the opposition, all fielding the best team of horses and riders available in their countries.

It seems to be fashionable now to condemn the Olympic Games as too commercial, too nationalistic, too drug-ridden and too much organised for the television. Although a lot of this is doubtless true the fact is that nearly every television viewer in the world seems to want to watch them. What I do know is that to be amongst them is an experience that cannot remotely be conveyed by watching television at home. Their vast size and scale, the feeling that the sport which accounts for your presence there is but one amidst an immense variety ranging from athletics to synchronised swimming, the mixture of nationalities, all together render that overworked word 'unique' as suitable as it will ever be.

Sporting stars of world fame wander about the Olympic Village in their tracksuits amongst competitors who will never be famous but who are thrilled just to be there. As the Games wear on tension relaxes and barriers between sports break down. On the aircraft home from L.A. I found myself sitting amongst the British judo team with Daley Thompson, ebullient after his gold medal, across the gangway. Kriss Akabusi, an old friend from the Army Physical Training Corps, rushed up for a chat. The 1984 Olympics, despite the Russian boycott, are a happy memory.

The various British equestrian teams were flung together in a way which rarely happens. Socially, the three day event team made every yard of the running. Although their competitors ride and prepare with the highest professionalism, the atmosphere is still basically amateur and redolent of the county set. They have organised an enthusiastic band of supporters prepared to travel at great personal expense to the Games and other championships and cheer their team on. The indefatigable and admirable Rosemary Barlow arrives in advance and busies herself in booking a room in the stadium which becomes a social base for all our equestrian teams, not merely the three day event team, and supporters throughout the competitions. The show-jumpers, made welcome as they are, often come from a different background and from a sport which is unashamedly professional and commercially based. Attempts to raise a show-jumpers' supporters club have occasionally been made, always unsuccessfully. But for the period of the Games chalk mixes happily with cheese.

The Americans organised the Los Angeles Olympics brilliantly, but there was one considerable snag – the distance between events. The riding stadium was on Santa Anita racecourse – a ninety minutes bus ride from the Olympic Village. The athletics stadium was an hour's drive away from the Village in the opposite direction. The other sports could only be reached after a long bus journey. The central bus station was in the Village. If you stayed at the athletics until the end of the day's programme you would arrive back at the Olympic Village to find that the last bus to Santa Anita had long since departed.

Travelling apart, the popularity of the Games meant that every seat at every event was fully booked, and if you wanted to escape from horses and watch something else you had, as well as organising transport, to ask someone to pull strings. I managed one afternoon at the athletics only because a most helpful young American volunteered to drive me there in his own car, and because I had been given a ticket, untruthfully stating that I was the father of one of the athletes, so could sit in the family stand.

The jingoism of the American crowds was a revelation. At times they became almost hysterical. Individually our hosts were hospitality and friendliness incarnate; en masse they could be frightening. An Englishman sitting next to me watching a judo contest involving an American, amidst the usual bedlam, remarked, 'Gosh, I can understand now why the Russians are so worried about this lot.' The intensity of feeling was such that I was not surprised at some of the very odd decisions given by refereees in the Americans' favour; the chances of a lynching must have seemed too high. The TV coverage was so American-orientated that the other competitors usually featured as no more than cannon-fodder over which the home competitors trampled to victory.

Even the show-jumping trial in the arena at Santa Anita, a non-event if ever there was one, took place before an enormous crowd, sitting all day in the broiling sun. They bellowed and screamed whenever an American rider appeared in the ring, apparently unaware that this performance was not really a contest at all, merely a warm-up. Even so, one of our riders, normally phlegmatic and with many years of experience behind him, suffered a bad attack of Olympic nerves and rode a disastrous round. After that young Steven Smith was promoted from the reserve to be a member of the four-man team for the Olympic Nations Cup event on the following day.

This was the first Olympic medal contest for the show-jumpers. The course was built by the ex-Hungarian American expert, Bert de Nemethy, and was brilliantly designed. He showed that it was possible to build a testing Olympic course without frightening the horses, by cunningly related distances between fences which were themselves imaginatively constructed – a course to test the rider as much as the horse. Our team had a reasonably good first round. Michael Whitaker's Amanda stopped once at a water-ditch but was otherwise clear; Tim Grubb did well; Steven gallantly but showed his inexperience. Ryan's Son, our last to go, was clearly feeling both the heat and his age and had three fences down. The Americans were sailing away in front and even at this stage did not look as if they could be caught – smooth, sleek thoroughbreds with smooth, sleek riders, jumping, it must be said, over fences which they knew but almost without a fault. The Germans, French, Swiss, Austrians, Dutch and ourselves were all struggling in their slipstream. The crowd was beside itself.

In the second round Michael and Amanda put us right back in the hunt with a brilliant clear. Tim Grubb was our second to go. He positioned himself at the entrance to the ring, actually under a part of the crowd, when the American jumping before him completed a clear round. The crowd stamped their feet on the wooden floor of the stand and went mad. So did Tim's terrified horse and a disastrous round followed. Our third to go was Steven Smith on a good horse of his father's and he came into the ring well knowing that on his shoulders rested our chances of a medal. His nerve held, as I was always confident it would, and he came back with only two fences down. Although the Americans were now home and dry for the gold medal, Steven's round had put us up with the Germans and the Swiss when all the third riders had gone.

The fourth horses of each team started their rounds and the Swiss had faults, as did the other contenders. Then in came Paul Schockemöhle, the German maestro, on the formidable Deister, the European champions. If they jumped a clear round the Germans would be sure of the silver medal. Paul went round smoothly and faultlessly; all seemed over for us. The last fence was a wide spread of rustic poles, and as he approached it something went ever so slightly wrong – dare I say it, of the European champion, that it was pressure? – and the far pole rolled – oh, so gently – to the ground. Our hearts leapt.

Cold reality soon brought us down again. It all now depended on Ryan's Son and John Whitaker. The veteran horse was clearly hating it, he was old, it was very hot and he had knocked over three fences in the first round. He could afford one fence down and we would win the silver medal; two down and we would win nothing. In a deathly hush they advanced upon the first fence – and down it fell. Now he had to do the impossible – jump thirteen more of these tricky, formidable fences, all clear. John proceeded to ride the most brilliant show-jumping round that I have ever watched. Relentlessly, calmly, with icy concentration he lifted that old, rather tired horse over fence after fence after fence until, as he cleared the last, our tension exploded in a mighty roar. Our no-hope team had won the Olympic team silver medal.

The eventers had won two silver medals to add to the show-jumpers' one, and the dressage riders had performed with credit. When we arrived at Heathrow there was an enthusiastic welcome home party and much mutual congratulation. All in all it had been fun.

By the 1988 Olympic Games in Seoul the amateur/professional distinction had effectively vanished. Riders, as far as the Games were concerned, were just riders; all were eligible. Our problem then was not the shortage of riders but shortage of adequate horses. As Bette Davis sang in a wartime film 'They're either too young or too old'.

We had one star, already among the two or three best show-jumpers in the world, Milton. With him in the team we were fairly sure of at least one medal, even a gold. Without him, with the horses available to us, we would be lucky to achieve any medals at all.

But his owners, Mr and Mrs Bradley, refused to let him go to the Seoul Olympics. No coherent reason was ever extracted from them. The flight there was a good deal shorter than the journey to Calgary, a show for which they regularly clamoured for their horse to be selected. The stabling and facilities in Seoul were of five-star quality. Their decision was a great disappointment. The sport from which they were making a great deal of money and to which, one might have thought, they owed something, badly needed the publicity fillip of an Olympic gold medal.

I was sorry for the rest of the team, whose tails were down as soon as this decision became irrevocable, and the main objective of their efforts largely disappeared from view. I was sorry for the many enthusiastic men and women who had worked voluntarily and hard for months to raise money in order to send the best possible equestrian teams to the Olympics. But Milton belonged to the Bradleys, and if they would not let the horse go to Seoul it was their decision and theirs alone. Whatever our personal feelings, we just had to make the best of it.

The Seoul Olympic Games were as memorable as those in Los Angeles but in a different way. This time there was no boycott. Instead there were the threat of riots, reports of students throwing Molotov cocktails, sword-rattling from North Korea, even wild talk of an invasion. The media in every Western country hyped up these threats, and however many soothing noises were made, a great many people changed their minds about taking their holidays at the Olympic Games. Where the Los Angeles hotels and stadia had been booked solid for months in advance, the opposite was true in Seoul.

This was sad for the South Koreans, who had spared nothing in trouble and expense. Not surprisingly security was an obsession. If you moved in any direction near the Olympic complex your progress would be immediately barred by a 15 foot wire fence through which you filtered slowly past its check points. Surrounded by (apparently) teenage soldiers in immaculate green uniforms and bearing sub-machine guns, you had to turn out your pockets, open your bag, take off your hat and produce several documents and authorisations before courteous young security guards bowed respectfully and let you through. It ought to have been infuriating but it wasn't. They were all so charming, so apologetic about inconveniencing you and yet so thorough and efficient that you could not possibly be impatient or rude to them.

Even walking the three day event cross-country course, a hot and dusty expedition, these delightful young men would constantly pop out of bushes and position themselves deferentially but immovably across your path. They would indicate that they did not wish you to proceed any further in your chosen direction but to make a highly unwelcome detour. Even then you forgave them. They were an object lesson in what can be achieved by good manners and charm but, it must be admitted, it did cross one's mind that those tommy-guns might be loaded.

South Korea had risen from the ashes of the 1950 war in astonishing fashion and Seoul was now a modern city except for its hotel accommodation. There was nothing between the Hilton and three others comparable and boarding houses, known as 'yogwans' to which Korean businessmen were in the habit of taking their secretaries or mistresses for a quick one during the luncheon interval. Our travel agency had put all who did not qualify for the Olympic Village into 'yogwans' – evidently the Hilton was too expensive.

Our 'yogwan' was run apparently by teenagers – or perhaps all Koreans look like teenagers – enthusiastic and anxious to please but speaking no word of any other language. The rooms were adequate but the Korean food provided there was to Western tastes inedible. After much gesturing the best we could achieve to launch us on our day were overcooked fried eggs swimming uninvitingly in fat.

Snacks at the stadium were obtained from stalls manned by sweet little Korean girls. Nothing on offer from them was even remotely edible except the sauerkraut sausage. 'Could we have bread too, please?' No comprehend. Puzzled shaking of heads, anxious looks. By the end of the fortnight they had learnt. 'No bled, no bled,' they would cry as soon as they saw us. So most of us ate nothing but sauerkraut sausage, with a nasty piece of meat at the 'yogwan' to round off our day. Good for the figure. No alcohol, either, just coke.

So much trouble had been taken by the South Koreans to entertain the world that it must have been disappointing for them that the world did not come. The specially designed pleasure park round the athletics stadium was a sea of oriental faces, apart from the occasional American. This meant that you could with ease penetrate into any of the stadia and I visited almost every event, some such as the boxing and athletics several times. But only occasionally was there a spark of the Los Angeles atmosphere, such as the splendid boxing final between a Korean and an American which the Korean won and the crowd, who obviously did not like Americans very much, went mad.

Otherwise enthusiasm was muted. Immense effort, vast expense and much goodwill had been lavished upon the Games. At the end they were counted a success – no riots, no Molotov cocktails, no invasion, great efficiency, but the champagne was flat. Prodigious feats were performed in the athletics stadium to polite clapping from Koreans who were not much interested, having no noticeable contenders themselves. Only the boxing and the martial arts, where they had, struck sparks. They had even less interest in the equestrian events, and the Korean authorities had to resort to 'rent-a-crowd' to make the attendance look respectable. Bored Korean children, whose parents had dozed off, crawled over one's knees during a tense jump-off in the show-jumping arena.

This time nothing went right for our show-jumping team. Lots of excuses – the going was too rough and too hard, horses too old to jump on such a surface or not sound enough, anyway not good enough. Above all, no Milton. Then in his prime, he would have been well-backed to win the gold. As it was, no medals.

The eventers again won two silver medals, and gallantly pretended that they did not mind once more failing to win a gold. Rosemary Barlow had overcome every obstacle to provide her hospitality room – at first there was no space, no possibility of a room, anyway no alcohol allowed in the stadium. She achieved space, a room and wine, and provided a welcome oasis during the long hot days.

There we had our final party, mainly to celebrate the eventers' medals. After a slow start it was warmed by the enthusiasm of their team and supporters. The show-jumpers went through the motions and stood there politely smiling as the cries of 'sooper' and 'absolutely farntarstic' trilled around them – all rather forced, and sadly typical of an enterprise on which so much money and effort had been lavished but which had resolutely refused to get off the ground.

Soon afterwards I gave up my equestrian responsibilities. Fourteen years was, I felt, quite long enough but there was another reason. Perhaps it is old age and a reluctance to come to terms with a changing world which makes me sad to see the dominating position that money now holds in equestrian sport. The sufferer is all too often the horse.

It may seem odd to have talked about the need for more money in racing and then deplore the effect it has on the competitive riding world. In racing, however, an improvement in prize money, in attendance at race meetings and in facilities to be found there can have no ill effect on the racehorse. Jockeys might perhaps ride more aggressively or use their whips more often if there was more money to be won, but if this danger exists at all it can be controlled. Otherwise the healthier racing's finances become, the more valuable the racehorses become, the better they are cared for and the greater the number that are put into training. A race is a race, whether it is the Cheltenham Gold Cup or a selling plate and the conditions the horses meet in it are of an established and fixed pattern.

Show-jumping has however become so commercial that the making of money is now an obsession. Even the TV commentators join in. A horse has a fence down – 'Oh, dear, that puts Tom out of the competition. But he won't be too sorry, there is only two thousand pounds prize money today, and Tom will be thinking that at least his horse will be fresh for the eight thousand on offer tomorrow.' And the commentator is quite right – that is exactly what Tom will be thinking.

Owners, riders, sponsors and organisers all stand to profit financially from lavishly endowed competitions which require horses to jump ever more often and ever higher. The process usually starts with a big international firm offering to put up a large sum of money for a new championship. Anyone who dares to mention that horses are jumping enormous courses quite frequently enough already is at once shot down by 'We can't afford to turn down an offer like that'. The suggestion that in that case there could be what we used to call in Whitehall a 'compensating reduction' by eliminating one of the existing championships is at once brushed aside – less money for someone.

As an example some years ago the firm of Volvo offered to finance a winter indoor show-jumping championship to run throughout the close season and culminate in a final in April. It was richly endowed and grandiloquently entitled by the FEI 'money men' – who seem to win every argument – the World Cup. The fact that the title was certain to confuse the general public with the genuine World Championship held in the summer turned out in the end not to matter, because the public have always ignored it. But a great many people make a great deal of money out of it, so much so that the top horses, instead of resting throughout the winter months now have to jump, with short intervals, all the year round. Other tests during the summer are then added. If it is Olympic year unnecessary and demanding qualifying rounds are inserted before the individual competition at the Games. Never in my dealings with the FEI has any effort been made to try and reduce the number of top class competitions in which the leading horses have to jump over ever higher and more testing obstacles.

Some riders wisely conserve their horses' energy. Too many others cannot resist the money on offer. Their horses jump too often and the strain under which they are placed burns them out. The horses may be appreciated as long as they remain in the top flight but the moment of discard comes all too soon and then they are forgotten. It is, of course absurdly idealistic not to remember that horses are usually bought in the hope that they will make their owner money, but now the hope, sadly, seems to have become an over-riding fixation. Show-jumpers have become tools, not friends and partners.

The three day event is far less commercialised and much less money is on offer. With the eventers the overwhelming desire for international prestige and national pride seems more important than the money to be won but, like show-jumpers, they must have sponsors, sponsors want success, and their sport's course is probably set in the same direction as that of show-jumping. I am no expert in the three-day event, just a fairly experienced horseman, but I do not find the contortions and pain which some horses are made to endure during the cross-country section a pleasant spectacle.

I am the first to admit that a certain level of hazard cannot be avoided now that the standard of preparation, of riding and of competition are so extremely high. If you watch Mark Todd, Ginny Leng or Ian Stark, for example, riding in an Olympic cross country you marvel how they and their horses often make a horrifying course seem easy.

But in the Olympic Games, and in other championships, Mark Todd and the other two are not the only competitors. The next rider to appear on the course may be a Turk or a Korean or an Egyptian. Often he, or his national federation, will have visited Ireland and bought for a very large sum of money a gallant, genuine Irish horse anxious to do its best. All too many times I have watched in horror the trouble, pain and fright to which some riders, manifestly far below the riding standard expected and quite incapable of managing a course of this difficulty, subject their luckless horses. Even at home, where standards are high, the Badminton 1992 cross country, run in unluckily slippery conditions, shocked many horse-lovers who are not necessarily squeamish.

After that Badminton some distinguished riders wrote defensively in the newspapers about how much they love their horses and how the death rate in racing is anyway far higher. With respect, not only is the racing situation, with 1100 meetings every year, not comparable but the death rate, though important, is not the point. It is the pain, the potential for injury and the strain leading to premature unsoundness – all adding up to an unpleasant spectacle which concerns.

Top international riders are by nature competitive and brave. But however much they care for their horses they are not the right people to advise on acceptable risks. I remember standing on the landing side of Bechers Brook discussing how to make it safer. Surrounding me were a number of experts, of which the most vociferous were jockeys, past and present. All these jockeys had ridden round Aintree often and some intended to go on doing so for many more years. All were totally dismissive, even scathing, about any suggestions for making the fence easier to jump. I much regret that I gave in to them; I should have known better. Two years later public opinion – on which all spectator sports must in the end depend – forced a change.

Since the 1992 Badminton there has obviously been some intelligent thought given by the Three Day Event authorities to reducing the risks. I hope that the successful 1993 Badminton will not encourage complacency, for I suspect that further steps will be necessary if a drastic alleviation is not one day to be enforced, as it was at Aintree.

By now most readers must be thinking that old age has made me soft. I can assure them that my softness is shared by many other horsemen and women. The FEI is already doing a great deal to eliminate cruelty and unfair practises. I believe it should go further and ask itself whether the questions now being asked of our willing but silent equine partner are still acceptable. I am not optimistic, for any effective action will cause an outcry. No squeals are louder than those that come from the pocket.

Finale

In a life marked by exceptional good fortune I have one particular blessing for which I have always been grateful. When one door closes I do not miss or repine for what went on behind it. I look forward to exploring the territory beyond the next door. I am sorry for people whose nature it is to yearn for their previous occupations and pastimes. Indeed very often I have been happy to move on.

When I had given up steeplechasing my eyes did not follow the galloping field in sorrow that I was no longer riding with them. More probably I would watch them hurtle flat out over the open ditch and feel an intense relief that I was standing safely on terra firma.

It was the same with athletics and with the Modern Pentathlon – much more enjoyable to watch the struggles of others from the grandstand, fun though it had once been. I was proud to have been an international show-jumper but when I finished I knew that my time was up. During my army service it was sometimes disappointing to have to move from an enjoyable command and find myself back in Whitehall, but the challenge ahead quickly made me forget it. And I finally left Whitehall with an overpowering feeling of relief. Indeed in the end, like a National Serviceman, I was counting the days. Now when I read in the Court Circular of *The Times* the news that the Army Board have entertained some foreign military potentate to a Dinner, I smile happily over my cornflakes in the knowledge that others have had to put on their white ties and sit through it.

It is pointless to look back, to regret missed opportunities or to cry over any milk that may have been spilt during one's life. I should have liked to have gone to university, I ought to have learnt languages, been taught how to play the piano, read more books and so forth. I wish, like some politicians, that I had 'spent more time with my family'. My sons are luckier; they both work from home and watch their children grow up, but the army was too demanding for that. No doubt all my life I have done those things that I ought not to have done and left undone those things that I ought to have done.

But – in Omar Khayyam's lovely words

> The Moving Finger writes, and having writ,
> Moves on; nor all your Piety nor Wit
> Shall lure it back to cancel half a line,
> Nor all your Tears wash out a Word of it.

The past is the past. It's over – fun to look back on, but there's nothing now you can do about it. Gone.

So I enjoy exploring the territory beyond the latest door to open. Presumably now there will only be one more. The pastels which Paul Maze gave me are busy and there is much else to do. As I sit at my desk I see outside my window lovely – and paintable – countryside. At my feet lies my old black labrador, as bloody-minded as his master, but devoted and faithful. Bustling about the house I can hear the happiest and most treasured gift of all, my dear wife. Now, I am in no hurry for the next door to open.

Index